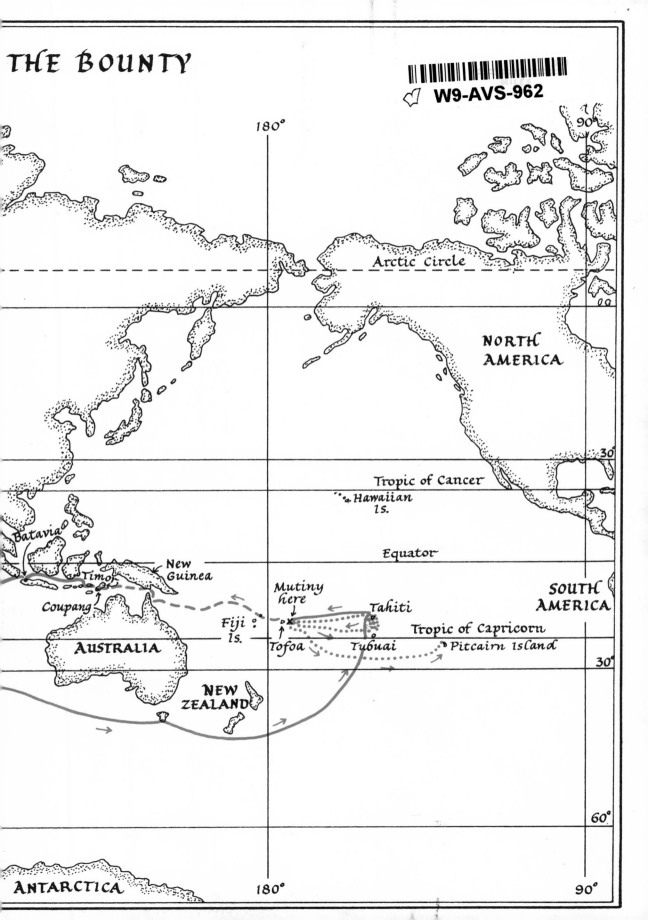

THE BOUNTY

90°

180°

Arctic Circle

NORTH AMERICA

30°

Tropic of Cancer

Hawaiian Is.

Equator

SOUTH AMERICA

Batavia

New Guinea

Timor

Coupang

Mutiny here

Fiji Is.

Tahiti

Tropic of Capricorn

Tofoa

Tubuai

Pitcairn Island

AUSTRALIA

30°

NEW ZEALAND

60°

ANTARCTICA

180°

90°

BLIGH

*A True Account of Mutiny Aboard
His Majesty's Ship Bounty*

CAPTAIN WILLIAM BLIGH

BLIGH

A True Account of Mutiny Aboard His Majesty's Ship
BOUNTY

SAM McKINNEY

With drawings by
NATHAN GOLDSTEIN

INTERNATIONAL MARINE PUBLISHING COMPANY

CAMDEN, MAINE

Published by International Marine Publishing Company.

International Marine Publishing Company offers software for sale. For information and a catalog, please contact TAB Software Department, Blue Ridge Summit, PA 17294-0850.

Questions regarding the content of this book should be addressed to:

International Marine Publishing Company
Division of TAB Books, Inc.
P.O. Box 220
Camden, ME 04843

55452

The paper used in this publication meets the minimum requirements of American National Standard for Information Sciences—Permanence of Paper for Printed Library Materials. ANSI Z39.48-1984.
Cartography by Alex Wallach
Duotone film prepared by Graphic Color Service, Waterville, ME
Printed and bound by Hamilton Printing Company, East Greenbush, NY

10 9 8 7 6 5 4 3 2

Library of Congress Cataloging-in-Publication Data
McKinney, Sam, 1927–
  Bligh : a true account of mutiny aboard His Majesty's Ship Bounty
/ Sam McKinney.
      p.   cm.
  Bibliography: p.
  Includes index.
  ISBN 0-87742-981-2
  1. Bounty Mutiny, 1789.   2. Bligh, William, 1754–1817.
3. Pitcairn Island.   I. Title.
  DU800.M33   1989
  996'.18—dc19   88-34626
                                                      CIP

CONTENTS

ACKNOWLEDGMENTS

I thank all those writers and historians who, through the years, have added to the lore, the legend and the history of the men of the *Bounty* and the British Navy under sail, and who—through their accumulated studies—have made this book possible. First among these is Owen Rutter, who so faithfully and meticulously reproduced Bligh's logs and Morrison's journal.

Other primary sources I have drawn upon liberally in my research for this book include Sir John Barrow (*The Mutiny of the Bounty*); George Mackaness (*A Book of the Bounty*); and J. C. Beaglehole (*The Life of Captain James Cook*). Complete references can be found in the Bibliography at the back of this book.

Special acknowledgment must also be given to N. A. M. Rogers, whose book (*The Wooden World, An Anatomy of the Georgian Navy*) provided me with so much information on conduct and practices aboard Royal Navy ships.

Gregory Foster, boatbuilder, designer and artist, was very helpful in supplying a critique of the *Bounty* launch.

To my own city library, the Multnomah County Library of Portland, Oregon, I owe a special debt of gratitude for allowing me to borrow Bligh's logs and Captain F. W. Beechey's log of H.M.S. *Blossom*.

And to Elizabeth Wiggans, Librarian at the National Maritime Museum, Greenwich, London, I am deeply indebted. Her patience and cooperation in drawing together information and illustrations vital to the accuracy of this book was invaluable.

In far-off New South Wales, Captain Ron Ware, a descendant of William Bligh, was kind enough to read my manuscript and provide noon positions for the launch voyage of his distinguished ancestor, a voyage he retraced himself in a replica of the *Bounty*'s launch. My thanks, too, to Luis Marden, chief emeritus of the for-

eign editorial staff for *National Geographic* magazine, who read the manuscript and provided invaluable critical feedback. I am deeply grateful for the efforts of these people and organizations; any inaccuracies remaining are mine alone.

Last (but far from least), my thanks to my editors at International Marine Publishing Company, Cynthia Bourgeault and Jonathan Eaton, for their support and encouragement.

INTRODUCTION:
CHRONICLES OF A MUTINY

> On the 16th of August 1787 I had the honor to receive my appointment from the Lords Commissioners of the Admiralty to command His Majestys Armed Vessel, forthwith to put her in commission and to use the utmost dispatch to complete her for a voyage to remote parts. . . .

With these words, the account begins of a voyage to the South Pacific under the command of 33-year-old Lieutenant William Bligh. By all rights, that voyage should have proceeded routinely. But 20 months later, after 29,000 miles logged across three oceans, Bligh's command was forcefully taken from him in the most famous—or infamous—mutiny in maritime history: the mutiny of the *Bounty*. It occurred off a remote volcanic South Sea island at dawn of April 28, 1789.

Immortalized by writers and by Hollywood films, the story of the *Bounty* mutiny has been enshrined as myth and legend. In this popularized form, the *Bounty* is a hell ship, and Bligh, its quintessential captain-as-brute. The mutiny itself, led by 25-year-old Fletcher Christian, is seen as a justifiable rebellion against the tyranny of a despotic commander and intolerable shipboard conditions. As legend it symbolizes the age-old struggle between the oppressed and the oppressor.

Indeed, the *Bounty* mutiny is a historical event that lends itself naturally to the dimensions and themes of a great morality play. The conflicts that traveled with the ship as it plodded across a vast ocean to its rendezvous with tragedy posed for its captain and crew, as they do for us today, unresolved questions of human conduct and action: What are the responsibilities of power? What are the limits of duty and obedience? When is an act of violence justified?

But the popularized legend of the *Bounty* stops short of such

1

philosophical speculation and settles instead for moral instruction. To make the point, events and characters must be simplified so there is no confusion between good and evil. The villain must fall and the hero must prevail, and the characters of Bligh and Christian have been shaped to fulfill these opposing roles. In reality, the *Bounty* story is much larger than its legend and much more interesting and complex than a simple contest between right and wrong. It is a story of men in conflict with the sea and with each other, men who nobly and successfully encounter the adversities of storm, exposure, sickness, and shipwreck—all things beyond their control—only to be doomed by forces they could have but failed to control: their pride, their ambitions, their lusts, and their vanities.

This book tells that larger story through the journals of the men of the *Bounty* and others who were swept into the vortex that centered around this mutiny at sea. The original written accounts of five men form the basis. They are:

Lieutenant William Bligh, captain of the *Bounty;*
James Morrison, boatswain's mate of the *Bounty;*
Captain Edward Edwards of H.M.S. (His Majesty's Ship) *Pandora;*
George Hamilton, the *Pandora*'s surgeon; and
Captain F. W. Beechey of H.M.S. *Blossom.*

These men—Bligh, Morrison, Edwards, Hamilton, and Beechey—might otherwise have served out their careers in obscurity, their journals long ago fallen to dust in the archives of the British Admiralty. Instead, they were participants, witnesses, and recorders of the *Bounty* story, and their journals—simple, unadorned records though they might be—stand among the classic works in the literature of the sea.

William Bligh, commander of H.M.S. *Bounty,* is, of course, the central figure in the story, and the most important document is his log, the official ship's log. It is characterized from opening statement to concluding sentence by precision, conviction, and authority. As were all Royal Navy logs, Bligh's was the record of the voyage, maintained in accordance to duty as required by the Lords Commissioners of the Admiralty. A ship's log was assumed to be a true and accurate record of a voyage unless proven to be falsely written. By its contents, a captain's performance could be evaluated. By its evidence, a ship's commander, any of his officers, and any members of the crew could be brought before a court-martial for judgment.

Owen Rutter, distinguished Bligh scholar, edited Bligh's journal for limited publication (300 sets of two volumes) by the Golden Cockerel Press in 1937. He states that the log "does not produce the impression of being an attempt to glorify, even to justify, the writer; it is obvious that he saw no need of self-justification, either at the time of the mutiny or at any other."[1]

Not everyone would agree that Bligh's log, or at least the post-mutiny entries, had no self-serving purpose. Rutter's conclusion, however, is unarguable: "Thus it [Bligh's log] transcends in interest and importance everything else that has been written on the subject of the *Bounty*."

Bligh's original log is a manuscript of nearly 900 pages of clean-lined script recording events and conditions observed, the number of sails carried, soundings of water depths, and the employment and health of the crew. On the left side of each page are orderly columns of figures that give day-to-day information on the ship's course, wind direction, air temperature, miles traveled, and positions of latitude and longitude.

Evidence of Bligh's abilities as a scientific observer are reflected in his voluminous remarks on such natural phenomena as geology, plant and animal life, and the cultural habits of the indigenous people he encountered, as well as his theories on nutrition and health.

Although it is known as the *Bounty*'s log, Bligh's log is in fact a record of his entire voyage—the execution and attendant circumstances of his command on the mission for which the Admiralty entrusted him. Thus, on the date of the mutiny, it shifts from H.M.S. *Bounty* to a small open boat; at Timor it shifts from the boat to shore and then gives way to a new log in the sailing vessel *Resource;* and at Java it shifts again, to a Dutch ship for the voyage home to England. Bligh kept his log sheltered in the open boat, and instead made his daily entries in a small notebook; these were transcribed into the log when the weather was fair and the boat relatively dry. The notebook still exists, and has been reproduced in a facsimile edition;* its water-stained pages call forth the image of a British commander reduced to cramped and desperate circumstances, yet unfalteringly discharging the daily duties of his post.

Upon his return to England after the mutiny, Bligh routinely submitted his log to the Admiralty, where it lay filed away for many

---

The Bligh Notebook: Rough account—Lieutenant Wm. Bligh's voyage in the Bounty's Launch from the ship to Tofua & from thence to Timor, 28 April to 14 June 1789 (Canberra: National Library of Australia, 1987). The second of this two-volume edition is a transcription of the notebook with an insightful introduction and valuable text notes by John Bach.

years. If the log had been publicly available earlier, a different Bligh from the Bligh of the legend might have emerged. But it was not until 1921 that the intact manuscript was transferred to the Public Record Office, and another 16 years before the Golden Cockerel Press limited edition appeared. By then the public image of a despotic Bligh was firmly fixed.

"The sea," observes Rutter in his introductory remarks to Bligh's log, "does not give up its treasures more slowly than Time its documents, and records long hidden in official archives or in private libraries have robbed many of fame too lightly won and caused posterity to reverse its verdict on as many whom their fellows had condemned.

"So it may be with William Bligh. . . . For a century and a half [now, two centuries] a single episode in his career has clung to his reputation like a burr. He had his faults, for he was mortal; yet he was a man who deserved well of his country. Thousands who are familiar with his name as the villain of a melodrama of the sea know nothing of his legitimate claims to distinction."[2]

I lay before the reader the written record of the man who commanded and then lost his ship, and leave it to you—if a judgment is wanted—to judge his conduct and his actions.

James Morrison was boatswain's mate on the *Bounty*. He wrote a journal that recorded all the major events of the *Bounty*'s voyage to Tahiti, the mutiny, the actions of the mutineers after taking the ship, and the later capture and return of certain crewmembers to England.

Morrison's journal is a book in its own right, and it is particularly important to the complete *Bounty* story because it reveals the character and personality of a Bligh not readily detectable in the *Bounty* log: the Bligh of apoplectic temper, who could release a torrent of rage and abuse on anyone who dared question his authority or failed to instantly follow his commands. This is the Bligh immortalized in the movie "Mutiny on the Bounty," in which Charles Laughton, standing on the quarter deck and trembling in a tantrum of fury, summons his lieutenant (portrayed by Clark Gable) with nothing more than the thunderous command of his name: "MISTER CHRISTIAN!" The Morrison journal gives sufficient evidence that such a picture of Bligh is not an exaggeration, that choleric outbursts of temper could be ignited in him by the merest hint of a challenge to his authority.

Was Morrison a reliable observer? Yes. No. Today, we would call him a "sea lawyer," the kind of man who could speak up against alleged injustice, a man not predisposed to lead a mutiny but one who could articulate the grievances that might have precipitated it.

He remained with Christian and his loyal supporters after the mutiny, but he later claimed that he was not a participant. A court-martial found him guilty as a mutineer and condemned him to death, but he received a King's pardon and returned to the sea, again in the service of the Royal Navy.

Twenty-eight years old at the time of the mutiny, Morrison was described in Bligh's log as follows: "Long Black Hair, has lost the use of the upper joint of the Fore finger of the Right hand . . . has been Wounded in One of his Arms with a Musquet Ball."

For a boatswain's mate, he was remarkably well educated. His journal shows him to be a gifted writer and an astute observer of human behavior. Nor is the journal his only piece of writing; his long dissertation on the habits and customs of Tahitian society, based on observations during his two years in residence on the island, formed one of the first ethnological studies of the island's culture. Morrison's journal, like the *Bounty* log, remained hidden for many years until publication in 1935 by Owen Rutter and the Golden Cockerel Press. The original manuscript is in the Mitchell Library (State Library of South Wales) in Sydney, Australia.

A shadow hangs over the Morrison journal concerning the unanswered question of exactly where and how it came to be written. As the later story will tell, Morrison was shipwrecked in the sinking of H.M.S. *Pandora,* the ship sent out to the Pacific under the command of Edward Edwards to capture the *Bounty* mutineers. After the wreck, the naked Morrison floundered in the water for an hour before he was rescued. Such an immersion would surely have destroyed any written material. Evidence suggests that Morrison wrote the journal after the shipwreck, while he was imprisoned awaiting a court-martial, but even this theory has its implausible element: How could a 383-page journal describing the people, dates, and daily events of a tumultuous three-year period have been so meticulously and accurately reconstructed?

Morrison offers no answer to this question. Rutter assumes that Morrison kept some form of a diary, which was taken from him before the shipwreck and later returned, and that this diary formed the basis for his complete journal. If, indeed, the journal was reconstructed during Morrison's imprisonment, then he had every reason to cast Bligh in a bad light (and himself as innocent), because Bligh had accused him of being an active supporter of the mutiny.

I have dwelt here for some length on the backgrounds of the Bligh log and the Morrison journal because they are central documents in the *Bounty* story and should be read in context and with an awareness of the perspectives of their authors. As with so many of the major links in the story, one must be careful when inter-

preting the writings of Bligh and Morrison not to be led too read-
ily to accusations of right and wrong or judgments of guilt and
innocence.

The log of Captain Edward Edwards and the eyewitness narrative of his surgeon, George Hamilton, continue the *Bounty* saga,
recording the tragic voyage of the *Pandora,* which ended in shipwreck and death. The two accounts were joined in a book edited
by Basil Thomson, published in 1915. Edwards's narrative—a
measure of the man himself—is sparse and emotionless as he
grimly follows in Bligh's track searching for the missing *Bounty*
mutineers. Fortunately for posterity, Hamilton's narrative fills in
the colorful and poignant details.

The concluding chapter to the *Bounty* story was written by Captain F. W. Beechey of H.M.S. *Blossom.* His book, *Voyage to the Pacific
and Beering Strait,* published in 1831, is the account of his 1825 visit
to Pitcairn Island, where he interviewed the last surviving mutineer and recorded the violent history of the doomed exile colony.

None of the five accounts introduced above is in print today.
The copies made available to me are rare library treasures, the
largess of unknown benefactors who, through their gifts, have allowed the retelling of this classic maritime epic. A sixth account,
by John Fryer, master of the *Bounty,* exists in a limited out-of-print
edition. Fryer's account, *The Voyage of the Bounty Launch,* deals only
with the open boat voyage and is essentially one long complaint
about Bligh; it is useful chiefly as a means of corroborating details
of the larger story, but lacks reliability as a principal source.

1

"THAT BASTARD BLIGH OF THE *BOUNTY*"

Bligh!

The name itself is an explosion, the exclamation point almost a part of its spelling. And yet Bligh's portrait (see frontispiece) shows an almost kindly face. The portrait is a pencil and water color executed by John Smart in 1803, when Bligh was 48 years old. Behind him lie 33 hard years at sea, but the face shows not a trace of this.

It is an intelligent face, the brown eyes kind, expressing a confident, knowing look. The mouth is almost cupid-like. The jaw line is strong, the cheeks full but not puffy or petulant.

Profession? I could not say just by looking at the portrait. I would rather imagine, however, that this is a man more accustomed to giving than taking orders.

He is Bligh of the *Bounty*. "That bastard Bligh of the *Bounty*," some would automatically say, knowing the man only by deed and reputation. But what is known of the man himself? The biographical data are not very revealing. Bligh's career followed the traditional route to naval command: early to sea, diligence in duty, and, eventually, the lucky assignment that gained him the influential patron so necessary for advancement through the ranks.

He was born in Plymouth on September 9, 1754, the first and only child of Francis and Jane Bligh. His father was a customs officer in this old Devon County port. Young William had a good education, and his father saw to it that he was well grounded in science and mathematics, two subjects most important to a professional career in the Royal Navy. The young Bligh also showed considerable ability as an artist.

At 16 he went to sea as an able-bodied seaman, and he was certified as a midshipman before he was 21. Already he was adept in navigation and cartography. He was a ship's master by 22. At the age of 27, Bligh married Elizabeth Betham, daughter of a wealthy and influential Scottish family. It was by all accounts a happy marriage, lasting 31 years and producing six daughters.

To understand the character and behavior of Bligh, it is necessary to know the mold from which he was cast. For Bligh, that mold was the institution of the British Royal Navy and his apprenticeship to its system under James Cook, one of the finest seamen it ever produced.

It was not a democratic system. Proud, arrogant, and mighty, the Royal Navy of Bligh's time, under King George III, was the military outreach of an island nation well on its way to a position of unequivocal world supremacy. Its collective systems of manpower, construction, supply, and administration formed the largest military organization in the Western world.

This great navy, quipped Winston Churchill—a one-time Lord of the Admiralty—was sustained by three things: "Rum, sodomy, and the lash." His comment, though facetious, succinctly expresses the popular conception of the British Royal Navy in the glory days of its wooden fighting ships—dramatic grist for fiction and films— when officers were expected to be harsh, and sailors, the dregs of streets and prisons, were oppressed, brutalized, and starved.

But reason suggests that this stereotype of the Royal Navy as an institutionalized example of man's inhumanity to man is not an accurate representation of the system. Though it often imposed a harsh and cruel servitude on its sailors, the navy was not a fleet of slave ships. It was composed of men, officers and crews alike, drawn from a social milieu which was itself for the great majority a difficult undertaking. The Royal Navy was but a creature of its time. For thousands of men, it offered escape from even worse conditions of numbing poverty or grueling labor in the fields or sweatshops.

By the simple fact that manpower was required to convert windpower into the energy that drove a ship, a sailor's life was not something to be needlessly wasted by sickness or death or incapacitated by unnecessary, vengeful punishment. In the late 18th century there were a number of influential exponents for a more enlightened view of shipboard management. Foremost among them was Captain James Cook.

Cook is generally recognized as history's most distinguished maritime explorer. His three great voyages (1768 to 1780) lifted the mist that hung over Balboa's Pacific and brought to light the vast area of the world's largest ocean. Other explorers had preceded Cook to the Pacific—Magellan, Drake, Le Maire, Wallis, Bougainville—but their expeditions were what might be considered "single track" voyages that stayed in the Southern Hemi-

A Ramsden sextant,
similar to Bligh's

sphere as they followed the trade wind routes of circumnavigation. Cook's mission was the exploration and charting of the entire Pacific, from the southern edge of its frozen margins to the limits of Arctic ice. His voyages were the first in the Pacific to have as their sole objective geographic and scientific exploration.

Cook's first voyage, from 1768 to 1771 in H.M.S. *Endeavour,* had as its principal, secret objective to search for the fabled *Terra Australis Incognita,* the "unknown southern land" that medieval minds assumed must counterbalance the landmasses of the Northern Hemisphere. A second objective was to set up an observation station on the recently discovered island of Tahiti and there observe the rare transit, in 1769, of Venus across the face of the sun—part of an intensive scientific effort spearheaded by England's Royal Society to determine the distance between the sun and the earth. Exacting survey and navigation skills would be required to locate accurately the island position selected for the observation.

Thus, the *Endeavour* was equipped and staffed for a major scientific voyage. Among the observers, naturalists, and artists appointed to the voyage by the Royal Society was the wealthy young Joseph Banks, a man of considerable ability as a natural historian, a patron of science, and, much later, the man responsible for the appointment of Bligh to command of the *Bounty.*

Cook's support from England's scientific organizations made him the first captain to use modern navigation methods and equipment, enabling him to undertake long-distance, accurate exploration. Before his time, a navigator could fix only the latitude of his position—his angular distance north or south of the equator. To get to a given destination he had first to sail to its known latitude, then sail due east or west until he made landfall. This "parallel sailing" was a crude system that made the time of the landfall doubtful, because the navigator could calculate neither the position of his ship nor the location of his destination east or west of the prime meridian of longitude (0° longitude, the meridian through Greenwich, England). Latitude could easily be calculated by simple sun or star sights. To determine longitude, however, the navigator needed an accurate timepiece, for location east or west of the prime meridian is a measure of time, which the art of navigation converts to distance.

The English government offered a prize of 20,000 pounds to the man inventing a clock that could accurately tell time aboard a ship at sea. John Harrison contrived such a clock in 1764, and Cook carried a refined version of that instrument, the first ship's chronometer. With this instrument, a sextant, and the newly published *Nautical Almanac* (a table of celestial positions), Cook was able to sail directly toward his intended landfall and survey and

A Kendall chronometer, the same model that was carried aboard the Bounty

chart coastlines more accurately than any explorer before him. Not incidentally, the successful observation of Venus' transit across the sun represents one of the milestones of 18th century astronomy. When the data from some 60 observations worldwide had been correlated and analyzed, the calculated distance from the earth to the sun was 153 million kilometers—respectably close to the 149.6 million kilometers accepted today.

On this voyage Cook discovered and charted the coast of New Zealand and the east coast of Australia, sailed to the north of Australia through Endeavour Straits, and returned to England by way of the Cape of Good Hope. He had reduced the possible area in which a supposed southern continent might be located, but he had neither discovered it nor disproved its existence. (Australia—or New Holland, as it was known at the time—was considered to be a large island, not to be confused with the mythical *Terra Australis Incognita,* the huge continental landmass that supposedly projected northward from the South Pole.)

His second voyage, from 1772 to 1775, explored along the ice rim of the Antarctic Circle. By this grand sweep of a huge oceanic region he was able to state with certainty that *Terra Australis Incognita* did not exist.

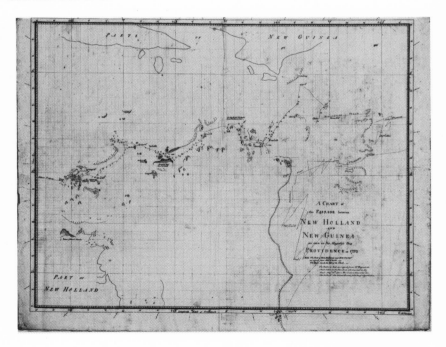

A later example of Bligh's cartography: a chart of Torres Strait drawn aboard H.M.S. Providence *in 1792. The track of H.M.S.* Pandora, *leading to her loss on the Great Barrier Reef (as described in Chapter 15), is shown at right. Small arrows give flood-tide current directions.*

Cook's final expedition (1776 to 1780) traversed five oceans to establish a record for the longest sailing voyage ever made. Always available to Cook for the difficult and often dangerous work of surveying was the 22-year-old William Bligh, sailing master of H. M. S. *Resolution.*

The primary objective of this voyage was the search for another geographical Holy Grail, the Northwest Passage. In October 1776, the *Resolution* cleared Cape Town and sailed eastward toward Tasmania and New Zealand. After charting new discoveries in the Central Pacific islands, Cook again visited Tahiti and then sailed northward, discovering the Sandwich [Hawaiian] Islands. He arrived off the northwest coast of America in late winter, 1778. The following August, Cook passed through Bering Straits and pushed the search for the passage to the edge of the Artic ice before giving up the quest. Thousands of miles of this hitherto unexplored northwest coast were charted under the skillful direction of the young cartographer Bligh.

Bligh would become, after James Cook, one of the most skillful practitioners of the arts of piloting and navigation. In the *Bounty* he would perform the remarkable navigational feat of sailing

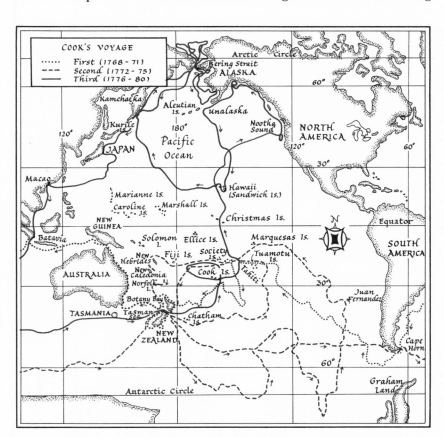

nearly 7,000 miles from the Cape of Good Hope, across the nearly empty Indian Ocean, to his first landfall: a small rock lying off the southern tip of Tasmania, then believed to be the southern terminus of Australia. Even more remarkable would be the use of his abilities as a navigator to pilot the open boat in which he and his loyal men were set adrift after his ship was taken from him in the mutiny, through a voyage across 3,618 miles of mostly uncharted waters. Bligh inherited his mastery from Cook.

But Bligh was observing much more than islands, headlands, coastal contours, and navigational techniques from 1776 to 1780. He was observing Cook's methods as a seaman, explorer, and surveyor. He was aware of his mentor's capable and humane diplomacy in all dealings with indigenous peoples. Unusual for his time, Cook proved—and Bligh noted—that such dealings could be conducted without bloodshed (though Cook himself was murdered by Sandwich islanders before the completion of his last voyage).

Aboard the *Resolution,* Bligh was trained in an altogether new system of shipboard life. Until the time of Cook, long sea voyages had exacted a huge toll in human life as crews were decimated by appalling conditions of sanitation and the uncontrollable advances of fever and disease. Medical theory in Cook's time connected disease with dirt, and the transmitting agency was believed to be the foul air of an unclean environment. Aboard the *Resolution,* Bligh saw how Cook maintained a clean ship. Seamen were forced to wash their clothes and bedding and bathe themselves. The enclosed lower deck areas of ships, notoriously foul breeding areas of disease and vermin, were aired in good weather and fumigated with acrid smoke or washed with strong solutions of gunpowder and vinegar.

Stalking all ships on long ocean passages was the horrifying sickness known as scurvy, a debilitating disease that first attacked the gums (causing the loss of teeth), then progressed to massive subcutaneous hemorrhaging. Death would follow as men collapsed in a state of weakness and bodily rot. Of the 1,900 men who sailed on the Anson expedition, for example—just 29 years prior to Cook's first voyage—1,300 died of scurvy and related diseases.

The cause, unknown for most of mankind's long association with ships and the sea, was a dietary deficiency of vitamin C. By the time of Cook's voyages, scurvy had been linked to diet, and the British navy was beginning to include such antiscorbutic foods as pickled cabbage (sauerkraut) and dried vegetable soup as a part of standard naval rations. That Cook so successfully avoided this disease on his long voyages was due to his insistence—backed with the threat of punishment—that his men eat these foods with their daily meals.

Breaking with the traditional watch system in which men were on duty four hours, then off duty four hours around the clock, Cook established a three-watch system of four hours of work followed by eight hours off, permitting much-needed rest.

Bligh watched and learned; he understood that discipline, diligence, authority, cleanliness, adequate rest, and a good diet lay behind Cook's great success as commander-explorer. What he perhaps failed to see was that these qualities stemmed from something yet more fundamental.

J. C. Beaglehole in his *Life of Captain James Cook* writes that Bligh was mentioned "a good deal in Cook's journal, never with dispraise. . . . He must, one can see from the records, have conducted himself expertly. . . . He was kind to his juniors. . . .

"One gathers, however . . . that there were men to whom he did not wish to be kind, and [he made] dogmatic judgments which he felt himself entitled to make; he saw fools about him too easily, and the thin-skinned vanity that was his curse through life was already with him. . . .

"Bligh learnt a good deal from Cook; but never learnt that you do not make friends of men by insulting them."[3]

Aboard the *Bounty,* Bligh enforced Cook's practical dietary and sanitation systems with a fanatical zeal that frequently led to outbursts of rage and insults. Like an angry housewife gone to sea, he continually fussed and fumed over the cleanliness of his ship and the food served to the crew. He summarized his constant and insistent effort to maintain the health of his crew in these remarks, written at the Cape of Good Hope after a difficult passage:

Seamen will seldom attend to themselves in any particular and simply to give directions that they are to keep themselves clean and dry as circumstances will allow, is of little avail. They must be watched like children. . . .

The Mode I have adopted has been a Strict adherence to the first grand point—cleanliness in their persons and bedding, Keeping them in dry Cloaths & by constant cleaning and drying the ship with Fires, to this I attribute their having kept free of Colds so wonderfully as they have done. A Great nuisance which is in general an Attendant in ships in a long continuance of bad weather is dirty Hammocks and Bags, this I think I perfectly got the better of, by having two sets, one of which was in charge to be got cleaned and dryed as a general Stock or property whenever they were done with, and by this Means I had it in my power to deliver Clean Hammocks and Bags as often as I saw it necessary. One person of a Watch was appointed to dry Cloaths by the Fire and a Man never came on Deck or went to sleep in wet apparel.

Commander Bligh of the Bounty

No foul Cloaths were ever suffered to be kept without airing, and in cleaning Ship all dark holes and Corners the common receptacles of all filth were the first places attended to.

After all that can be done perhaps Ships may be subject to Fevers and Fluxes; but the Scurvy is realy a disgrace to a ship where it is at all common, provided they have it in their power to be supplied with Dryed Malt, Sour Krout, and Portable Soup.... Chearfullness with exercise, and a sufficiency of rest are powerfull preventitives to this dreadfull disease.... To assist in the first particulars every opportunity I directed that the Evenings should be spent in dancing, and that I might be secure in my last I kept my few Men constantly at three Watches, even in the Worst of Weather, and I found them additionally alert on a call when their immediate Service was required....

In other ways as well, Bligh demonstrated his enlightened style of ship management. The movie version of Bligh portrays him as a commander who took sadistic pleasure in the physical punishment of his crew. The log, a record of all punishment administered, presents an opposite portrait: a man who, compared with other commanders of his time, made infrequent use of the lash. An entry made off the Patagonian coast of South America reads:

Untill this Afternoon I had hopes I could have performed the Voyage without punishment to any One, but I found it necessary to punish Matthew Quintal with 2 dozen lashes for Insolence and Contempt.

But counterbalancing these enlightened qualities are the temperamental flaws that Beaglehole describes so trenchantly. In his enforcement of rigorous shipboard standards, Bligh's "thin-skinned vanity" would not tolerate the slightest disobedience or questioning. Insult his men he did, with a tongue that cut far more cruelly than the lash.

An example is the pumpkin incident described in Morrison's journal. When the crew refused to accept spoiled pumpkins as a substitute for their daily ration of bread, Bligh's reaction was not only rage, but vindictiveness as well: "You damn'd infernal scoundrels; I'll make you eat grass or anything you can catch before I have done with you."

Even more crucial was the episode of the coconuts, recorded by Morrison on the eve of the mutiny (and related in Chapter 7 of this book): a single eruption of Bligh's temper, which, perhaps more than any other single incident, stands as an explanation if not an excuse for Christian's mutiny.[4]

Bligh's ability to command in situations that demanded the best of courage and leadership was unparalleled. In the *Bounty*'s 16-month voyage to Tahiti, through the winter weather of the North Atlantic, the terrible storms of Cape Horn, and the long, gale-driven passage across the Indian Ocean, only one ship's spar was lost and only one man died. Later, when Bligh was deprived of his ship and set adrift with 18 men in an open boat, he sailed that boat across thousands of miles of uncharted waters—again, with the loss of only one man. The voyage was an ordeal of survival that succeeded only through his sheer determination and skill. Pushed to his limits by challenge, danger, and hardship, Bligh more than equaled his mentor, Cook. In the tedium of mundane shipboard life he reverted to the quarrelsome, acid-tongued, petty tyrant of Morrison's description.

Perhaps Bligh was his own severest critic, driven by the compulsion to prove to himself, over and over again, that he was qualified to command, that indeed he was no ordinary commander but a man who could claim himself successor to the great Cook. Such a man needed the backdrop of epic events for his relentless self-testing, for the proof and recognition of his ability to command. When events were removed from the large scale of wind, storm, and heroic challenge, a frustrated Bligh wasted his abilities in petty squabbles, yielding to the gnawing need to reaffirm the authority of his command.

The sea itself, with all its demons of adversity, was Bligh's great self-chosen crucible. By the sea and his conquest of it he wished to be judged, not by the measure of his fellow man. Stepping beyond human boundaries and judgments, Bligh—a tragic hero like Captain Ahab pursuing the white whale—went too far and lost all.

For all his bluff and posturing, however, Bligh was also a very mortal man of flesh and human sentiment. To round out our picture of a complex, enigmatic commander, here is a love letter written to his wife years after the mutiny, when he had been married 20 years and had fathered six daughters:

My Dearest Love . . . I shall be in constant flutter & expectation until I hear from you. I always pray for your health & happiness. May this letter give you every comfort & joy. Bless My Dear Harriet, My Dear Mary, My dear Betsy, My Dear Fanny & Jenny & my Dear Duck. No creature can be so happy as I am at being so near you & the hope of seeing you soon. I ever am, my Dear Betsy, Your affectionate William Bligh.[5]

2

THE *BOUNTY* AND HER MEN

Had its mission been successful, the *Bounty* would have carried out the first British commercial voyage to the Pacific Ocean. The objective was to transplant breadfruit trees from Tahiti to the British West Indies, where it was thought that the introduced plant could provide a source of cheap, nutritional food for slave labor. The American food supplies that had fed plantation slaves had been halted by the Revolutionary War, and thousands of workers had died from malnutrition-related diseases.

Cook had returned from his Pacific voyages with glowing reports of the large, starchy fruit of the breadfruit tree, which was a major food source for the Tahitian people. Describing the wonders of the plant, he wrote:

" . . . If a man plants ten of them in his lifetime, which he may do in an hour, he will as completely fulfill his duty to his own and future generations as the native in our less temperate climate can do by ploughing in the cold winter, and reaping in the summer's heat. . . .

"And from this we may observe, that the inhabitant of Otaheite [Tahiti], instead of being obliged to plant his bread, will *rather* be under the necessity of preventing its progress. . . ."[6]

Hoping that the breadfruit tree would eliminate their dependence on imported food, plantation representatives petitioned King George III to support an expedition that would transplant the exotic trees. The petition was accepted, and Joseph Banks (by this time Sir Joseph Banks, president of the Royal Society) was given responsibility for the planning and organization of the voyage.

Banks, you recall, had sailed on Cook's first Pacific voyage, and he had personally paid the expenses of the naturalists and artists who accompanied that important expedition. Although he had

The breadfruit tree

16

not sailed with Cook again, he was familiar with the details of the second and third voyages. In particular, he knew that a young man by the name of William Bligh had ably served Cook as sailing master, navigator, and cartographer. Bligh, having been forced ashore at half pay by peacetime naval personnel reductions, had taken a post as master of the merchantship *Britannia,* owned by the prominent West Indies merchant Duncan Campbell, an associate of Banks. Banks recommended that the 33-year-old Bligh be appointed commander of the impending voyage.

Meanwhile, the Royal Navy had purchased the merchantship *Bethia,* and under Banks's supervision it was outfitted for its new mission at Deptford Dock on the Thames River. What was done to the rather small *Bethia* (215 tons; length on deck, 91 feet) at Deptford Dock might have, unwittingly, started the chain of events that would make the renamed vessel, H. M. S. *Bounty,* one of the most famous ships in maritime history.

The ship was converted from a cargo vessel to a floating greenhouse designed to contain and transport over a thousand potted plants, along with the crew and supplies necessary for a two-year voyage.

First consideration was given to the survival of the breadfruit plants. All the interior space from the stern cabin forward to the quarterdeck companionway was appropriated for their storage. A lead-covered deck beneath the rows of pots formed a drainage system, allowing the fresh water used for watering the plants to be recovered. Large gratings and skylights were opened in the deck for ventilation and sunlight. With this layout, the living accommodations aboard the ship were substantially reduced.

Thus, the voyage of the *Bounty* began with the handicap of a reduced crew. The ship would sail with only one commissioned

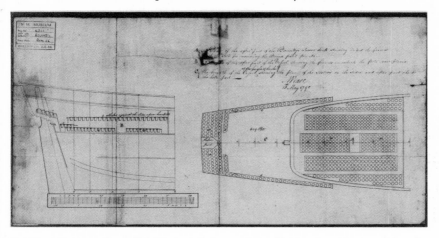

Profile and plan views of the Bounty's *lower deck, showing how the potted breadfruit plants were to be stowed*

18

officer, its captain. In addition, it would sail without the Royal Marines, men normally carried aboard to support the solitary authority of the captain's decisions. With its reduced crew, the *Bounty* did not warrant the command of a full-ranked captain. To his disappointment, Bligh commanded with the rank of lieutenant.

To cut yet another man from the crew, Bligh was assigned the additional duties of purser. It was a bad marriage of duties. The ship's commander was responsible for the health and welfare of the crew. The purser's first duty was to account to the navy for the food and supplies consumed by that ship's crew. The rancor over the cheese incident, described ahead, illustrates the problems inherent for Bligh in his combined role. This dual assignment was to add one more note of discord to the volatile subject of food, which was to provoke so much trouble aboard the *Bounty*.

These decisions and alterations had been made in Bligh's absence. He arrived with the *Britannia* on July 31, 1787, and on August 16 he was appointed commander of the *Bounty*, receiving a first lieutenant's commission after 17 years of naval service. James Cook had been 39, with 13 years of naval experience, when he assumed his first command.

Sailing under Bligh in the *Britannia* was Fletcher Christian, age 22. He had joined the navy as a midshipman, and, like Bligh, had been forced ashore by the peacetime manpower reductions. Through family connections he looked for a new post, and that

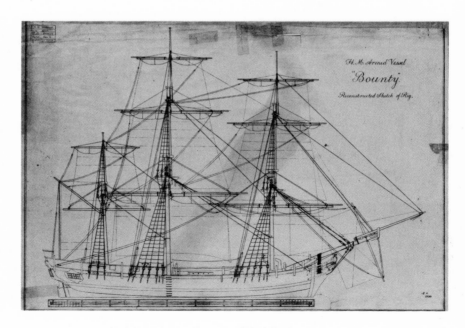

The Bounty's *rig as modified for her voyage*

search led him to Bligh, who appointed him *Britannia*'s second mate. Such linkage was a part of the traditional system called "interest," in which friendship, family, and patronage were the doorways to career advancement. Bligh had received his command of the *Britannia* through Duncan Campbell (his wife's uncle) and his command of the *Bounty* through Banks. By the same processes, Christian was presented to Bligh and their destinies linked.

In the journals of Bligh and Morrison, very little is revealed about the character of Fletcher Christian. He stands completely shadowed by his blustery commander, his name infrequently mentioned, his actions and conduct only rarely referred to. Christian himself kept no journal, wrote no letter. Thus, his character has to be assembled from scant biographical data, the limited observations of others, and speculation.

He came from a Cumberland family of landowners and lawyers; thus he came to Bligh from a gentleman's educated background. A younger classmate of his at the grammar school he attended for eight years was the future poet William Wordsworth. His elder brother Edward was a barrister, and the family's ambitions for Fletcher lay in that direction. But law did not appeal to young Christian. Instead, in what may have been a rather romantic inclination, he went to sea. Probably he came to Bligh less hardened to rough and sometimes arbitrary naval discipline than sailors of greater experience and less fortunate origins.

Something in Christian's character or ability must have appealed to Bligh. In addition to accepting him as second mate on *Britannia,* he chose him as master's mate on the *Bounty* and then jumped him to the position of acting lieutenant and second in command.

It is not difficult to imagine in Christian a compelling urge to escape his elder brother's shadow. Perhaps going to sea was for him an attractive solution to a younger sibling's age-old problem: how to end an unwanted competition and begin instead to define one's intrinsic worth in a self-chosen arena. It was Christian's misfortune that his escape landed him as junior officer under the talented and formidable Bligh. Why did Christian follow Bligh from the *Britannia* to the *Bounty?* The obvious answer would be to further his naval career at a time when naval posts were difficult to obtain. And perhaps Bligh the temporary commander of a merchantship was a different captain from Bligh the career naval officer in command of the *Bounty.* In his *Life of Captain James Cook,* J.C. Beaglehole contrasts conditions in the navy with those in the merchant service in the mid 18th century: "The navy was a different matter. Its physical conditions were worse; its pay was worse; its food was worse, its discipline was harsh, its record of sickness ap-

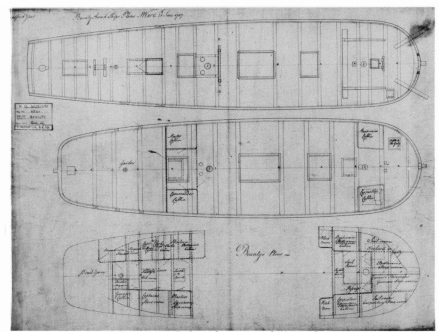

The Bounty's *deck and accommodations plans*

palling. . . . Officers entered the navy voluntarily, from higher social classes, to make a career; but it was commonly thought in the
profession that they should not enter later than their early adoles-
cence, to be inured to its rigours soon enough for other modes of
life to be deprived of attraction."

Perhaps, too, Christian both shrank from and needed the guid-
ance of men stronger than himself. His career was molded out-
wardly by others who—as elder brother or father figure—could
give course and shape to his life. Not a leader himself, he was de-
pendent on leadership from others, and relied heavily on their
praise and support. When support turned to acerbic criticism, he
crumbled. Cast—largely by accident—as leader of a mutiny, his
leadership disintegrated in a bloody trail of death and violence
that dogged him across the Pacific, concluding with his own murder on the lonely island that had been his prison and became his
grave.

Forty-six men—including Bligh and Christian—sailed with the
Bounty on October 4, 1787, when it cleared Deptford for the run
down channel to an anchorage at Spithead, off Portsmouth. All
members of the crew sailed as volunteers, as distinct from the
"pressed men" who were sometimes forced into service by the
Royal Navy. Perhaps it was for this reason that the Admiralty felt

the usual shipboard contingent of marines was unnecessary. All members of the crew had been personally approved by Bligh with the exception of David Nelson and William Brown, who had been selected by Banks as botanist and botanist's assistant. Nelson had sailed on Cook's third voyage, and Peckover, the gunner, had sailed on all three. The old sailmaker, Lawrence Lebogue, and Able-bodied Seaman Thomas Ellison had sailed with Bligh in the West Indies merchant trade. Others among the ship's junior officers lacked experience, and the majority of the men aboard were under 30. Peter Heywood's family were close friends of Bligh's in-laws, the Bethams. Bligh had met George Stewart's family several years before. John Hallett was the brother of a friend of Mrs. Bligh. Able-bodied Seaman Robert Tinkler was John Fryer's brother-in-law. Thus, the world of a ship, with its divisions of rank, skill, social class, status, and age—a microcosm of late 18th century England—took form around its mission.

That world, the life of a ship, writes N.A.M. Rogers, " . . . can only be understood in relation to these overlapping patterns. In their dealing with one another, in tension and accommodation, in fear and affection, in persuasion and command, men acted within the constraints imposed by the complex internal structure of shipboard society."[7] The men of this world were, by job description and name, the following (for a more detailed description of what these jobs entailed, see Appendix 1):

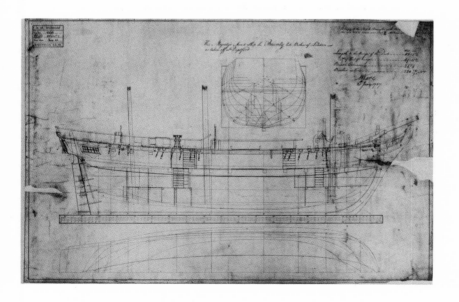

Lines and profile plans for His Majesty's Armed Vessel Bounty

COMMANDER	WILLIAM BLIGH
MASTER	JOHN FRYER
BOATSWAIN	WILLIAM COLE
GUNNER	WILLIAM PECKOVER
CARPENTER	WILLIAM PURCELL
SURGEON	JOHN HUGGAN
SURGEON'S MATE	THOMAS LEDWARD
MASTER'S MATE	FLETCHER CHRISTIAN
MASTER'S MATE	WILLIAM ELPHINSTONE
MIDSHIPMAN	THOMAS HAYWARD
MIDSHIPMAN	JOHN HALLETT
ACTING MIDSHIPMAN	GEORGE STEWART
ACTING MIDSHIPMAN	PETER HEYWOOD
ACTING MIDSHIPMAN	EDWARD YOUNG
QUARTERMASTER	PETER LINKLETTER
QUARTERMASTER	JOHN NORTON
QUARTERMASTER'S MATE	GEORGE SIMPSON
BOATSWAIN'S MATE	JAMES MORRISON
GUNNER'S MATE	JOHN MILLS
CARPENTER'S MATE	CHARLES NORMAN
CARPENTER'S CREW	THOMAS MCINTOSH
SAILMAKER	LAWRENCE LEBOGUE
ARMOURER	JOSEPH COLEMAN
MASTER-AT-ARMS	CHARLES CHURCHILL
CLERK-STEWARD	JOHN SAMUEL
BOTANIST	DAVID NELSON
BOTANIST'S ASSISTANT	WILLIAM BROWN

ABLE-BODIED SEAMEN: Thomas Burkett, Michael Byrne, Thomas Ellison, Thomas Hall (ship's cook), Henry Hillbrant (served also as ship's cooper), Robert Lamb, Isaac Martin, William McCoy, John Millward, William Muspratt, Matthew Quintal, Richard Skinner, Alexander Smith, John Smith, John Sumner, Robert Tinkler, Matthew Thompson, James Valentine, and John Williams.

For some of those men, the retreating coastline they would leave behind on the gray, December day of the *Bounty*'s departure was the last they would ever see of England. Others would see it again in chains.

3

OUTWARD BOUND

October 4, 1787–March 18, 1788

While his first naval command, H.M.S. *Bounty,* lay at the Deptford Dock undergoing reconstruction of her interior arrangements, Bligh prepared her for the long, stormy voyage ahead. He ordered the masts shortened so that she would be more seaworthy. He also thought the ship overballasted for storm sailing, and reduced the ballast weight from 45 to 19 tons. Her underbody was sheathed with copper to protect her from the marine borers and fouling organisms of tropical waters.

The alterations were time-consuming and, to Bligh, a growing source of anxiety as it had been decided that he should take the most direct sailing route to Tahiti, which would call for a late-season passage around Cape Horn. Finally, on October 4, the ship moved downriver to the navy's supply docks, where it took on provisions. With his ship now ready for sea, Bligh was ordered to sail to Spithead (off the harbor of Portsmouth), there to receive his final orders. Wind and weather were against the *Bounty* as she sailed down the English Channel, and Bligh was not able to reach Spithead until November 4.

"I think I cannot have much worse weather in going round Cape Horn," he wrote in a letter to Sir Joseph Banks, "and it is with pleasure I tell you I think the ship very capable."[8]

Further frustrating delays followed before Bligh was given his final orders on November 24. They read in part: "You are directed to put to sea in the vessel you command, the first favorable opportunity of wind and weather, and proceed with her as expeditiously as possible round Cape Horn to the Society Islands . . . where, according to the accounts given by the late Capt. Cook, and persons who accompanied him during his voyages, the bread-fruit is to be found in the most luxuriant state."[9]

Bligh immediately requested that he be given discretional orders on the Cape Horn route because of the lateness of the season. Weeks passed with no response. To Duncan Campbell he wrote:

If there is any punishment that ought to be inflicted on a set of Men for neglect, I am sure it ought on the Admiralty for my three weeks' detention at this place during a fine fair wind which carried all outward bound ships clear of the Channel but me, who wanted it most. This has made my task a very arduous one indeed for to get round Cape Horn at the time I shall be there. I know not how to promise myself any success & yet I must do it if the ship will stand it at all or I suppose my character will be at stake. Had Lord Home sweetned this difficult task by giving me promotion I should have been satisfied.[10]

Finally, on December 18, his request was granted in a reply which read:

"The season of the year being now so far advanced as to render it probable, that your arrival, with the vessel you command, on the southern coast of America, will be too late for your passing round Cape Horn without much difficulty and hazard; you are *in that case,* at liberty (notwithstanding former orders) to proceed in her to Otaheite, round the Cape of Good Hope."[11]

Clearly the Admiralty intended that Bligh first make his best attempt at the shorter Cape Horn route, altering his route only if conditions proved impossible. Bligh attempted to sail immediately, but contrary winds again caused delays, and it was not until December 23 that he was able to make this log entry:

At 4 A.M. hove Short [on the anchor] & got up Yards and Topmasts and at ½ past 6 Weighed and lay too untill day light. Then I made Sail. . . .

The voyage of the *Bounty* had begun. On board were stores and supplies for 18 months, trinkets and trading items for the purchase of the breadfruit trees, and knives, nails, hatchets, and other items. The ship was armed with four 4-pound guns and 10 half-pound swivel guns. On deck was stowed a 23-foot launch, an 18-foot cutter, and the jolly boat, a third ship's boat.

On December 24 Bligh worked clear of the land, but the ship was hit by a gale. The log described this stormy Christmas Eve spent in misery and danger:

Squally with Sleet, One of the People in furling the Main Top sail fell Over & was saved by Catching hold of the Main Mast Stay by Which he came down not at all hurt . . . a Very heavy Sea Struck on the Larboard Quarter & carried away a Sweep and Spritsail Topsail Yard. . . . Some of the bread has got damaged. . . . Ordered all Wet Cloaths to be taken by the Fire to dry.

On Christmas Day the storm moderated, and the crew was served an extra allowance of rum and a beef and plum pudding for dinner. On the 27th:

Very hard Gales and high Sea with Severe Squalls. . . . A Storm of Wind with most Violent Squalls. . . . Shiped a very heavy Sea which broke the foremast Chock of the Boats to peices and Stove all the Boats that it was with the utmost difficulty and Risk that they were saved from being Washed Overboard. . . . A Sea Struck us in the Stern and Stove it all to peices between the Cabbin Windows . . . with difficulty the Time Keeper & my Instruments were saved. One Azimth [azimuth] Compass was broke all to peices. The gale encreased with such fury on us that I could not with any safety attempt to bring the Ship too, and therefore anxiously waited for a few Minutes abatement of the Gale to accomplish it, which as it did not take place we had no alternative but to keep before the Sea. The Situation in the Morning was of a very serious Nature, but fortunately no sea Struck us while we were repairing the damage, which was owing to a want of firmness in the Joiners Work in the Middle part of the Stern opposite the Coating of the Rudder. . . . Our Bread [ship's biscuit, or hardtack] I apprehend is much damaged altho we used our Utmost to clear the Water out of the Cabbin; but so much was in it, that it required some time to carry it clear off. . . . The great hardship in small Ships such Weather as this is that we cannot light a fire to dress Victuals, and which has been our Case today. I therefore Ordered Grog to the People in addition to their Beer to make up for their Wet uncomfortable Situation.

The storm destroyed a large quantity of the ship's bread and carried away seven casks of beer that had been lashed on deck. When the weather moderated, the boats were repaired, fires were lit, and two men from each watch were assigned to drying clothes and bedding. All hands were employed in breaking and drying spoiled bread to save what they could of their food. A cask of cheese was found to be rotten, and shortages were discovered when a cask each of beef and pork were opened. Such problems as spoiled food and shorted supplies were endemic to the naval supply system of Bligh's time. Food contractors ashore consistently supplied ships with less than the agreed upon qualities and quantities, thereby enriching their own pockets at the expense of the crews.

The high peak of Tenerife in the Canary Islands was sighted on January 5 of the new year, 1788. The next day the ship came to anchor in the harbor of Santa Cruz, where work was immediately begun to repair the damage done by the storms.

During the four-day layover at Santa Cruz, Bligh—the constant surveyor and observer—logged a description of the harbor, the conditions of the anchorage and the landing beaches, the island's industries, its climate and diseases, and the prices of agricultural products. He sent his botanist inland "to range the hills and examine the country in search of plants and natural curiosities."

From Tenerife, he wrote to Duncan Campbell, saying:

> . . . I have the happiness to tell you my little ship does wonderfully well. . . . I have her now the completest ship I believe that ever swam, and she really looks like one fit to encounter difficulties, and is looked at as such, knowing our voyage. . . . My men are all well and cheerful and . . . behave very well.[12]

A small quantity of beef and some potatoes and pumpkins, along with fresh water and 863 gallons of wine, were loaded aboard the ship at Santa Cruz. It would seem that such an amount of wine, enough to supply each man in the crew with 19 gallons, was excessive. It was not. Wine and beer were taken aboard because they kept better than plain water, which quickly went bad in wooden casks. On January 10, the *Bounty* set sail and headed south on what Bligh hoped would be a nonstop run down and across the Atlantic, around Cape Horn, and then across the Pacific to Tahiti.

A day out of Santa Cruz, Bligh put the crew on the three-watch system pioneered by Cook instead of the customary "four on, four off." Wrote Bligh:

> I have ever considered this among Seamen as Conducive to health, and not being Jaded by keeping on Deck every other four hours, it adds much to their Content and Chearfulness. Sometime for relaxation and Mirth is absolutely necessary, and I have considered it so much so that after 4 O'Clock, the Evening is laid aside for their Amusement and dancing. I had great difficulty before I left England to get a Man to play the Violin and I prefered at last to take one two thirds Blind than come without one. [The blind fiddler was Able-bodied Seaman Michael Byrne.]

After cutting the crew's workload by one-third, he made an equal one-third cut in their daily bread ration. This seemingly contradictory action was perfectly logical to Bligh. The long voyage had only begun. A late season attempt at rounding Cape Horn was a foreboding event. Bligh considered the conservation of all his resources—manpower, food, and equipment—essential for survival in the weeks ahead.

Sultry calms, light and variable winds, and rain were encountered as the *Bounty* sailed south toward the equator. All empty water casks were filled with rainwater. The continual dampness caused everything to mildew, and Bligh ordered the ship to be aired and cleaned daily. Fires were lit below deck, and the ship was washed in vinegar. During every interval of dry weather, the hatches were opened and clothing was washed and dried. Cleanliness, rest, and a reasonably balanced diet: these were the conditions Bligh insisted on maintaining in his ship. In his log entry for January 11 he congratulated himself on his efforts:

. . . Few Seamen & Officers I may venture to Say can ever boast of more Comforts at Sea.

Bligh's log paints a picture of the *Bounty* as a tidy, contented ship with basic human needs well attended to and even a fiddler to dance to during the evening watch. But Morrison's journal gives a somewhat different version. Two incidents, both food-related, recorded in Morrison's entry for January 1788, mar the otherwise idyllic portrait of shipboard life.

When a cask of cheese was opened, two cheeses were found missing. Bligh, said Morrison, declared that they had been stolen, but " . . . the Cooper [Henry Hillbrant] declared that the Cask had been opened before . . . and the Cheeses sent to Mr. Bligh's house."

The incident was a clear manifestation that Bligh's double role as commander and purser entailed incompatible obligations. Crew complaints about food allotments were usually lodged against the purser. The purser was responsible for the purchase of all food supplies, and it was generally assumed that he was more interested in filling his pockets with the profits of shady deals and shorted allotments than the stomachs of men with food. But what was expected behavior from a purser was not from a captain, and no member of the crew would have thought much of a captain making off with a cheese for his own and privileged use. Here, apparently, was Bligh the purser catching Bligh the commander in an act of theft. He covered the incident with bluff and bluster and, according to Morrison, ordered the cheese allowance to the men cut until the deficiency was made up. Then, continued Morrison, he told the cooper that he " . . . would give him a dam'd good flogging If He said any More about it." The reduction in cheese allowance, according to Morrison, was promptly effected by Mr. Samuel.

The second event, alluded to in Chapter 1, concerned the pumpkins that had been purchased at Santa Cruz. As the ship approached the heat of the equator, the pumpkins began to spoil. Bligh ordered that they be served to the crew in lieu of bread. The crew refused the exchange offered of one pound of pumpkin for two pounds of bread. On being informed of the crew's decision, Bligh exploded: "You dam'd Infernal scoundrels, I'll make you eat Grass or any thing you can catch before I have done with you." According to Morrison, Bligh told the crew that " . . . every thing relative to the provisions was transacted by His Orders, and it was therefore Needless to make any Complaint for they would get no redress, as he was the fittest Judge of what was right or wrong," and that "He would flog the first Man severely who should dare attempt to make any Complaint in future and dismissed them with severe threats."

Bligh probably felt justified in enforcing what in the navy was referred to as a "table of equivalents." Seamen objected to any change in their fare, but changes were sometimes necessary. To minimize the impact, departures from the usual allotments were expected to follow the table of equivalents (two pounds of potatoes or yams in place of one pound of bread, for example). Apparently in this instance the crew considered their captain and purser's idea of equivalency mistaken. Morrison wrote that the officers were subjected to the exchange as well, and "felt it more severely, than the Men, who had, previous to the sailing of the Ship from Spithead, laid in large quantities of potatoes which were not yet expended."

Nearly a month out of Santa Cruz the *Bounty* picked up the southeast trade wind, and she crossed the equator February 8 with all sails set. The traditional rough ceremony for those who had never crossed the line was observed—except, wrote Bligh, for ducking, " . . . which I never would allow for of all the Customs it is the most brutal and inhuman. Twenty Seven Men & Officers were therefore Tarred & Shaved with a peice of Iron Hoop, And the Officers to pay two Bottles of Rum & the Men One, which I promised to Answer for, and gave every One a half pint of Wine as soon as the Business was over, & dancing begun."

The voyage continued south, and the ship, hundreds of miles from land, existed within the unchanging routine of duty watch, sleeping, and eating. The heat increased, and awnings were strung overhead as the crew made up chafing mats and reef points out of old rope. Every day, Bligh's unrelenting program of sanitation was enforced: a rigid routine of airing the ship and scrubbing below decks with vinegar and water. The log dwells on these small details of the passage:

Empd [employed] making Matts & Points & Clean'g below. Served Sour Krout to the People & boiled some Pease which will be continued Constantly. Very Fine Wr [weather] & Clear. No Birds or Fish. Fore Topmt Steer'g Sail set and Ship kept 7 points off the Wind.

Scrubbed & Cleaned all Hammocks & bedding. Washed & dryed all Officers Cabbins and every part below.

On February 17 the *Bounty* came up with the ship *British Queen*, and Bligh passed his letters over to that ship to be carried back to England. In one of these letters, addressed to Duncan Campbell, he wrote:

We are all in good spirits and my little ship fit to go round a half-score of worlds. My men all active good fellows, and what has given me much pleasure is that I have not yet been obliged to punish any one. My officers and young gentlemen [the midshipmen] are all tractable and well disposed, and we now understand each other so well that we shall remain so the whole voyage, unless I fall out with the doctor [John Huggan], who I have trouble to prevent from being in bed fifteen hours out of the twenty-four.[13]

On Sunday, March 2, after all hands were mustered for divine services, Fletcher Christian was formally appointed as lieutenant, thus making him second in command of the *Bounty*. Said Bligh:

I now thought it for the Good of the Service to give Mr. Fletcher Christian an Acting Order as Lieut. I therefore ordered it to be ready by all hands.

The appointment apparently did not seem out of line to Morrison, who made no comment on the matter. Christian thus became a lieutenant, though only an acting one. Bligh could not grant him a commission; that would await Admiralty review at the completion of the expedition. The immediate practical effect of the appointment was that Christian would command the third watch, releasing the master and the gunner from the necessity of alternating watches.

The ship was approaching the unseen coast of Brazil, and Bligh ordered soundings to begin. No bottom was found at 240 fathoms.

Soundings were found in 83 fathoms off the coast of Patagonia on March 10. On this same day, for the first time on the voyage, a seaman was punished. Commented Bligh:

Untill this Afternoon I had hopes I could have performed the Voyage without punishment to any One, but I found it necessary to punish Matthew Quintal with 2 dozen lashes for Insolence and Contempt.

The flogging of a man—a repugnantly brutal act to our age—was not only a common punishment in the Royal Navy of the 18th century, it was often the only form of punishment available to a commanding officer. The various laws which officers were expected to enforce and men were expected to obey were laid out in a compendium of customs and regulations known as the Articles of War. For many crimes, the specified punishment was death. The articles did not specify appropriate punishment for lesser infractions such as Quintal's "Insolence and Contempt."

"A flogging," says N. A. M. Rogers in his book *The Wooden World, an Anatomy of the Georgian Navy,* "was itself too severe and formal a punishment for many everyday offences, but a captain had no instructions as to how else he might deal with them." For incompetence or insubordination, he points out, a petty officer could be reduced in rank, but there was no way to "disrate" the lowly seaman.

Rogers does not defend flogging, but he does give perspective to the entire issue of naval discipline and punishment. The term "discipline" meant training, the condition of a crew that made its members capable or incapable of handling duties and responsibilities. It was not a code of behavior imposed by authority. Discipline " . . . was something inherent in the nature of seafaring, and common to all ships and seamen everywhere. It owed almost nothing to the authority of officers, and almost everything to the collective understanding of seamen. A ship at sea under sail depended utterly on disciplined teamwork, and any seaman knew without thinking that at sea orders had to be obeyed for the safety of all. This was not a matter of unquestioning obedience but of intelligent cooperation in survival.

"The clear impression given by the admittedly vague descriptions of offences in ships' logs is that they were chiefly the sort of antisocial behaviour which made life more unpleasant, more arduous or more dangerous than it need have been, and they were generally punished only at sea, where there was a real functional need of discipline. The fact was that living, and still more sailing, in the crowded and dangerous environment of a ship required a high degree of self-discipline, and those who had not learnt it, or would not learn, were a burden on their shipmates. In this, as in other aspects, discipline in the Navy appears on examination to have been largely an organic response to the nature of life at sea, overlaid with a ramshackle legal structure, and not an attempt to sustain an artificial authority by force."[14]

Disobedience was simply dangerous. Obedience through discipline (training and efficiency) was a matter of individual necessity for the survival of all. The duty of the officers was to impose it, the duty of the crew was to accept it. For both parties, the concept of obedience and discipline rested on unstated consent, not on force supported by licensed brutality.

There were, of course, many instances in which ship captains did exceed these standards through cruel, capricious, and arbitrary treatment. Such treatment broke the essential and orderly

Flogging Matthew Quintal, March 10, 1788

bonds of mutual consent and safety. These men—incompetent and sometimes even deranged—commanded disorderly and dangerous ships.

Contrary to legend, Bligh was not one of these. In fact, a case can be made, as the later narrative seems to bear out, that he was too lenient. That he used the lash not too much, but too little. Leadership required that some men—like Quintal—had to bleed. Behind Bligh's quickness to impose verbal lashings might have been an aversion to the price of discipline: punishment that drew blood.

4

TURNED BACK BY THE HORN
March 18–April 22, 1788

Cape Horn is an island that stands at the stormy junction of the Pacific and Atlantic oceans. Located at the extreme southern tip of South America, the island is 1300 miles farther south than the Cape of Good Hope, its African counterpart. It is one of thousands of islands that make up the larger landmass of Tierra del Fuego, a steep-sided, snow-capped archipelago separated from the South American mainland by the Strait of Magellan.

The waters around the Horn lie squarely within the belt of prevailing westerly winds known as the "Roaring Forties." Air that subsides in the high-pressure regions of the horse latitudes, a broad band centered at about 35° south, then flows toward lower-pressure regions to the south and is deflected eastward by the earth's rotation. With no landmasses as obstacles, the prevailing westerlies rule unopposed over the cold and inhospitable Southern Ocean. The winds commonly blow between 18 and 30 knots throughout the year, but in the southern winter they are frequently much stronger. The seas they generate march around the bottom of the world in an unlimited fetch, often reaching terrifying proportions.

In 1520, Ferdinand Magellan sailed the first ship from the Atlantic to the Pacific through the protected strait between South America and Tierra del Fuego that now bears his name. Francis Drake made the second passage in 1578, also through the Strait of Magellan. Until William Schouten sailed around Cape Horn in 1616, it was believed that South America was joined to the South Pole by land. His ship, the *Hoorn,* gave the cape its name.

In the third awful week of the *Bounty*'s attempt to round the Horn, Bligh compared the conditions he was encountering with those experienced by British Captain George Anson. Nearly 50 years had passed since Anson's fleet of seven ships had mounted its assault on the Horn. For two months they fought the storms of the cape, suffering every kind of disaster a vengeful sea can deliver and every kind of shipboard sickness, accident, and death. Two of Anson's ships were blown back into the Atlantic and ran for home. One was wrecked. The remaining four made it around the Horn, but at a terrible cost in human life. The *Centurion* alone, Anson's flagship, lost 300 men, almost all to scurvy.

By March 18 the *Bounty* was approaching Cabo Blanco off the Patagonian coast, 600 miles north of Cape Horn. The tropical climate had been left astern, and the ship approached the coast through gales and fog. At night, off the unseen coast, soundings were taken at half-hourly intervals in a complicated, time-consuming process that involved slowing the ship so the leadline could be dropped. Bottom was usually recorded at depths of around 300 feet.

A few days later, off the entrance to the Strait of Magellan, the first of the Cape Horn gales struck the ship, and the *Bounty*'s battle with Cape Horn began. The gale was " . . . so quick upon us," wrote Bligh, "that we had scarce time to secure our Sails, the Wind also was very violent and the Sea in the Course of a few hours became breaking and very troublesome to us. . . . The Gale encreased with much violence and continued so the whole Night with an exceeding high Sea. . . . The Air is now become very Sharp, and some of my people begin to feel rheumatic pains. . . ."

This was Bligh's first attempt to round Cape Horn. With Cook, aboard the *Resolution,* he had traveled around the Cape of Good Hope on both the outward and return voyages. Bligh's intended westward course confronted head-on the prevailing westerly winds.

Bligh was aware of what awaited him at the Horn and was as prepared as possible for the contest. His preparations had begun while still docked at the Deptford yard, when he had shortened the *Bounty*'s rig. Down the long track of the Atlantic he had carefully maintained his ship and had husbanded his critical resources of human health and energy. No finer seaman ever challenged Cape Horn. Optimistically, he confronted the first gale and, as he wrote, " . . . being prepared we cared little about it. . . ."

On the morning of March 23, autumn in those southern latitudes, a dog and a goat aboard the ship gave warning of nearby land by reacting to its offshore smell . . . Tierra del Fuego. Bligh set his course for Le Maire Strait, which separates the high peaks of Staten Island from the southeasterly tip of Tierra del Fuego. Headwinds met him, however, as he started toward the strait, and forced him to alter course eastward and around the outside of

Staten Island. The island was rounded in a gale of snow, with the sails triple reefed, and the ship was kept well offshore to avoid the strong, opposing Cape Horn currents. The log records the next several days and nights spent struggling against unremitting winds and seas:

It blew a Storm of Wind and the Snow fell so heavy that it was scarce possible to haul the sails. . . . the Storm exceeded anything I had met with and a Sea higher than I had ever seen before. . . . The ship falling heavy to windward, the Sea become so very high, and the Weather side of it like a Wall.

The air temperature dropped into the thirties, while the rain, snow, and fog continued. Bligh ordered fires to be kept constantly burning so the men could dry their clothes. The heavy smoke be-

low decks caused many men to become sick. With the ship burying its bow in water, Bligh relinquished his own cabin " . . . to the use of those poor fellows who had Wet Births [sic] . . . ."

It was not much of a cabin to give up, barely a closet with a berth. Still, it was the captain's cabin, a place private and sacrosanct. Bligh did not allow the privileges of command to stand above the more urgent needs of his crew.

By the third week crew injuries were beginning to mount. The gales grew even more violent—so severe, wrote Bligh, "that I dare scarce show any Canvas to it. The motion of the Ship is so very quick and falls so deep between Seas that it is impossible to stand without man ropes across the Decks. . . . We are obliged to pump Ship every hour. . . . Men who were obliged to be aloft felt the Snow Squalls so severe as to render them almost incapable of getting below, and some of them sometimes for a While lost their Speech." Bligh himself had to be lashed to the mast in order to take his observations.

These men were locked in the battle of human flesh and a wooden ship against the elements of wind and sea. They bore it well, and, wrote Morrison, "thought Nothing of Hardship and Notwithstanding fatigue and increasing bad weather they Carried on their duty with alacrity and Cheerfulness; anticipating the Pleasure and profit[15] they hoped to reap by the success of the Voyage."

Morrison's journal then gives this vivid account of the *Bounty* and its men during their Cape Horn encounter:

"Wheat & Barly were now boild evry Morning for breakfast, . . . but of this the quantity was so small that it was no uncommon thing for four Men in a Mess to draw lots for the Breakfast, and to devide their bread by the well known Method of 'Who shall have this'.[16]

"The quantity of Wheat boild was one Gallon for 46 Men, of which they all partook, and of Barley two pounds for the like number—the division of this scanty allowance Caused frequent broils in the Gally, and in the present bad Weather was often like to be attended with bad Consequences and in one of these disputes the Cook Thos. Hall got two of His ribbs broken, & at a Nother time Churchill got his Hand Scalded and it became at last Necessary to have the Masters Mate of the Watch to superintend the division of it.

"The Weather Continued to grow Worse evry day, hail rain sleet & snow or rather large flakes of half formed Ice alternately following each other in heavy squalls, which often reduced us under bare poles & and battend Hatches, as the sea made fair breaches over us running in a Manner Unknown in Northern Climes frequently obscuring the sun when 20 degrees above the Horison, tossing the ship so violently that the people could not stand the deck without the assistance of a rope or something to hold by; at several times with this violent Motion and sudden Jerking Mr. Huggan the Surgeon was flung down the after ladder into the Cockpit and dislocated his shoulder, and a few days after Richd. Skinner Met with the same fate in the same place, and Peter Link-letter got a hurt in his back by being thrown down in the fore Cock pit, of which he always complain afterwards—Yet notwithstand-

A loose tarpaulin on the ship's launch

ing the severity and inclemency of the Season and the Continued Gales & repeated Squalls, which seemd to break with redoubled violence & threaten us every Moment with distruction such was the alacrity and carefulness of Officers & Men, that we never lost a spar, or a Yard of Canvas. . . .

"Sweet Wort [a hot infusion of barley used as an antiscorbutic] was Now Made from Malt, & a pint a Man served hot evry day, which was very acceptable & Nourishing in our present situation; but the intense cold, and being continually Wet, the hard duty & continual fatigue which the rigourous Season required, this and the uncomfortable situation of the Men between decks which were always filld with smoke while the Hatches were fast, soon began to lay hold of their constitutions & several fell sick. The straining of the ship tho perfectly sound, kept the hammocks always wet, which made them very uncomfortable, Not only for the Sick but for the Well.

"As the people began to fall sick the duty became heavyer on the Well but was still Carried on with alacrity & Spirit; and the behaviour of the Seamen, in this trying Situation, was such as Merrited the entire Approbation of the Officers, and Mr. Blighs thanks in a Publick speech.

"After a fatiguing, and innefectual tryal, it was found that the Passage round Cape Horn was not practicable at this season of the year, tho we had reach'd the 62nd deg: of South Lattitude & 79th of West Longitude;[17] yet we found that we lost ground [were blown back], and tho the Ship was an excellent Sea Boat, it was as much as she could do to live in this tremendous sea where the Elements seem to wage Continual War. . . . On the 18th of April Mr. Bligh ordered all hands aft and after returning them his thanks for their unremitted attention to their duty, informd them of his intention to bear away for the Cape of Good Hope; as it appear'd to him an Impossibility to get round Cape Horn. This was received with Universal Joy and returned according to Custom with three Cheers. . . ."

Yet it was not quite over, Morrison tells us, for after the ship had run nearly 120 miles to the east, the wind backed from the west more to the north, inducing Bligh to heave to on starboard tack and try again. "But these flattering appearances soon vanished . . . for it shifted again to the Wd. and blew with redoubled fury and we again bore away on the 22nd."

For a month, Bligh had tried to drive the *Bounty* westward around the Horn. Eight of his men had been injured and incapacitated. Reluctantly he concluded it "improper and even unjustifiable to persist any longer in a passage this way to the Society Islands."

The defeat for being driven back by the Horn he bore himself; the credit for trying so hard for so long, he gave to the crew. Under double-reefed sails, the *Bounty* turned eastward on a course that would carry it back across the Atlantic to a port of refuge at the Cape of Good Hope. Bligh had been beaten by the Horn, but it was a defeat in the kind of contest that seemed to bring out the best in the man. He and his skills had been pushed to the outer limits of human ability. By leadership and command he had held a ship and its company together where others before him had failed, losing neither a man nor a spar in the month-long battle with the winds of Cape Horn.

5

ACROSS THREE OCEANS
April 22–October 26, 1788

Bound for Cape Town

Gales, rain, and fog followed the *Bounty* on the long, dreary passage from Cape Horn to the Cape of Good Hope. It was a lonely voyage with only a few bird and whale sightings to break the tedious days of nearly continuous wet and cold weather. The invalids mended, and Bligh's rigorous program of ship cleaning was maintained in spite of the weather. The men were given all the "Sour Krout, Mustard & Vinegar" they could eat, their hot breakfast of boiled wheat, and plenty of "Sweet Wort." At frequent intervals all hands were turned out for dancing to the tune of the near-blind Irishman's fiddle.

Repairs were begun on the *Bounty* as soon as she arrived in Cape Town. Behind her was a voyage of some 15,000 miles through mostly stormy seas. Bligh encountered the captain of a Dutch ship, who reported that he had buried 30 men on a voyage considerably shorter than that of the *Bounty*.

With his outstanding health record, Bligh had earned the self-congratulatory comments he recorded in his remarks after arrival at Cape Town:

Perhaps a Voyage of five Months which I have now performed without touching at any one place but at Tenarif, has never been accomplished with so few accidents, and such health among Seamen in like continuance of bad Wr.

Then, in a letter of June 20 to Duncan Campbell, he reported on his failure to round Cape Horn, which he attributed to the frustrating delays that had postponed his departure from England.

"I do not repine," wrote Bligh, "but if the cruel inattention of the Admiralty had not detained me I should certainly have made my passage round the land. . . ."[18]

Upon arrival in Cape Town, Able-bodied Seaman John Williams was punished with six lashes "for neglect of duty in heaving the lead." Repairs then began on the ship; during the 38-day layover in Table Bay the *Bounty* was caulked and painted, and her rigging was overhauled. The work went slowly because of the wet and windy weather. Each day while at anchor, the crew was served fresh meat and vegetables.

Bligh took advantage of the five weeks in port to investigate the country and gather seeds and plants for later cultivation in Tahiti. In his journal observations he comments on the shore fortifications, the nature of the crops grown, and the deplorable conditions of the Cape Colony slaves.

The ship was reprovisioned with the following:

> 9,200 pounds of bread and biscuits
> 7,166 pounds of flour
> 34 gallons of oil
> 69 bushels of beans
> 776 gallons of wine
> 1,656 pounds of fresh meat
> 119 pounds of raisins
> 256 cabbages
> 256 bunches of greens
> 300 pounds of gun powder

Reprovisioning

On July 2 the *Bounty* departed, rounding the Cape of Good Hope to begin a winter passage eastward across the Indian Ocean. The longest leg of the voyage now lay ahead: 6,000 miles of open ocean between the Cape of Good Hope and Tasmania (called Van Dieman's Land at the time), the next landfall. In praise of his men, who had suffered the winter weather of both capes, Bligh wrote that they " . . . will be the only people that ever Navigated these Seas a whole Winter in such tempestuous Weather and with so few advantages."

The strong winds of the "Roaring Forties" carried the *Bounty* on a stormy, 49-day passage across the Indian Ocean. Bligh had previously made this passage in 1776–77 with Cook aboard the H. M. S. *Resolution,* but that voyage had been made in the calmer summer months. This time he was at sea in midwinter.

July 21: . . . [It] blew a most severe Storm, and before We could get the Sails in it drove us Fore Castle under. . . . Set the Fore Staysail and the Ship lay well too. Gave every Man a Dram and sent them below by a good fire.

The crew was constantly employed in setting the sails, reefing them, and setting them again as storm after storm and gale after gale blew the ship eastward.

August 5: Hard Gale and the Sea breaking frequently over us. . . . Covered the boats to prevent their filling with Water. The Sea flying over our Lower Yards.

August 14: Strong gale and high breaking Sea. Several heavy ones made way over us this Morning & Stove the Quarter Boards in."

Today we can only marvel at such a voyage—endless days and even more endless nights of cold, wet weather, watch in, watch out, wet deck to wet berth and back again, a routine that must have reduced mind and body to the barest functions of brute survival. And that survival depended upon the will and skill of one man, who, by any fault in action or decision, could have sent them all to a cold sea grave.

For Bligh, the cloudy, rainy days of this long passage made the taking of navigational sights very difficult. Nevertheless, he ran a remarkably true and direct course to the small off-lying Mewstone Rock at the southern tip of Tasmania—"perfectly," he wrote, "to my most sanguine expectation." Working to the eastward of Tasmania (believed at that time to be a part of Australia), the *Bounty* came to anchor August 21, 1788 in Adventure Bay, where Bligh had previously anchored with Cook. By Bligh's reckoning, he was 6,690 miles east of the Cape of Good Hope. Ship and crew were in remarkably good shape after this long voyage. Only one man had been injured, and the only equipment loss was one broken spar.

Crews were sent ashore to resupply the ship with wood and water. The surf in Adventure Bay, however, was so high that the boats had difficulty landing, and the wood had to be rafted out to the ship. Fishing and hunting were poor, but the crew cut bundles of grass for the shipboard livestock. Needing lumber for repairs, they dug a saw pit on the shore and set to work cutting planks.

During this layover Bligh confined the carpenter, William Purcell, to the ship for his "insolent and reprehensible Manner" while working ashore with the wood-gathering party. Bligh did not elaborate on the incident. Morrison did, with this somewhat prophetic comment: "Here also were sown seeds of eternal discord between Lieut. Bligh and some of his Officers."

Not only was the carpenter confined, said Morrison, but Bligh also "found fault with the innatention of the rest [of the officers],

The saw pit at Adventure Bay

to their duty, which produced continual disputes evry one endeavouring to thwart the others in their duty, this made the men exert themselves to divert the storm from falling on them by a strict attention to their duty and in this they formed their account and rejoyced in private at their good success."

It was not unusual for discipline to become lax while a ship was in port or at anchor; indeed, it was a constant problem for the British Admiralty, then and throughout the 19th century. The hard, demanding routines of sea were broken, together with the connecting link of an all-absorbing need to survive in the face of elemental and inhospitable forces. At Adventure Bay, Bligh seems to have turned over the responsibilities for shipboard affairs to his subordinates, assuming that his orders would be carried out while he himself went ashore to investigate the countryside. Later, during the long layover in Tahiti, his interests as a scientific observer would override his obligations to his ship, with even graver consequences of dissension and dissipation among the crew.

It is both to Bligh's credit and discredit that he extended his duties so wholeheartedly to include detailed observations of the social and physical world he encountered. His voyage with Cook had trained him as an observer and recorder, and it can be assumed that he—as well as the Admiralty—considered his observations a natural and expected adjunct to his position. He was exploring a still largely unexplored part of the world, and any information he could gather would be added to the growing worldly knowledge of 18th century England. No doubt Bligh hoped thereby to gain stature in the estimation of the British Admiralty. But Bligh's notes reveal more than base ambition; it was also simple curiosity that impelled him to keep elaborate and detailed notes on such subjects as natural history, geography, and geology and—during his long layover in Tahiti—human society and customs. Curiosity, and the pride of an artisan practicing a craft at which he knows he excells.

In his shore rambles at Adventure Bay, Bligh diligently recorded his observations of plant and animal life and soil conditions. He wrote descriptions of the various types of trees (noting they would not serve for masts), measured the jawbone and tail of a dead oppossum, and described in detail its teeth and claws. The colors and sizes of all the birds and fish seen were also recorded. Bligh described the few natives he encountered as " . . . perhaps the most wretched & Stupid People existing, yet they are with this no doubt the most inoffensive." Assisted by David Nelson, the *Bounty*'s botanist, Bligh supervised the planting of fruit trees and various vegetables.[19]

The ship was loaded with 41 tons of fresh water and 30 tons of wood for fuel (this wood coming aboard with " . . . many Scorpions and Santapies [centipedes] & a large kind of black Ants full One Inch long"). Just before the *Bounty* sailed, shore crews were ordered to gather large quantities of a bush that provided both leaves for tea and branches for brooms.

On September 4 the *Bounty* departed Adventure Bay on the last leg of the outward voyage, which would carry it through the southern Pacific Ocean to Tahiti, still 5,500 miles ahead.

The course took the ship around the southern end of New Zealand in rough, wet weather, as Bligh made his easting in the prevailing westerlies and open waters of the high latitudes before turning north to intercept the easterly trade winds of the reef-studded tropics. On September 19 a group of uncharted small islands was observed. Taking credit for their discovery, Bligh named them the Bounty Isles, the name still in use.

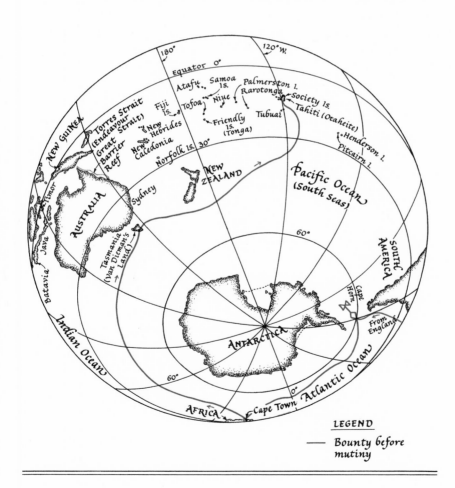

LEGEND

— Bounty before mutiny

Slowly the ship pushed northward. The weather moderated and became warmer. Seabirds and whales were sighted daily. By October 9 the air temperature had climbed into the sixties, and a wind "as steady as a Trade" pushed the ship through a smooth sea. But even as the grim climate of the higher latitudes softened, a series of troubles visited the *Bounty*.

On October 8, John Fryer refused ("for reasons best known to himself," said Morrison) to sign the routine monthly books which dealt with the ship's expenses and other matters unless Bligh gave him a good conduct report. It was a mild form of blackmail on the part of Fryer, indicative of a growing rancor between them, that Bligh would not accept. He wrote:

As I did not approve of his doing his duty conditionally I sent for him and told him the Consequence when he left me abruptly saying he would not sign the Books upon such conditions. I now ordered the Hands to be turned up. Read the Articles of War, with particular parts of the Instructions relative to the Matter, when this troublesome Man saw his error & before the whole Ships Company signed the Books.

According to Morrison's account of the affair, Fryer said to Bligh, "I sign in obedience to your Orders, but this may be Cancelled hereafter."

Fryer's portrait, which appears in an illustrated edition of Sir John Barrow's *Mutiny of the Bounty*,[20] suggests a constant complainer. The eyes look furtive; the mouth is given an acerbic downturn at the corners. One imagines a dry, quarrelsome, and flinty personality behind the face. Fryer and Bligh never got along. Perhaps Fryer was secretly rankled by the promotion of Christian to second in command; no doubt he felt professionally slighted by Bligh's frequent desire to serve as his own navigator, thereby preempting to an indeterminable extent the most jealously guarded duty of the master. Probably he considered himself equally as competent as Bligh to command, second-guessed his commander's decisions, and was not reluctant to express his own ideas of how the ship should be managed. For his part, Bligh judged Fryer insubordinate and incompetent. Their mutual dislike grew as the voyage progressed, finally reaching open enmity.

On October 10, Able-bodied Seaman James Valentine died. Valentine had been ill while the ship was at anchor in Adventure Bay. He was bled by the surgeon, but later the arm became infected. The infection eventually healed, only to be followed by a chest condition that caused coughing and shortness of breath. He was again treated by the surgeon but died of what was diagnosed as asthma.

"He had no Effects of any Value," wrote Bligh. "I therefore directed the few Shirts and Trowsers that belonged to him to be given to the two Men who had attended him during his illness with great care and Affection." The next day, his body was committed " . . . to the deep with all the decency in our Power."

A few days later three men complained of rheumatic pains. Bligh initially thought it a symptom of a "Scorbutic Complaint" and ordered that their salt meat provisions be replaced with flour and malt. Concerned, he intensified the ship cleaning routine. Clean hammocks were issued to all crew, and fresh seawater was pumped through the ship. Grog rations were stopped as punishment to two men who refused to take part in the evening dancing, a ritual Bligh steadfastly considered conducive to good health.

The surgeon told Bligh that the rheumatic pains were a symptom of scurvy. Bligh examined the men, found no evidence of swollen gums, loose teeth, or bad breath (normal symptoms of scurvy), and discounted the diagnosis.

"Mustered all hands," he wrote, "& saw them clean and I think I never saw a more healthy set of Men and so decent looking in my life."

The sick list grew. Was Bligh unable to accept that an outbreak of scurvy was possible aboard his well-ordered ship? Certainly scurvy was anathema to his systematic and demanding standards of shipboard diet and cleanliness, as well as heresy to his pride and ego, and these factors may have prevented him from assessing the true condition of the crew.

On the other hand, the surgeon's diagnosis was open to question as well. He, too, reported sick, but Bligh discovered that he was intoxicated and wrote, "It was now four days since he had seen light and in bed all the time intoxicated, I therefore ordered his Cabbin to be cleaned and searched, and all liquor to be taken from him which was accordingly done, but the operation was not only troublesome but offensive in the highest degree."

Morrison's journal states: "Several of the seamen particularly the oldest began to complain of Pains in their limbs and some simptoms of the Scurvy began to make its appearance and weakness and debility began to be observed through the Ships Company. . . ."

His journal also records the growing dissension aboard the *Bounty* in this October entry:

"Mr. Bligh and His Mess mates the Master & Surgeon fell out, and seperated, each taking his part of the stock,[21] & retiring to live in their own Cabbins, After which they had several disputes & sel-

dom Spoke but on duty; and even then with much apperant reserve."

On October 25, 5,563 miles out from Adventure Bay, Bligh's navigating skill enabled him to make an exact landfall on the tiny island of Maitea, barely three miles in circumference and 75 miles distant from Tahiti. He congratulated himself on the accuracy of his navigation, writing:

I could not suppose myself above a quarter of a degree wrong and concluded I should certainly meet with it [Maitea] in the Morning which I did.

The crew readied the ship for the next day's arrival at Tahiti, and were themselves inspected by the surgeon for venereal disease. Commented Bligh:

As I have some reason to suppose the Otaheitans have not been visited by any ships since Captn. Cook, I hope they may have found means together with their natural way of living, to have eradicated the Venereal disease. To prove this and free us from any ill founded Suppositions, that we might renew the Complaint, I have directed the Surgeon to examine very particularly every Man and Officer & to report to me his proceedings. This was accordingly done and he reported every person totally free from the Venereal complaint.

On Sunday, October 26, 10 months out of England, the *Bounty* came to anchor in Matavai Bay, concluding a voyage of 27,086 nautical miles.[22] The *Bounty* and her weary crew had arrived in paradise and to an anchorage behind Point Venus, from which Cook had observed the planet Venus 19 years before.

6

BOUNTY IN PARADISE
October 26, 1788–April 4, 1789

It is the stuff of a Hollywood film. A sailing ship crosses a wide, lonely sea. The men aboard—months and thousands of miles from home—have suffered all the privations of the long voyage. Their food has been plain, rough, and monotonous. For days and nights, through the cold of winter and then the heat of the tropics, these men have endured the psychological strain of a harsh discipline as they lived, worked, slept, and ate in the cramped quarters of a constantly rolling and pitching ship.

And then the green-clad slopes of a mountainous island rise out of a tropical sea. Inside a calm bay protected by an encircling ring of coral, the ship comes to anchor a few yards off a clean, sparkling beach. Within minutes, the ship is surrounded by handsome laughing men who deliver fresh fruit and flowers to the ship and bring with them the gift of their women.

The men of the *Bounty* were not the first to discover the delights of Tahiti, or Otaheite, as it was called at the time. That pleasure fell to the men of H.M.S. *Dolphin* (Samuel Wallis, captain), who landed there in 1767. They were followed by the French ship *La Boudeuse*, commanded by Louis de Bougainville. He called it *New Cytherea* after the Aegean island hallowed by Aphrodite, the Greek goddess of love. Cook stopped at Tahiti on all three of his Pacific voyages, with Bligh accompanying him on the last visit.

A complex religious system was the basis of the island's social structure, governing all aspects of conduct both sacred and profane. Social classes were rigid, and the highest chiefs claimed direct descent from the gods.

Everyday life for the Tahitians was easy. The sea provided abundant fish, and the land provided crops and material for clothing and shelter. To northern Europeans, who had to struggle to survive, it was a paradise.

53

The reading public of England became aware of Tahiti through the published records of Cook's voyages. These created, in essence, a neoclassical picture of the noble savage living an idyllic life. When certain sketches of Tahitian scenes and people drawn by Cook's artists were redrawn, the natives were shown greeting the ships in clothes that resembled the figures of a Grecian urn.

Cook also brought back artifacts and natural specimens, and these were eagerly sought by private collectors and museums. London society could not see enough of Omai, the Tahitian boy Cook brought home. A play portraying Omai as the idealized savage (against the backdrop of an exotic setting) ran for 50 performances.

But London society was romanticizing a doomed culture. The first ships to visit Tahiti left behind tools, metal, guns, and disease. The island's population, variously estimated at 50,000 to 140,000 in the time of Cook and Bligh, was within three generations reduced to a mere 6,000.

A story is told that the scientist Sir Joseph Banks, who visited Tahiti with Cook, dried his botanical specimens between sheets of paper on which had been printed Milton's great epic poem, *Paradise Lost*.

At dawn of Sunday, October 26, 1788, as the *Bounty* moved toward her anchorage in Matavai Bay, she was accompanied by vast numbers of islanders who had come out to greet the ship—so many, commented Bligh, that "in ten minutes, I could scarce find my own people."

Understanding that the ship was from "Pretanee" (Britain), the islanders asked about Cook. Bligh had issued orders to the crew that no one was to mention Cook's death. Nelson, the botanist, who had accompanied Cook's third expedition, told the islanders that Bligh was Cook's son. Thus, in the mantle of Cook, Bligh returned to Tahiti.

With the false modesty that so often concealed Bligh's high opinion of himself, he wrote in his log entry that day:

I do not wish that any Account of mine may be supposed to be given with greater certainty and with a View to supersede such [previous] descriptions. I only do it as my duty, having so much time before me, as perhaps many circumstances may occur that may lead to facts which otherwise may never be known.

"Such descriptions," of course, were the observations recorded by the three voyages of Cook to Tahiti. As "son of Cook," his duty—as he saw it—was to add to the knowledge acquired by his mentor. Twelve years had elapsed since Bligh had last been in Tahiti. During his stay there in the *Bounty,* he would be able to observe the first effects of European influence on the island people, stemming from that earlier encounter. Already, for example, guns were being used in tribal skirmishes, and iron tools were replacing native stone implements. Though his medium of expression was only a ship's log, Bligh's observations on native customs during the 23 weeks the *Bounty* remained at anchor would ultimately constitute a detailed ethnographical treatise on Tahitian culture.

But the man he attempted to emulate, Cook, had had a staff of men to oversee ship, crew, and scientific work. Bligh was one man attempting to direct all three. The spread of his responsibilities was too large. In addition, in order to obtain permission to transplant the breadfruit trees, Bligh had to participate in a number of diplomatic formalities with island chieftains. All of this involved long periods of time away from the ship, and in Bligh's absence, with his attention on other matters, shipboard discipline lagged. In Tahiti, the men of the *Bounty* enjoyed a surfeit of sensual delights—food, women, sun, and rest—beyond their wildest imagination. It was not a place easily forgotten.

"Huzza for Otaheite!" was the cheer Bligh claimed he heard as the *Bounty* sailed away with its crew of mutineers. He went to his death still apparently believing that the lure of the island was the reason his crew mutinied—memories of a place, he wrote, where "they need not labor and where the allurements of dissipation are beyond anything that can be conceived." He was probably partly right.

Nothing in the record, however, suggests that Bligh in any determined way attempted to withhold from his men the "allurements of dissipation" that were everywhere about them. Upon anchoring, crewmembers were given all the food they could eat, and every night the island women were allowed to remain aboard with the men.

Bligh went ashore, where he was entertained at the house of a minor chief. There, he wrote, " . . . the Ladies, for they deserve to be called such from their natural and unaffected manners and elegance . . . cloathed me in the Otaheite stile. . . ."

Bligh also wrote:

Among the Women who were now come on board to the Men, I found one who had been on board the Resolution in 1777. She was a shrewd Girl, & among other questions put to here, were, if the Venereal disease was still among them. I was instantly answered in the affirmative, and such a string of descriptive circumstances of the havock it had made came out, as shocked me to the greatest degree. Many fine Girls she said had died of it, and de-

scribed the many forms this dreadful disease puts on as left me no room to doubt of the truth of the relation: however I have not as yet seen any afflicted in a manner as to judge if it at present exists, or is my knowledge of the language sufficient to enquire if they had discovered a cure for the complaint.

When the ruling chief, Tinah (also called Otoo) and his wife, Iddeeah, were ushered aboard the ship, he and Bligh ceremoniously joined noses and exchanged names, "He taking the Name of Bligh, which they could pronounce no way but Bry, and I that of Tinah." To the chief, Bligh gave hatchets, files, knives, a saw, and shirts; to his wife, earrings, necklaces, and beads.

A few days after the *Bounty*'s arrival, Bligh describes how he was formally welcomed by the chief:

As soon as I got there [the chief's house] a large peice of Cloth 41 Yards long and two Wide was spread on the ground, and then Cloathing me in the manner of the Cheifs with a peice stained of a red colour wrapt round my shoulders and waist, two large Hogs about 200 lbs. each and a Quantity of baked breadfruit and Coca Nutts were presented. A Great number of people were now gathered on each side of the Cloth, and I was desired to walk from one end to the other and then back which I did and seemed to please them very much, and the word Tyo or Friend was several times exchanged between us.

Ashore, Bligh assisted in the cultivation of a garden because of his desire to introduce to the island what he thought would be valuable food plants. Cook on his three visits to the island had also attempted to introduce new food sources, along with a breeding stock of cattle, sheep, ducks, geese, turkey, and peacocks. Many of the animals, Bligh was disappointed to discover, had been killed.

In none of his early visits ashore did Bligh mention the *Bounty*'s mission. He felt some caution was necessary in negotiating the removal of large numbers of the breadfruit tree, which was a main food source for the island people. A circuitous approach seemed appropriate. In a conversation with the chief while visiting the nearby village of Pare (Oparre) on November 1, Bligh pointed out that King George had sent many gifts and that courtesy required the chief to send presents in return. Otoo immediately agreed and listed the many things he could give, including the breadfruit plant. That, said Bligh, was exactly what the king would like, and the chief offered all that was wanted. Cleverly, Bligh had concluded the negotiations. Instead of having to trade for the plants, he was now performing a service for the chief by transplanting the breadfruit to England as a gift to King George.

Walking back from Pare, Bligh was moved by the beauty, charm, and grace of the Tahitian society. In his log entry for November 1, he writes:

> About a quarter of a Mile farther towards the Hills through the delightful Breadfruit flats of Oparre, we again stopped at the side of a Serpentine River where they said our Ducks and Geese swarmed in. Here a lane was made by the Natives, and I was in view of a House on the other side about 50 Yards distant. It had a beautiful and picturesque appearance, as had all the country about it, to which, no description could do justice. . . .
>
> These two places [Oparre and Matavai] are certainly the Paradise of the World, and if happiness could result from the situation and convenience, here it is to be found in the highest perfection. I have seen many parts of the World, but Otaheite is capable of being preferable to them all, and certainly is so considering its natural State.

In the next paragraph in the log, Bligh expresses concern about " . . . what we may have done . . ." to destroy the condition of that natural state. The natives were fascinated by British things, particularly ships and guns. Bligh drew them a picture of a ship of one hundred guns. Was it as big as a mountain? he was asked. Wrote Bligh:

> Otoo desired one of these large ships might be sent out, and myself or Toote [Cook] to come to Matavia. He also gave me commission [orders to buy] for Cloaths, Spy Glasses, Hatchets, Files, Gimlets, Highbacked Elbow Chairs and Beds and Bed places, so that whatever good we may have done them, we have given them a Taste for luxury and indolence. . . .

Remembering Cook's violent death in the Sandwich Islands, Bligh wanted to remind the Tahitians of the killing power possessed by the ship's guns. Morrison recorded that when visitors came aboard, "they were entertained by Mr. Bligh, who gratified their curiosity by firing a Gun, at which they appeared much amazed & always stopd their ears & fell down as soon as they saw the Flash, and a Pistol was to all appearances as much dreaded as a four pounder. Mr. Bligh took the opportunity at such times, to shew them the effects of round and Grape Shot, which to them appeared Wonderful, and they always exclaim'd in amaze when they saw the shot fall, scarcely giving credit to what they saw."

On November 2, the main and the mizzen topsail, along with some smaller sails, were taken ashore by a party commanded by Christian, and tents were erected for the protection of the breadfruit plants. There, Nelson, the botanist, and his assistant Brown would work. With the consent of Otoo, Bligh fixed a boundary around the tents within which the islanders were forbidden to enter. Christian and six other men—Midshipman Heywood, Peckover (the gunner), and four crewmen—were permanently assigned to live at the shore station while the plants were being gathered.

Unfortunately, neither Bligh's log nor Morrison's journal provides much information about this shore camp, which was set up for the all-important task of gathering breadfruit trees under Nelson and Christian's supervision. From the brief references provided, it can be assumed that native labor was engaged to dig and transport the plants to the camp. Bligh writes with considerable pride about the efficiency with which these plants were collected and, later, delivered aboard in good health. One can judge, therefore, that Christian here performed well and that Bligh—by and large—had nothing to complain about in the conduct of his second-in-command, but Christian's precise role in the collection of the plants remains indistinct. Morrison says only that Christian was sent ashore with his men "as a guard in case the Natives should behave amiss," and in his post-mutiny log entries Bligh, retrospectively, shares the success of this phase of the mission with Nelson alone.

In the many fictionalized versions of the Bounty story, it was during this time ashore that Christian is supposed to have fallen deeply in love with one of the island women, and his desire to return to this woman is postulated as one of the contributing causes of the mutiny.

Christian's brother, Edward, later claimed in a long treatise he wrote in defense of his brother that though it had been claimed that Christian had "a favourite female at Otaheite, it is proper that it should be known that although Christian was upon shore, and had the command of the tent all the time that Captain Bligh was at Otaheite with the *Bounty*, yet the officers who were with Christian upon the same duty declare that he never had a female favourite at Otaheite, nor any attachment or particular connection among the women. It is true that some had what they call their girls, or women with whom they constantly lived all the time they were upon the island, but this was not the case with Christian."[23]

"They appeared much amazed & always stopd their ears. . . ."

At least one crewmember would later assert in an affidavit collected by Bligh that Christian did indeed have a favorite female consort, but it is equally plausible that the pervasive ambience of Tahiti made a deeper impression on Christian's sensibilities than the charms of any particular woman.

A few men aboard the ship were put on the sick list from overeating the abundant food available to them, and the carpenter suffered a nail puncture in his knee. Then a more serious event occurred. The gudgeons of the large cutter were stolen, and Alexander Smith, under whose watch the theft occurred, was punished with 12 lashes for negligence and inattention. Several chiefs and their wives on board at the time attempted to prevent the punishment. The women, commented Bligh, " . . . showed every degree of Sympathy which marked them to be the most humane and affectionate creatures in the World."

In punishing Smith, Bligh might have been overreacting to what Europeans thought of as the bane of the islands: thieving. European society was built on laws that protected personal property. Communal Tahiti had no such laws; wives, children, property, and possessions were shared. One was free to take what was wanted or needed. The islanders thought nothing of prying nails out of ship decks to obtain much-wanted metal. Such thefts had to be stopped by punishment or threat of punishment. Petty thievery had at times driven Cook to distraction during his stops at Polynesian islands. It was the theft of a ship's boat, Bligh remembered, that had precipitated Cook's murder. Smith's lashing was intended to demonstrate that thieving was a punishable crime aboard a King's ship.

There were also lighter moments, however—as illustrated in a scene that took place the next day aboard the ship. Bligh's barber had brought with him a "tete," a head used by hairdressers to show different hair fashions. After dressing the head "with much taste and neatness," Bligh attached it to a stick wrapped in cloth to give the appearance of a body. Then the head-on-a-stick was shown to the natives.

One half of them realy beleived it was an English Lady and asked if it was my Wife, and one Woman ran with a basket of Breadfruit and a peice of Cloth and presented it as a present. . . . Some joined Noses with it and others kissed it.

Later, the women asked Bligh to explain how English women delivered their children. He explained the process, he said, "with the knowledge I had of the matter," and then asked the same question of the Tahitian women. He received a graphic demonstration of childbirth, with the chief's wife representing the woman in labor:

One of her attendants seated himself . . . and Opening his knees took her between them in a sitting posture with her legs under her so as to rest upon her heels. Her arms were brought round under his, and his hands spread over the Upper part of the Belly, which they described were occasionally as the pains came on pressed downwards, and in this Manner the Mother was held until the efforts of nature delivered her.

He was also told that a firstborn girl was frequently killed by twisting " . . . its neck as soon as it came from its Mother." Bligh the observer expressed no shock at this disclosure, only regret that he could not speak of the practice "with certainty. . . ."

When the subject of religion came up with a native priest, Bligh was asked if the English had a God.

Having replied of course in the Affirmative, I was asked if he had a Son and who his Wife was. I told them he had a Son but no Wife. Who were his Father and Mother then? was the next question. I said he never had either Father or Mother. At this they laughed exceedingly. You have a God then who never had a Father or a Mother and has a Child without a Wife. . . . Did he not lie with a Woman to get him? I said no. Who was then before Your God and where is he? Is he in the Winds or in the Sun? Many other like questions were put to me concerning the Divine Omnipotence, & I answered them in as explanatory a manner as the little knowledge I have of the language would allow me, but it was too Scanty to enable me to enter into a discussion of their tenets. I only thought this matter worthy of remark to show their Ideas and their mode of investigating a truth, and I shall renew it again when I think there is a less chance of my being misunderstood and I can understand them with greater certainty.

Inquiring about the rituals of death, Bligh learned:

. . . The practice of embowelling was used to the Superior Chiefs, and the mode of doing it, was by a Man wrapping his two forefingers round with cloth and introducing them at the Anus, the bowells were extracted. The Chief thus embowelled was kept as long as the Sinews held the bones together, at the expiration of which they were put into the Earth but the inferior Order of People after a month or two were buried . . . and indeed it is reasonable to suppose so, otherwise the whole country would become covered with Dead bodies which is not the case.

Bligh was a crusty sea captain, married, a father and devout Anglican as well as the King's representative of the Church of England. For all this, he was remarkably open-minded in his observations of Tahitian religious beliefs and sexual mores. In one log entry he records, without critical comment (spicy later reading for the Admiralty), how the king's wife kept a lover and that " . . . both men cohabitated with the Wife in the same hour, and in the presence of one another."

Although Bligh's descriptions are from the vantage point of an 18th century European, assured of his own cultural superiority and hence in a position to be tolerant and understanding, his empathy for the Tahitians is also genuine. All around him, Bligh saw how men of his own culture, so-called Christians, were behaving as they gorged themselves on the pleasures of Tahiti—a woman or a fat pig for the price of a nail—and introduced to the island wants alien to its culture. The natives were like children before this invasion. Bligh seems to have been touched by their guilelessness, saddened by the knowledge that his own visit was disrupting their gentle tranquility.

One of Bligh's parting observations was a comment on the rapid change in technology that had affected the island society during the *Bounty*'s visit:

It is now a rare thing to see them use any other than Iron Tools. In their natural State they used a peice of Split Bamboo for a Knife, a hard black Stone brought to a blunt edge for a hatchet, and a Splintered peice of the same for a Drill, and their teeth were always sufficient to clear a Cocoa Nut of its Rind to give them food and drink. But now they will do nothing without a Knife and a Hatchet. . . .

And then, in describing an amusing yet poignant vignette, he added:

They are immoderately fond of our Apparel and wear with great pride an old Shoe and an old Stocking, altho it is with the utmost difficulty they can keep the Shoe on their foot, and render them the most laughable Objects existing.

By the latter part of November, the weather had become cloudy with occasional showers. The men aboard ship were employed in painting and rigging repairs. The ship's cutter was hauled up on

"They wear with great pride an old shoe. . . ."

the beach, and worm damage was repaired by pouring boiling water over the infested parts and painting the hull with white lead. Ashore, the accumulated breadfruit trees now numbered 600 plants ready to be transferred to the ship.

The sick had recovered, but four cases of venereal disease were reported. By all the evidence of Bligh's journal, he believed his men had been infected through intercourse with island women. Apparently, he accepted the accuracy of the ship's doctor's report that the crew on the eve of their arrival in Tahiti had been free of infection.

On December 5—a day of fresh gales and seas breaking over the outer barrier of the bay—the carpenter, William Purcell, refused to follow an order. Bligh had asked him to cut a large stone for the natives, to be used for sharpening their axes. Bligh wrote that the carpenter answered, "I will not cut the stone for it will spoil my Chisel, and tho there is law to take away my cloathes, there is none to take away my Tools." Said Bligh:

This Man having before shewn his Mutinous and insolent behavior, I was under the necessity to confine him to his Cabbin.

Saturday, December 6, 1788:

I experienced a scene to day of Wind and Weather which I never supposed could have been met with in this place. . . . By Sun set a very high breaking Sea ran across the Dolphin Bank, and before seven O'Clock it made such way in the Bay that we rode with much difficulty and hazard. Towards Midnight it encreased still more, and we rode until eight in the Morning in the midst of a heavy broken sea which frequently came over us. The Wind at times dying away was a great evil to us for the Ship from the tremendous Sea that broke over the Reefs to the Eastward of Point Venus, producing such an outset thwarting us against the Surge from the bank which broke over us in such a Manner, that it was necessary to batten every part of the Ship. In this state we remained the whole Night with all hands up in the midst of torrents of Rain, the Ship sending [scending] and rolling in a most tremendous manner, and the Sea foaming all round us so as to threaten instant destruction.

The islanders on shore became very anxious for the safety of the ship. In the morning, the chief and his wife paddled a canoe through heavy surf to the ship, where they embraced Bligh "with a flood of tears, [and] said they had prayed to the Eatua [God] for my safety, but that they feared the Ship would be lost." Others

swam out to the ship, among them a woman who expressed grief through the Tahitian practice of self-inflicted injury. Describing the act, Bligh wrote:

The strongest and only established proof among these people of their sincerity on those occasions is the Wounding of themselves on the Top of the Head with a Sharks tooth until they bring on a vast profusion of blood, and having a knowledge of this I was prepared to prevent this Woman from doing it; but I had no sooner come to her than the Operation was performed before I was aware of it, and her face was covered with blood in an instant.

Her husband, equally concerned, told Bligh, "You shall live with me if the Ship is lost, and we will cut down Trees to build another to carry you to Pretanee."

On December 10 the ship's surgeon died. Bligh ascribed his death to "drunkenness and indolence." Exercise, he wrote, "was a thing he could not bear an Idea of, or could I ever bring him to take a half dozen of turns on deck at a time in the course of the whole Voyage. Sleeping was the way he spent his time . . . and [he] was so filthy in his person that he became latterly a nuisance." Permission was granted to bury the surgeon ashore.

Fearing the troubles that could arise in trading negotiations, Bligh had issued an order that no one was to engage in private bartering "for curiosities" with the islanders. Trading for private food stores was at first allowed, just as Cook had done, but it wasn't long before the trading got out of hand and began to undermine Bligh's ability to trade for ship's provisions. Fryer alone had accumulated 40 hogs; Bligh seized them and had them killed for the ship's use.

When Fryer complained, wrote Morrison in his account of the affair, Bligh replied that "evry thing was his, as soon as it was on board, and that He [Bligh] would take nine tenths of any mans property and let him see who dared say any thing to the contrary, [and then those hogs of the seamen] were seized without ceremony. . . ."

Still the practice continued, so Bligh ordered the mate of the watch to keep a record of all hogs brought on board. This stopped the traffic in hog trading until the natives adopted the method of smuggling the hogs on board cut up in pieces and hidden in baskets of breadfruit and coconuts.

Though Bligh's reason for curtailing private trading was sound, his tactics were not. "It became," concluded Morrison, "a favour for a man to get a Pound extra of His own hog."

The price of living in paradise was about to be reckoned. As the year drew to a close, things began to go increasingly amiss.

On Christmas Day, 1788—the second Christmas of the voyage—the *Bounty* sailed out of Matavai Bay toward the safer anchorage of Toaroah Harbor at Pare, a short distance down the coast. Fryer had been sent ahead in the launch to reconnoiter, and returned a favorable report. All the plants collected to date were put aboard the ship, to be off-loaded again at Pare, and the launch was sent ahead to sound the entrance to the harbor. While discharging its duty, however, the launch, under Christian's command, fell into the windless lee of the *Bounty*, which then sailed past it and grounded on an unseen coral "rock" that had escaped Fryer's earlier attention. The ship was pulled off without damage (though with "some trouble," said Morrison) but Able-bodied Seaman William Muspratt, who had been in the launch, was punished with a dozen lashes for "neglect of duty." One imagines Bligh comparing Christian and Fryer's performance with his own open-boat pilotage as master under Cook.

Three days later another seamen, Robert Lamb, was given 12 lashes for allowing his cleaver to be stolen. Bligh told the witnessing island chiefs that their people would receive the same punishment if they persisted in stealing and were caught.

Four men suffering from venereal disease were placed on the sick list. Flies had become troublesome, " . . . more numerous than in any part of the World," commented Bligh. Squally, rainy weather interfered with the work that had to be completed before the ship could sail. With few shipboard duties possible, the crew was given additional time ashore.

Then, during the morning watch of January 5, three seamen (Charles Churchill, the above Muspratt, and John Millward) deserted in the *Bounty*'s small cutter, taking with them a small supply of arms and ammunition. Churchill's chest, which he had left behind, was examined, and in it was found a list that contained the names of three of the men stationed at the shore camp. Bligh was furious. Storming ashore, he confronted Christian with the accusation that some of the men under his charge at the shore camp were involved in the desertion. "They persisted in their Innocence," wrote Morrison, "and denyd it so firmly that He [Bligh] was inclined from Circumstances to believe them and said no more to them about it."

Though the records are silent on the matter, these troubled days must have helped drive the wedge between Bligh and Christian. Perhaps, even, the "I am in Hell" period of agony that Christian complained of on the morning of the mutiny had its origins

in these last dark, brooding wet weeks before the *Bounty*'s departure from paradise.

Bligh entered this complaint in the log—the first explicit report of his growing dissatisfaction with his men:

> Had the Mate of the Watch [Hayward] been awake no trouble of this kind would have happened, I have therefore disrated him and turned him before the Mast. Such neglectfull and worthless petty Officers I beleive never was in a Ship as are in this. No Orders for a few hours together are Obeyed by them, and their conduct in general is so bad, that no confidence or trust can be reposed in them, in short they have drove me to every thing but Corporal punishment and that must follow if they do not improve.

Hayward was placed in irons for failing to prevent the desertion.

The island chiefs were immediately notified and dispatched with the master, Fryer, to search for the men. The missing boat was soon returned with the report that the three deserters had taken a canoe and fled to a small offlying island. Bligh warned the chiefs that unless they assisted in the search for the men he would " . . . proceed [against the chiefs] with such violence as would make them repent it." Then, weighing this threat against the need to maintain goodwill in order to acquire additional breadfruit plants, he added in his log: " . . . I shall proceed to no extremities until I have the Plants on board."

Other problems were reported. Nearly a ton of bread had spoiled in the damp, tropical climate and had to be condemned. Rats had destroyed the supply of hops. Six men were now down with venereal disease. Cockroaches appeared everywhere in the ship. Morrison's journal vividly describes the invasion of the insects:

" . . . The ship began to swarm with Cockroaches to get rid of which evry Method was tried but to no purpose after repeated washing & Carrying evry Chest & box on shore where the cloaths were cleard of them they appeared as plenty in two or three days as ever, the Cables appeared alive with them and they seemed to Encrease instead of deminish tho great quantitys were destroyed evry day. Hot water was now applied twice a Week and the Cables & evry part of the Ship from stem to stern washd with it but to no purpose they flew to the Hold rigging & mast head and returned as before. . . ."

Then it was discovered that the reserve sails aboard the ship were "very much Mildewed and rotten in many places." Bligh had reason to be furious: thousands of miles from home, the new sails, which might be crucial to the return voyage, had been allowed to rot through neglect. Fryer and William Cole were blamed:

> If I had any Officers to supercede the Master and the Boatswain, or was capable of doing without them, considering that as common Seamen, they should no longer occupy their respective Stations. Scarce any neglect of duty can equal the criminality of this, for it appears that altho the Sails have been taken out twice since I have been in the Island, which I thought full sufficient and I had trusted to their reports, Yet these New Sails were never brought out, or is it certain whether they have been out since we left England, yet . . . they reported to me to be in good Order.

Morrison, the boatswain's mate, was silent about the incident, saying only that the hot water used to combat cockroaches had found its way into the sailroom and storerooms, "but had done no other damage than Watering every thing in them. The Hot water was now disused & the sails . . . were got on Shore & Washd with Salt water dry'd & Made up while the Carpenters Caulk'd over the Store & Sail rooms."

It was not until January 23 that the whereabouts of the deserters was known. With night and bad weather coming on, Bligh and a crew set out to capture them, led by native guides. Landing in the dark, Bligh walked along a rocky beach until he came to a house where the three men had taken refuge. They surrendered without a fight, and with the three deserters under guard, the entire group took shelter for the night. The next morning all returned to the ship, and the deserters were put in irons.

The following day, Bligh read the Articles of War, including Chapter XVI, which, in part reads: "Every person in or belonging to the fleet, who shall desert or entice others so to do, shall suffer death, or such other punishment as the circumstances of the offense shall deserve. . . ."

The three *Bounty* men were not the first to desert their ship for the soft shore life of Tahiti. Cook had recorded desertions on all three voyages, and each time the escaped men had been dragged back to their ship to suffer punishment. In no case, however, was that punishment death. Although the Articles of War might imply otherwise, a Royal Naval commander could not himself sentence a man to death, no matter what the crime. A court-martial was required for handing down such a sentence, and the convening of a court-martial required at least five officers of post-captain rank. (Bligh's was at the time probably the only British ship in the South Pacific.) Moreover, courts-martial of the time rarely extracted the

extreme penalty of hanging in cases of desertion for the simple reasons that desertions were fairly common, most men were caught, and the life of a working sailor was not something to be sacrificed merely to uphold the letter of the law.

Bligh would have been within his rights to have jailed the deserters until such a time as a court-martial could be convened. Such an action, however, would have reduced his crew by three men. Commented Bligh:

As this affair was solely caused by the neglect of the Officers who had the Watch, I was induced to give them all a lecture on this occasion, and endeavoured to show them that however exempt they were at present from like punishment, yet they were equally subject by the Articles of War. . . . An Officer with Men under his care is at all times in some degree responsible for their conduct; but when from his neglect Men are brought to punishment while he only meets with a reprimand, because a public conviction by Tryal will bring both into a more severe and dangerous situation, an alternative is often laid aside through lenity, and sometimes necessity, as it now is in both cases.

Churchill was given a dozen lashes; Muspratt and Millward received two dozen each. Then they were put back in irons for further punishment. The three men, perhaps unaware of the constraints on Bligh's authority as judge and executor, wrote him a letter in which they thanked him for his leniency and asked that he inflict no additional punishment. It read:

"Sir,

We should think ourselves wholly inexcusable if we omitted taking this earliest opportunity of returning our thanks for your goodness in delivering us from a trial by court martial, the fatal consequences of which are obvious; and although we cannot possibly lay any claim to so great a favour, yet we humbly beg you will be pleased to remit any farther punishment, and we trust our future conduct will fully demonstrate our deep sense of your clemency and our steadfast resolution to behave better hereafter."[24]

The appeal was signed by Churchill, Muspratt, and Millward, but Bligh disregarded it. An example had to be set with severe punishment. A few days later, the men were further punished with the same number of lashes.

On the last day of the month, another seaman, Isaac Martin, was given 19 lashes for striking a native. "I had ordered him two dozen," wrote Bligh, "but by the desire of Tinah he came off with less . . . but it was so violent a transgression among these friendly people, and so great a violation of my orders without any real cause, but a supposition that the Native had Stolen a peice of Iron Hoop from him, that nothing but the intercession of the Cheifs cleared him. . . ."

On the dark and cloudy night of February 6, someone cut two of the three strands of the *Bounty*'s anchor cable. The culprit was never found. (After the mutiny, James Morrison returned to Tahiti with the *Bounty* mutineers, where he was told that the cable had been cut by an island man as a reprisal against Bligh for having placed Midshipman Thomas Hayward in irons.) To prevent another attempt, Bligh had a platform built over the bow so that the anchor line could be constantly watched by a sentinel.

Bligh reading the Articles of War

The wet weather of January continued into February. Slowly the ship was being readied for sea. Men were employed in caulking the hull, repairing casks and the rigging, and taking aboard supplies. Ashore, other men sawed planks and made hay for the shipboard animals. The forge was in constant operation as natives brought the blacksmith pieces of iron to shape and sharpen. The armourer's services could be bartered for provisions, and were good diplomacy besides. The battle with the cockroaches continued, and the ship was periodically washed with boiling water and fumigated with tobacco smoke. Bligh continued his observations of the native culture. He witnessed a funeral, and in a long ceremony he was made an island chief.

During the night of March 2, a native stole an empty water cask, part of an azimuth compass and a seaman's bedding from the shore camp. Hearing of this, Bligh stormed ashore and, said Morrison, "rebuked the Officers at the tent [including Christian] for neglecting their duty. . . ."

According to Morrison, Bligh "then went in a passion to Matte [a Tahitian chief] and insisted on having the theif delivered up & in a short time the theif & Cask were both brought to the tent and Matte told Mr. Bligh to shoot him, which he said would make the others afraid to steal." The man was taken aboard ship and Bligh ordered that he be given 100 lashes. Said Bligh: "He bore it surprizingly and only asked me twice to forgive him altho he expected he was to die. His Back became very much swelled but only the last stroke broke the Skin."

He was then placed in irons—Bligh's intent being to release him when the ship sailed—but five days later he escaped. Bligh held Stewart, the mate of the watch, accountable. Again, he formally recorded his grievances with his junior officers:

I had given in Written orders that the Mate of the Watch was to be answerable for the Prisoners and to visit and see that they were safe in his Watch, but I have such a neglectfull set about me that I beleive nothing but condign [well-deserved] punishment can alter their conduct. Verbal orders in the course of a Month were so forgot that they would impudently assert no such thing or directions were given, and I have been at last under the necessity to trouble myself with writing what by decent Young Officers would be complied with as the common Rules of the Service.

Heavy rains continued to slow the work aboard ship. Rivers were flooded, and the outfall of rainwater from the swollen streams was so great that the bay near the ship changed from salt to brackish.

As March ended, the *Bounty* was nearly ready to depart. All the island cats and dogs were removed from the ship, and great care was taken to prevent stowaways from hiding aboard. The crew began the tedious task of transporting and stowing over 1,000 breadfruit trees aboard the ship. Morning and night the ship was crowded with natives bringing farewell presents of fruit and hogs.

The *Bounty,* indeed, must have resembled a floating farm. Morrison described it as "lumbered with Hogs Cocoa Nuts & Green Plantains for Sea stores. . . ." Bligh recorded that the ship carried the pork salted at Tahiti, 25 hogs, 17 goats, and "as much fruit as I could Stow . . ." along with 47 tons of water. Below decks was the precious cargo of 774 pots, 39 tubs, and 24 boxes which contained in all 1,015 breadfruit plants.

The night before he sailed, Bligh reported "No mirth or dances on the Beach as usual in the Evening. All sorrow at our departure." Tinah and his wife, said Bligh, showed "a great degree of Grief and they were inconsolable for some time. . . ."

On April 5 the ship cleared the harbor accompanied by a fleet

Stowing breadfruit

of canoes. Bligh put the last of the islanders ashore in Matavai Bay, hoisted in his boats, and "bid farewell to Otaheite, where for 23 Weeks we were treated with the greatest kindness. . . . Whatever Ship comes after me, will, if they conciliate the Affections of these People, receive the same kind of treatment." He had done well. He had circumvented the pitfalls of island diplomacy with a skillful blend of gifts, patience, measured firmness, and show of force, as he had learned from Cook. He had what he had come for, and he had not worn out the welcome for future British ships.

Homeward bound! It is the course the sailor dreams of, works for. West by northwest the *Bounty* steered as the high peaks of Tahiti dropped astern. A "Double Allowance of Grog was Given to all hands . . ." wrote Morrison. He then added this observation, significant because it summarizes the mood of the crew on the eve of its dissolution:

"Evry body seemd In high spirits and began already to talk of Home, affixing the length of the Passage and Count up their Wages and One would readily have Imagined that we had Just left Jamaica instead of Taheite so far onward did their flattering fancies waft them."

7

MUTINY ON THE *BOUNTY*

April 4–April 28, 1789

From Tahiti, Bligh set a course westward in accordance with his orders to pass through Endeavour Straits, between the northern cape of Australia and the island of New Guinea. His eventual destination was the West Indies. The west-about route, though longer, avoided subjecting the breadfruit trees to the rigors of Cape Horn, and passed through numerous tropical islands where plants could be gathered to replace any that might die.

From the indolence and surfeit of a South Seas island paradise, the crew now confronted the demands of a voyage that would take them halfway back around the world. Below decks were a thousand valuable plants, intolerant of salt water or spray. Daily they had to be watered, aired, and nurtured. Watches were resumed and order was imposed as the functioning society of a ship regrouped around its constituent parts—captain, officers, and crew. The tedium of ritual and duty marked the slow advance of time.

Remarks 9th April 1789:

About Nine O'Clock in the Morning the Weather turned very Squally and a large Body of black heavy clouds collected in the East. Soon afterwards a Water Spout appeared, the Column of which was seen to great advantage . . . I had scarce made these Observations when I observed it advancing rapidly towards me, the sea in the Vortex giving great proof of the Strength of the Whirlwind. I therefore took in all the Sails but the Foresail and stood across it and it passed within 10 Yards of our Stern, without our feeling the least effect from it. . . .

On April 11, after an afternoon of severe squalls and lightning, several small islands (Aitutaki, in the Cook Islands) were sighted. A single canoe bearing four men put out from one of the islands

and came alongside the ship. The men presented Bligh with a shell necklace plaited with human hair. Among the gifts Bligh gave the natives was a mirror which " . . . they handled and examined as a Monkey would do."

Log of the *Bounty,* April 12:

Dark Gloomy Wr. . . . Punished Jno Sumner with 12 lashes for Neglect of duty. . . .

On April 23, the *Bounty* arrived at the island of Anamoka (Nomuka, in the Tonga or Friendly Islands), where a brief layover was planned to refill the water casks and take on additional provisions. According to Morrison's account, a party was sent ashore under the command of Christian to gather wood. Natives surrounded the men, attempted to steal an ax, and became so troublesome that the party was unable to work. Christian reported the situation to Bligh, who, Morrison stated, "dam'd him for a Cowardly rascal, asking him if he was afraid of a set of Naked Savages while He had arms; to which Mr. Christian answered 'the Arms are no use while your orders prevent them from being used.' "

Bligh excused the men, saying that "they could not comply with every part of their duty and keep their tools in their Hands, and they therefore merit no punishment." His wrath again fell on Christian: "As to the Officers," he wrote, "I have no resource, or do I ever feel myself safe in the few instances I trust them."

Just before the *Bounty* departed from Anamoka, natives stole an anchor from a ship's boat ashore. Able-bodied Seaman McCoy was held accountable for the theft, and two island chiefs visiting aboard the ship were seized as hostages until the anchor was returned. It was not, and the ship got underway with the chiefs still prisoners under armed guard.

Bligh sent them to the messroom, reported Morrison, "and set them to peel Cocoa Nuts for His Dinner," thus insulting them perhaps more deeply than he realized. He then turned to the crew and "passed the Compliment on officers & Men," wrote Morrison, "that they were a parcel of lubberly rascals and that he . . . with good sticks would disarm the whole of them, and presenting a Pistol at Wm. McCoy threatend to shoot him for not paying attention."

Bligh seemed not at all interested in maintaining diplomatic relations with the island chiefs of Anamoka. The chiefs were allowed to return to the island in a canoe, but, pointed out Morrison, "seeing that they could not revenge the insult . . . it was the oppinion of most on board that if a Weak mand Ship Came in their Way they would remember this days transaction and make them suffer for it." The incident may have been a factor in the treatment Bligh and his loyalists would soon receive on neighboring Tofua.

Give Bligh his due credit. He had reason to be short tempered . . . to a point. He had aboard his ship the precious cargo of breadfruit plants. Water was critical to their survival, and so the filling of the ship's casks at Anamoka was more important than the establishment of friendly native relations. By his own testimony, he no longer felt confidence in the abilities of his officers to carry out his commands. Surrounded by what he saw as incompetence, Bligh felt he had to supervise everything personally.

His breadfruit safely aboard, Bligh could now relax the patient diplomacy that was alien and probably stressful to his nature. With no curious islanders looking on, sometimes grieving when punishment was meted out, and drawing unpredictable conclusions, he could impose a simpler order within his wooden world, furthering his mission and at the same time whipping his officers back into shape. The men must relearn discipline while he relaxed his. And the goad for ship's discipline was his tongue, the deepest effects of which he was ever unaware.

Meanwhile—evidently unbeknownst to Bligh—Christian was sinking deeper and deeper into a private hell. Unable to command under Bligh and unable to oppose him, he stood alone in the gathering tensions aboard the *Bounty*. To Christian, Bligh must have appeared a perfectionist who was by nature unable to delegate real responsibility. Any task Christian carried out seemed certain to engender a stinging and arbitrary rebuke. The implied promise of his appointment as second in command 13 months before had turned sour; he served an irascible master, and the reef-strewn waters of Bligh's irritability were impossible to negotiate. Criticism might be occasioned by any blunder, no matter how petty, or even by following orders to the letter. Bligh's log and Morrison's journal

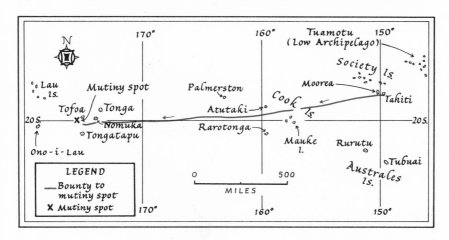

pay no more attention to Christian in this period than at Tahiti. It seems clear, however, that Christian was presiding over his own dissolution. If he had lost his authority as a leader, he yet had the lonely consolation of his pride. That pride contained the smoldering ego of a desperate man.

On April 27, the *Bounty* lay rolling in the calm of a flat, glassy sea. The island of Tofua was in sight, and from its volcanic summit rose a tall column of incandescent ash. Ocean and ship reflected the red haze of the flaming island. That afternoon, according to Morrison, Bligh again publicly insulted Christian. Morrison's journal describes that final humiliating scene:

"Mr. Bligh Came up, and taking a turn about the Quarter Deck when he missed some of the Cocoa Nuts which were piled up between the Guns upon which he said that they were stolen and Could not go without the knowledge of the Officers, who were all Calld and declared that they had not seen a Man toutch them, to which Mr. Bligh replied 'then you must have taken them yourselves', and orderd Mr. Elphinstone [the master's mate] to go and fetch evry Cocoa nut in the Ship aft, which He obeyd. He then questioned evry Officer in turn concerning the Number they had bought, & Coming to Mr. Christian askd Him, Mr. Christian answered 'I do not know Sir, but I hope you dont think me so mean as to be Guilty of Stealing yours'. Mr. Bligh replied 'Yes you dam'd Hound I do—You must have stolen them from me or you could give a better account of them—God dam you, you Scoundrels, you are all thieves alike, and combine with the men to rob me—I suppose you'll Steal my Yams next, but I'll sweat you for it, you rascals, I'll make half of you Jump overboard before you get through Endeavour Streights'—He then Calld Mr. Samuel [Bligh's clerk] and said 'Stop these Villians Grog, and Give them but Half a Pound of Yams tomorrow, and if they steal then, I'll reduce them to a quarter'. The Cocoa Nuts were Carried aft & He Went below, the officers then got together and were heard to murmur much at such treatment, and it was talked among the Men that the Yams would be next seized, as Lieut. Bligh knew that they had purchased large quantitys of them and [they] set about secreting as many as they Could."

Nothing of this incident appears in Bligh's log. The day closed, a day in which the ship had made little way and the only punctuation in the interminable frustration of hot sun and a sailing vessel without wind had been provided by Bligh's explosion. Bligh went to bed. Fletcher Christian held the morning watch. If the plan he improvised that night had gone right, he would never again have seen Bligh. He planned to leave the ship and escape to the nearest island on a hastily assembled raft of planks. It was an impossible plan; the nearest island, Tofua, was miles away. That Christian, an experienced ship's officer, could even contemplate such a plan shows how desperate he was to rid himself of his tormentor. The plan failed, and instead he found himself at daybreak the leader of an unplanned mutiny.

Let Morrison describe this critical event (Morrison claimed to have heard the story from Christian at a gathering of the ship's remaining crew immediately after the mutiny):

Christian, "finding himself much hurt by the treatment he had received from Mr. Bligh, had determined to quit the ship the preceeding evening, and informed the Boatswain, Carpenter, Mr. Stuart and Mr. Hayward of his resolution who supplied Him with some Nails, Beads and part of a roasted pig with some other articles. . . . He also made fast some staves to a stout Plank which lay on the larboard Gangway, with which he intended to make his escape; but finding he could not effect it in the first and Middle Watches, as the people were all a stirring, he went to sleep about half past three in the Morning. When Mr. Stuart calld him to relieve the Watch he had not Slept long, and was much out of order, & Stuart begd him not to attempt swimming away, saying 'the People [that is, the rank-and-file crew] are ripe for any thing', this made a forcible impression on his mind & finding that Mr. Hayward the Mate of his Watch (with whom he refused to discourse) soon went to sleep on the Arm Chest which stood between the Guns and Mr. Hallet [second mate of the watch] not making his appearance, He at once resolved to seize the ship. . . ."

Enlisting seven men (Quintal, Martin, Churchill, Thompson, Smith, Williams, and McCoy), Christian got the keys to the arms chest from Coleman by claiming a musket was needed to shoot a shark, armed these men as well as others who may or may not have known why they were being armed, and took the ship.

Years later, Alex Smith (who after the mutiny changed his name to John Adams), the last living mutineer, told essentially the same story to Captain F. W. Beechey when Beechey's ship, *Blossom*, called at Pitcairn Island, where some of the mutineers had eventually taken refuge. Adams, wrote Beechey, recalled that the night of April 27 (the eve of the mutiny) "was one of those beautiful nights which characterize the tropical regions, when the mildness of the air and the stillness of nature dispose the mind to reflection. Christian, pondering over his grievances, considered them to intolerable, that anything appeared preferable to enduring them, and he determined, as he could not redress them, that he would at least escape from the possibility of their being increased. Absence from England, and a long residence at Otaheite, where new connexioins were formed, weakened the recollection of his native country, and prepared his mind for the reception of ideas which the situation of the ship and the serenity of the moment particularly favoured. His plan ... was to set himself adrift upon a raft, and make his way to the island then in sight [Tofua]. As quick in the execution as in the design, the raft was soon constructed, various useful articles were got together, and he was on the point of launching it, when a young officer [Midshipman George Stewart] ... to whom Christian communicated his intention, recommended him, rather than risk his live on so hazardous an expedition, to endeavour to take possession of the ship, which he thought would not be very difficult, as many of the ship's company were not well disposed towards the commander, and would all be very glad to return to Otaheite, and reside among their friends in that island."

According to Adams, Christian then began to organize the mutiny, "resolving, if he failed, to throw himself into the sea; and that there might be no chance of being saved, he tied a deep sea lead about his neck, and concealed it within his clothes. Christian went to every man of his watch, many of whom he found disposed to join him, and before daylight the greater portion of the ship's company were brought over."[25]

Bligh awoke on the morning of April 28, 1789, no longer in command of his ship. In his log, he recorded his last hours aboard the *Bounty:*

Just before Sun rise Mr Christian, Mate, Chas. Churchill, Ships Corporal, John Mills, Gunners Mate, and Thomas Burkett, Seaman, came into my Cabbin while I was a Sleep and seizing me tyed my hands with a Cord behind my back and threatned me with instant death if I spoke or made the least noise. . . . Mr. Christian had a Cutlass in his hand, the others had Musquets and Bayonets. . . . I was forced on Deck in my Shirt, suffering great pain from the Violence with which they had tied my hands. I demanded the reason for such a violent Act, but I received no Answer but threats of instant death if I did not hold my tongue. . . .

The Boatswain was now ordered to hoist the Boat out, with a threat if he did not do it instantly to cake care of himself. . . . 'Hold your tongue Sir or you are dead this Instant' was constantly repeated to me. . . .

The Boatswain and Seamen who were to go in the Boat, collected twine, canvas, lines, Sails, Cordage and eight and twenty Gallon Cask of Water, and the Carpenter got his Tool Chest. Mr. Samuel got 150 lbs. Bread with a Small quantity of Rum and Wine. He also got a Quadrant and Compass into the Boat but [was] forbid on Pain of death touching any Map whatever, Ephemeris Book of Astronomical Observations [an almanac], Sextants, Time Keeper or any of my Surveys or drawings. . . .

Much altercation took place among the Mutinous Crew during the whole business, some Swore 'I'll be damned if he does not get home if he gets anything with him' (meaning me). Others, when the Carpenters Chest was carrying away, 'Damn my Eyes he will have a Vessel built in a Month', while others laughed at the Situation of the Boat being very deep, and not room for those that were in her. As for Christian, he seemed to be plotting instant destruction on himself and every one, for of all diabolical looking Men he exceeded every possible description.

I asked for Arms but they laughed at me and Said I was well acquainted where I was going and therefore did not want them. Four Cutlasses were however thrown into the Boat after She was veered astern.

When the Officers and Men were put into the Boat . . . they only then waited for me, and the Ships Corporal informed Christian of it, who then told me 'Come, Captn. Bligh, your Officers and Men are now in the Boat and you must go with them. If you attempt to make the least resistance you will instantly be put to death', and forcing me before him, holding by the Cord that frapped my hands behind my back and a Bayonet in his other, with a Tribe of Armed Ruffians about me I was forced over the side where they untied my hands, and being in the Boat we were veered astern by a Rope. A few peices of Pork were now thrown into us and some Cloaths, and after having undergone a great deal of ridicule we were at last cast adrift in the open Ocean. . . . Huzza for Otaheite was frequently heard among the Mutineers.[26]

In Morrison's account of the mutiny, he stated that he had taken no part in it and that he would willingly have assisted in retaking the ship had such an effort been possible. He wrote:

"As I saw none near me that seemed inclined to make a push, and the Officers busy getting the boat in order, I was fain to do so too, and the Boat was got out, when evry one ran to get what He could into her and get in themselves as fast as possible. The officers were hurryd in as fast as possible, and when Mr. Bligh found that He must go, He beggd of Mr. Christian to desist, saying 'I'll Pawn my Honor, I'll Give My Bond, Mr. Christian, never to think of this if youll desist': and urged his wife and family, to which Mr. Christian replyd 'No, Captain Bligh, if you had any Honor, things had no[t] come to this; and if you Had any regard for your Wife & family, you should Have thought on them before, and not behaved so much like a villain'. Lieutenant Bligh attempted again to speak, but was ordered to be silent; the Boatswain also tryd to pa-

"If you attempt to make the least resistance you will instantly be put to death."

cify Him [Christian] to which He replied 'Tis too late, I have been in Hell for this Fortnight passd and am determined to bear it no longer, and you know Mr. Cole that I have been used like a Dog all the Voyage.' The Master begd to be permitted to stay, but was ordered into the Boat, and Mr. Christian gave Churchill order to see that no arms went in the Boat. . . . The Lieut. [Bligh] then Beggd that some of the people would stay, and askd Mr. Christian to let the Master to stay with them but he answered, 'the men may stay but the Master must go with you.' Mr. Bligh then said 'Never fear my lads you cant all go with me my lads. I'll do you Justice if ever I reach England. He was then brought to the Gangway and cast off his hands and he went into the boat. . . ."

Morrison described the loaded boat with its 19 men aboard as "almost sunk a long side." It had, he said, only seven inches of freeboard.

In the final scene of this shattering event, Bligh stood in the dangerously overloaded boat and, said Morrison, " . . . beggd for His Commission [his lieutenant's commission] and Sextant; the Commission was Instantly Given him with his Pocket Book and Private Journal by Mr. Christians order, and He took His own Sextant which Commonly Stood on the Dripstone Case [the dripstone being a water purifier] and Handed it into the Boat with a Daily Assistant, saying 'there Captain Bligh this is sufficient for evry purpose and you know the Sextant to be a good one'."[27]

By 8 A.M., the boat was cast off, and the men aboard it started rowing toward the island of Tofua, some 25 miles away.

In all the tumult and confusion of the morning, it had been difficult to determine which men were active participants in the mutiny and which were innocent bystanders. It was obvious to all that the launch could carry only so many. Some men who were not participants in the mutiny stayed behind on the ship because they were afraid of embarking in the overloaded boat. Some men were forced below and simply left behind against their wishes. Some men called out to Bligh as he was departing to remember that they had not been a part of the mutiny. Surprise, confusion, and shock at the sudden turn of events obscured the lines of participation. Many aboard the *Bounty* were guilty of the worst sea crime. Some were not. Said Morrison: "The behaviour of the Officers on this Occasion was dastardly beyond description none of them ever making the least attempt to rescue the Ship which would have been effected had any attempt been Made by one of them as some of those Who were under arms did not know what they were about and Robert Lamb who I found Sentry at the Fore Hatchway when

I first Came on Deck went away in the Boat & Isaac Martin had laid his Arms down and gone into the boat but had been ordered out again.

"Their passive Obedience to Mr. Christians orders even surprized himself and he said immediately after the boat was gone that something more than fear had posessd them to suffer themselves to be sent away in such a Manner without offering to make resistance."

Much later, back in England, the long and complicated court-martial proceedings would attempt to reconstruct that morning of the mutiny. Where each man stood and what he did would help determine his verdict, innocent or guilty.

Almost as soon as the launch pulled away from the *Bounty,* Bligh began to assemble the case for the prosecution of the mutineers by writing out a description of each man, by means of which they might be recognized and apprehended. Portions of his descriptions, reproduced below, give an excellent picture of the makeup of the crew of a British naval ship in that era.

FLETCHER CHRISTIAN, 24:
> 5 ft. 9 in. High. Dark Swarthy Complexion. Hair—Blackish or very dark brown. Make—Strong. A Star tatowed on his left Breast, and tatowed on the backside. His knees stand a little out and he may be called a little Bowlegged. He is subject to Violent perspiration, particularly in his hands, so tht he Soils anything he handles.

GEO STEWART, 23:
> 5 feet 7 in. High. Slender Made, Narrow chested and long Neck. A Star tatowed on the left Breast and One on the left Arm with a heart and darts. Small Face and black Eyes.

PETER HEYWOOD, 17:
> 5 ft. 7 in. Fair. Well proportioned. Very much tatowed. . . . At this time he had not done growing and Speaks with the Manks or Isle of Man Accent.

EDWD YOUNG, 22:
> Dark Complexion and rather a bad look . . . Make: Strong. Lost several of his Fore teeth and those that remain are rotten.

CHAS CHURCHILL, 30:
> 5 ft. 10 in. High. Fair. Top of the Head Bald. Strong Made, the Fore Finger of his left hand crooked and his hand shews the marks of a Severe Scald.

JAS MORRISON, 28:
> 5 ft. 8 in. Sallow. Slender. Long Black Hair, has lost the use of

the upper joint of the Fore finger of the Right hand . . . has been Wounded in One of his Arms with a Musquet Ball.

JOHN MILLS, 40:

5 ft. 10 in. Fair. Strong made, Raw Boned. A Scar in his Right Arm pit Occasioned by an Abcess.

JNO MILLWARD, 22:

5 ft. 5 in. High. Dark Hair, Strong Made, very much tatowed in different parts of the Body.

MATW THOMPSON, 40:

5 ft. 8 in. Very Dark. Slender . . . has lost the joint of the Great Toe of his Right Foot and is tatowed. . . .

WILLM MCCOY, 25:

5 ft. 6 in. High. Fair. Strong. A Scar where he has been Stabbed in the Belly. . . .

MATW QUINTAL, 21:

5 ft. 5 in. Fair. Strong made. Very much tatowed on the back-side and Several other places.

JNO SUMNER, 24:

5 ft. 8 in. High. Fair. Slender . . . a Scar upon the left Cheek and tatowed in several places.

THOS BURKITT, 26:

5 ft. 9 in. High. Slender. Very much tatowed. Fair Complexion, very much pitted with the Small Pox.

ISAAC MARTIN, 30:

5 ft. 11 in. High. Sallow Complexion . . . Raw Boned, tatowed. . . .

WILLM MUSPRATT, 30:

5 ft. 6 in. High. Dark. Slender. A very Strong Black Beard with Scars under his Chin, is tatowed on several places of his Body.

HENY HILBRANT, 25:

5 ft. 7 in. High. Fair. Strong . . . his left Arm shorter than the other having been broke; speaks bad English; is tatowed in several places.

ALEX SMITH, 22:

5 ft. 6 in. High. Complexion—Brown. Strong made, very much pitted with the Small Pox, and very much tatowed on his Body, Legs Arms and Feet, and has a Scar on his Right Foot where he has been cut with a Wood Axe.

JNO WILLIAMS, 25:

5 ft. 5 in. High. Dark. Black Hair, Slender Made, has a Scar on the back part of his head, is tatowed. Native of Guernsey and Speaks French.

RICHD SKINNER, 22:

5 ft. 8 in. High. Fair. Very well made, has Scars on both

Ankles and on his right Shin, is very much tatowed and by Trade a Hair Dresser.

MICHL BYRN, 28:

5 ft. 6 in. Fair. Slender . . . is almost Blind and has the marks of an Issue on the back of his Neck. Plays the Violen.

THOS ELLISON, 17:

5 ft. 3 in. Fair. Dark Hair, Strong Made, has got his Name Tatowed on his Right Arm and Dated Oct. 25th. 1788.

WILLM BROWN, 27:

5 ft. 8 in. High . . . a Remarkable Scar on One of his Cheeks which contracts the Eyelid & runs down to his throat. . . . Is tatowed.

JOSH COLEMAN, 40:

5 ft. 6 in. Strong. Fair. Hair—Grey. A Head tatowed on One of his Arms.

THOS MCINTOSH, 28:

5 ft. 6 in. Fair. Slender . . . is pitted with the Small Pox. Is tatowed.

CHAS NORMAN, 26:

5 ft. 9 in . . . is pitted with the Small Pox; has a remarkable Motion with his Head and Eyes.

"Joseph Coleman, Michl Byrne, Thos McIntosh and Charles Norman are deserving of Mercy," wrote Bligh, "being only detained against their inclinations."

"These men," he noted with his characteristic perversity, were the "most able Men on board the Ship." This was to be their fate:

Five would be murdered by Tahitian men on Pitcairn Island; four would be drowned at sea; seven would be tried by court-martial and acquitted or pardoned; three would be tried, found guilty, and hanged; three more would be murdered; one would fall to a drunken death; and two would die of natural causes.

An hour after Bligh and his men had been cast off in the launch, a breeze came up. The *Bounty*'s sails were trimmed and the ship set a course toward Tahiti, leaving behind a trail of the potted breadfruit plants, which were thrown overboard. By noon, the launch and its abandoned men had disappeared from sight.

Leaving behind a trail of breadfruit plants

8

POSTCRIPT TO A MUTINY

In the Georgian navy in which William Bligh served, the concept of mutiny did not conform to our modern definition.

We think in terms of what naval historian N. A. M. Rogers calls " . . . the Cecil B. de Mille school of history, whose notion of mutiny is of the violent seizure of a ship from her officers, on the high seas." Mutinies of this type did sometimes occur aboard merchant-ships, but such a mutiny aboard a naval ship was, Rogers points out, "virtually unknown."

In Bligh's time, the word most often applied to single acts of insubordination and, sometimes, group action by a crew attempting to achieve specific correction in such matters as pay or shore liberty. Today, we might think of such group action as a strike or work stoppage.

When such mutinies did happen, Rogers explains, they "conformed to certain unwritten rules which, if written, would have stated these limitations:

"No mutiny shall take place at sea, or in the presence of the enemy.

"No personal violence may be employed (although a degree of tumult and shouting is permissible).

"Mutinies shall be held in pursuit only of objectives sanctioned by the traditions of service."[28]

There is a contradiction here. Mutiny is defined as something that shall not happen, but when it does, it shall only be for some justifiable purpose. Nothing justified the taking of a ship from its rightful commander by force. What gave the *Bounty* affair such notoriety was that it was an event without precedent, a shattering occurrence that threatened the stability and order of the British Naval system. The "why?" of the mutiny is still debated today. A definitive answer is impossible, but a review of the record offers some grounds for speculative conclusions.

The *Bounty* departed from Tahiti during the sixteenth month of her voyage. By that time, 10 men had been punished with the lash. The offenses ranged from insubordination—punished in each case with 12 lashes—to desertion, punished with 48 lashes. The record, very moderate for the time, is as follows:

Matthew Quintal *Two dozen for insolence and contempt*
John Williams *Six for neglect of duty*
Alexander Smith *One dozen for insolence and disobedience*
Matthew Thompson *One dozen for insolence and disobedience*
Robert Lamb *One dozen for neglect of duty*
Charles Churchill *Two dozen for attempted desertion*
William Muspratt *Four dozen for attempted desertion*
John Millward *Four dozen for attempted desertion*
Isaac Martin *Nineteen for striking a native*
John Sumner *One dozen for neglect of duty*

Two men had died, one from an undiagnosed illness, the other from extreme alcoholism. Crew injuries had been limited to a nail wound in the carpenter's leg, plus a few bruises and broken ribs from the ship's violent action in storms. Scurvy had been contained, venereal disease had affected only a few men, and the only other illnesses were routine colds and a few rheumatic complaints.

For most of the voyage full rations were served to the crew, and during the long layover in Tahiti the men were allowed to gorge themselves on the native fare. Water was never rationed.

During the cold, wet weather of the passages, fires were kept constantly going and men were assigned to dry the crew's clothing.

Early in the voyage, the usual watch routine of "four on, four off" had been replaced by Cook's innovative system of having the men work only four hours out of each 12-hour period. In Tahiti, liberal shore time was granted, and all crewmen were allowed to keep aboard ship their choice of women.

Why, then, with this record of good health and minor punishments, did this tragic event occur?

In the aftermath of the mutiny, Bligh quickly reached his own conclusions. Here, he wrote, "We may observe to what a height the baseness of human Nature may arrive at, not only ingratitude in its blackest die, but eternal criminality against their Country and connections."

Bligh believed that Tahiti, with its soft life and easy women, was the cause of the mutiny, adding, however, that

. . . no cause could justify such an effect. . . . I can only conjecture that they have Ideally assured themselves of a more happy life among the Otaheitans than they could possibly have in England, which joined to some Female connections has most likely been the leading cause of the Whole business.

. . . . What a temptation it is to such Wretches when they find it in their power, however illegally it can be got at, to fix themselves in the midst of plenty in the finest Island in the World where they need not labour, and where the alurements of disipation are more than equal to any thing that can be conceived.

Bligh traced the beginning of the mutiny back to February 6 when the ship's anchor cable had been nearly cut in two—by crew members, he incorrectly believed. He saw this as a deliberate act to wreck the ship so that its crew could remain in Tahiti.

The act suggested to him that the mutiny "had been long planned." He wrote:

With such deep laid plans of Villany and my mind free of any Suspicions it is not wonderful I have been got the better of. But the possibility of such a Catastrophe, was ever the farthest from my thoughts. Christian was to have dined with me and Supped the preceding Evening [the day of the coconut altercation] but he desired to be excused as he found himself unwell, about which I was concerned rather than suspecting his integrity and honor.

But there were no "deep laid plans of Villany," no great plot. One man, driven to desperation and inspired by an acting midshipman's passionate but ambiguous comment ("the People are ripe for any thing"), organized an impromptu revolt to rid himself of the man who ruled over his life and asserted authority in strict and demeaning terms. His original seven co-conspirators were able-bodied seamen, some or all of whom we may assume were motivated mainly by a desire to return to Tahiti. We know from Bligh's log that John Mills, the gunner's mate, and Thomas Burkett, an able-bodied seaman, were also active participants. The others who remained with the ship included the three young acting midshipmen (at least two of whom, Stewart and Heywood, were confined below decks during the mutiny by Morrison's account); the carpenter's mate and crew, Norman and McIntosh (both of whom, says Morrison, Christian ordered to remain aboard); the armourer, Joseph Coleman (also detained by Christian); Morrison; and several other able-bodied seamen. All other officers, but only four able-bodied seamen, accompanied Bligh. It would be all too easy to draw false conclusions; we can conclude with certainty only that the active mutineers, apart from Christian, were seamen—not officers. Cole, Purcell, Hayward, and Stewart might empathize with Christian, and might even abet his effort to desert, but no mature and stable officer could help but recoil at the enormity of the prospect of mutiny. Knowing this, Christian would not even have approached them; he found the help he needed in the forecastle.

This Bligh did: In the pursuit of duty, which he held above all else, he drove his men not with the lash but with the violence of his temper. The sting of the lash is quick and painful. And then over. Continual verbal insults, like the slow dripping of the Chinese water torture, can destroy completely. Bligh worked on Christian that way, and somewhere between the islands of Tahiti and Tofua, Christian broke and a mutiny occurred. Was Christian's rebellion justifiable?

Perhaps, in terms of how he had been persecuted and if the original plan of his solitary escape from the ship had been followed. When that failed, he resorted to an act of criminal conspiracy with others to obtain his own ends. Because of that, careers were ruined, a ship was lost, men died, and others became outcasts. In the end, Christian relinquished his brief freedom and paid for his act with his own life.

In his *Mutiny of the Bounty,* published in 1831, Sir John Barrow summarized the mutiny as follows:

"Many useful and salutary lessons of conduct may be drawn from this eventful history, more especially by officers of the navy, both old and young, as well as by those subordinate to them. In the first place, it most strongly points out the dreadful consequences that are almost certain to ensue from a state of insubordination and mutiny on board a ship of war; and the equally certain fate that, at one time or other, awaits all those who have misfortune to be concerned in a transaction of this revolting nature. In the present instance, the dreadful retribution which overtook them [the mutineers], and which was evinced in a most extraordinary manner, affords an awful and instructive lesson to seamen, by which they may learn, that although the guilty may be secured for a time in evading the punishment due to the offended laws of society, yet they must not hope to escape from the pursuit of Divine vengeance. . . ."[29]

Divine vengeance, shipwreck, the sea, sickness, the hangman's noose, stones, the ax, and the musket . . . these devices claimed the lives of 71 men, some guilty, some innocent, as the result of Christian's act. In the wake of that act lies the larger story of the mutiny of the *Bounty.*

9

A MORSEL OF BREAD,
A SPOONFUL OF RUM

April 28–May 2, 1789

A crime in itself, 19 men—nearly two tons of human flesh—were abandoned at sea in a small, open boat by the *Bounty* mutineers. In addition to Bligh, they were:

John Fryer   *Master*
Thomas Ledward   *Surgeon's Mate*
David Nelson   *Botanist*
William Peckover   *Gunner*
William Cole   *Boatswain*
William Purcell   *Carpenter*
William Elphinstone   *Master's Mate*
Thomas Hayward   *Midshipman*
John Hallett   *Midshipman*
John Norton   *Quartermaster*
Peter Linkletter   *Quartermaster*
Lawrence Lebogue   *Sailmaker*
John Smith   *Able-bodied Seaman*
Thomas Hall   *Able-bodied Seaman*
George Simpson   *Quartermaster's Mate*
Robert Tinkler   *Able-bodied Seaman*
Robert Lamb   *Able-bodied Seaman*
John Samuel   *Clerk*

To sustain them, they had the following provisions:

150 pounds of bread (ship's biscuit)
16 pieces of pork
6 quarts of rum
6 bottles of wine
28 gallons of water
4 empty breakers (small casks)

Fortunately, they had a remarkably seaworthy boat. Noted watercraft historian Gregory Foster has studied the lines of this boat, which are on file with the National Maritime Museum in Greenwich, England. In a letter to the author, he points out that "even overloaded, running in high seas, Capt. Bligh soon came to rely on this boat's inherent good behavior. It did not play tricks with him.

"It was also an excellent sailing boat. For a 23-foot boat to average close to four knots on a 3,600 mile run, mostly under a double-reefed lug foresail, is more than a respectable performance. It is astounding."

The *Bounty*'s launch was a skeg-built boat 23 feet long, by 6 feet 9 inches beam, by 2 feet 9 inches depth (from rail to keelson). "Ordinarily," Foster writes, "the boat's draft to the bottom of her skeg would have been 2 feet, but with 19 men and supplies on board, the boat drew over 3 feet, leaving a bare 7 to 8 inches of freeboard. The success of the boat's design is not to be found in any extremes or unusual features, but, rather, in its very moderate proportions, normal shape, and sturdy construction.

"Ironically," he adds, "the *Bounty* launch would not pass present day Coast Guard stability standards for a passenger-carrying vessel."

Inside, the boat had six thwarts, a bow platform, and sternsheets with raised floor aft. Normally, Foster explains, "The launch would have been rowed by five or six pairs of oars, double-banked with two men on each thwart pulling one oar apiece." In addition, it would have carried a typical ship's boat rig of the time, which

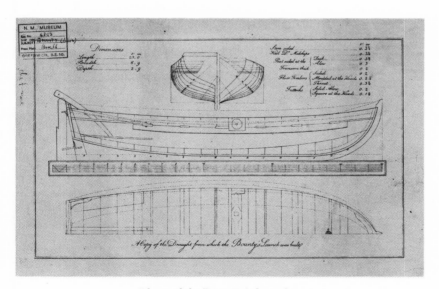

Plans of the Bounty's *launch*

was a two-masted lug rig without a jib. Both sails would have been loose-footed.

"This amazing little vessel," says Foster, "proudly stands at the head of a tradition which produced the most seaworthy rowing and sailing boats ever known. By the late 1700s, this tradition had reached a state-of-the-art that would have to be considered the golden age of European and American boat design and craftsmanship. Thousands of longboats, launches, pinnaces, cutters, yawls, and jollyboats were being produced, each to nearly standard specifications, by leading maritime nations for the use of both naval and merchant shipping.

"Services these ships' boats were called upon to perform included carrying out and retrieving the huge anchors of the mother ship, often towing her, lightering passengers and cargoes, coastal charting and sounding, military expeditions, ship-to-shore and ship-to-ship contacts, and as lifeboats.

"As much as we must admire Bligh for his legendary seamanship and navigational abilities, our respect must be equally to the sweet and solid masterpiece of the boat which, in Bligh's own words, 'performed so well, that I no longer dreaded any danger in that respect'."

And so began an impossible voyage through the largely unknown and uncharted island- and reef-studded waters of the Pacific, the Coral Sea, Australia's Great Barrier Reef, Torres Strait, and the Arafura Sea to the Dutch colony on Timor, a tiny speck of an island nearly four thousand miles away.

What other options had Bligh? None. Tahiti would have been an impossible destination. It was upwind from his position—a direction he could not sail—and it was also the assumed destination of the mutineers. But even Timor, the nearest European outpost, was, for Bligh, but the first step in the long voyage ahead. From Timor he hoped to secure passage on a ship for England—England and the courts of law where justice would be done.

He had reached such a resolve within minutes of being evicted from his ship:

I had scarce got a furlong on my way when I began to reflect on the vicisitudes of human affairs; but in the midst of all I felt an inward happiness which prevented any depression of my spirits, conscious of my own integrity and anxious solicitude for the good of the Service I was on. I found my mind most wonderfully Supported, and began to conceive hopes notwithstanding so heavy a Calamity, to be able to recount to my King and Country my misfortune.

Reflecting back, he added:

What Mans situation could be so peculiarly flattering as mine twelve hours before? I had a Ship in the most perfect of order and well Stored with every necessary both for Service and health; by early attention to those particulars I had acted against the power of Chance in case I could not get through Endeavour Straits as well as against any Accident that might befall me in them, and to add to this I had very successfully got my Plants in the most flourishing and fine order, so that upon the whole the Voyage was two thirds completed and the remaining part no way doubtfull.

By an act of villainy, he had lost the ship that was to complete that voyage. Very well, then: by sheer determination he would continue it in an open boat.

Once away from the ship, he put the events of the morning out of his mind to concentrate, instead, on surviving the situation that now confronted him. The boat was immediately rowed toward Tofua, where Bligh hoped he could find a supply of breadfruit for food, and water. An afternoon breeze allowed the sails to be set, but it was after dark before they reached the island. The shore appeared too rocky and steep to hazard a night landing, so the crew was forced to spend the night in the boat with two oars working to keep it off the beach.

By dawn the boat was underway again as Bligh searched along the island for a landing. A small cove with a surf breaking on its rocky beach was discovered around 10 a.m. The boat could not be beached, so a stern anchor was set about 20 yards off, and the crew waded ashore. Some men were sent inland to search for food and water, but they returned with only a few quarts of rainwater collected from holes in the rocks. Before leaving the cove, Bligh issued a morsel of bread and some wine to each man for dinner.

That afternoon, the launch worked its way south along the island, making a difficult beach landing in order to gather a few coconuts that grew on the summits of the high cliffs back from the shore. Twenty nuts were obtained and hauled to the boat through the surf with ropes. The boat then returned to the cove, where all the men spent their second night on board, stretched out as best they could in the cramped space.

The next morning (April 30) an attempt was made to put to sea, but heavy winds forced the boat to return to the cove. A morsel of bread and a spoonful of rum were issued to each man. Bligh and a few other men climbed the cliffs back from the cove on a second foraging expedition. The group hiked to within a few miles of Tofua's steaming volcano, where the land, said Bligh, was "all cov-

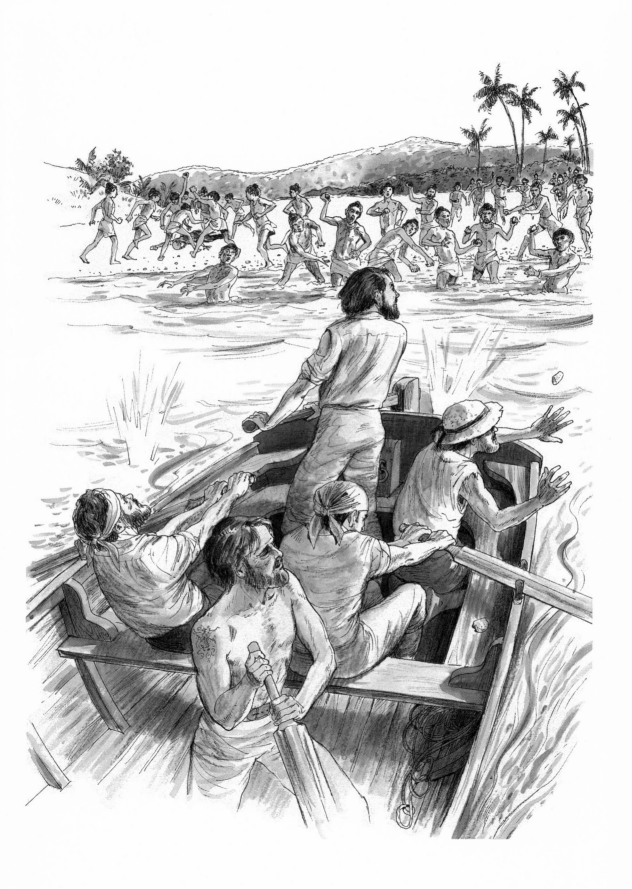

ered with lava and had a horrible appearance." Using coconut shells as containers, they lugged nine gallons of water back to the boat.

Bligh was hoping to encounter natives from whom he might be able to obtain supplies. A few deserted huts had been seen on the inland walk, but there was no other evidence of habitation. That night half the crew slept in the boat and the other half huddled in a cave at the head of the cove.

The next afternoon a party was sent out to search for water, but it returned in the evening without success. Searching for water again the next morning (Sunday, May 2), the party met two native men, a woman, and a child, who were brought to the camp. Soon afterward a group of 30 islanders appeared, and Bligh was able to trade buttons and beads for breadfruit, coconuts, and plantains. Water, however, was not available in any quantity.

Before long a large number of natives had gathered on the beach and, wrote Bligh,

We heard nothing but the knocking of Stones together which they had in each hand, which I knew very well would be the method of Attack.... They were always anxious for me to sit down, but I as constantly refused, for it occurred to Mr. Nelson and myself that by that means they intended to seize hold of me. We eat our miserable dinner in some quiteness.

After Dinner we began by little and little to get our things into the Boat which became troublesome on account of the Surf and I carefully Watched the Motions of the Natives who I found still encreasing in Numbers, and that instead of their intention being to leave us, fires were made and places were fixed for their residence during the Night. Consultations were also held among them & every thing assured me we should be attacked and I sent the Master orders to Keep the Boat well in upon the Beach when he saw us coming down that we might easily get in.

Quietly, so as not to incite an attack, Bligh instructed the crew to load everything into the boat and prepare for an escape. With the sound of the clacking stones growing louder, Bligh walked toward the boat, holding as hostage one of the native chiefs—"every one in a silent kind of horror," he wrote. The chief broke away, and Bligh and his men scrambled through the surf to the boat and climbed in. John Norton ran back up the beach to cast off the stern line.

"I did not conceive that the power of a Man's Arm could throw stones with such force and exactness...."

The attack began as about 200 men began to haul in on the stern line. Norton was knocked to the ground, where he was beaten to death with stones as several men fought for his pants over his dying body. For Bligh, the entire scene reawakened memories of the murder of James Cook on the beach of Hawaii. In his journal entry, Bligh wrote:

I once before sustained an Attack of this Nature with as small a Number of Men against a multitude of Indians. It was (after the death of Captain Cook) on the Mora at Owhyee. . . . Yet, notwithstanding, I did not conceive that the power of a Man's Arm could throw stones from 2 to 8 lbs. Weight, with such force and exactness as these people did. Here unhappily I was without Arms and the Indians soon discovered it.

Bligh cut the stern line, and the boat was pulled out into the deep water on the anchor line. The men began rowing frantically away from the beach, with a canoe carrying 12 natives in close pursuit. Paddling close to the launch, the natives threw large stones at the crew. Bligh and his men were helpless to defend themselves from the stones as the more maneuverable canoe circled the launch at a safe distance. As a desperate ploy, Bligh threw overboard some clothes, which the natives stopped to collect. In the gathering darkness, the launch escaped.

It had been a lucky deliverance. Unarmed, Bligh did not want to hazard another encounter with hostile natives. Even " . . . supposing our lives were safe," he reflected, "Our Boat, Compass and Quadrant would be taken from us, and thereby I should not be able to return to my King and Country to give an account of the transaction."[30]

Night had fallen. The boat was sailing southward along the western shore of Tofua, a dark sky reflecting the smoldering glow of the island volcano. The men in the boat were caring for the wounds and bruises sustained in the attack. Vivid in their minds was the horrible memory of John Norton's head being smashed by stones as he lay helpless on the beach. All hands now looked to Bligh and asked him " . . . to take them towards home."

There would be no relief, he told them, until they reached New Holland in Timor, 1,200 leagues (3,600 miles) to the west, where, Bligh said, "I had no Idea of the part of the Island the settlement was at. . . ."

After the supplies were inventoried, each man agreed to live on "One Ounce of Bread per day and One Jill [four fluid ounces] of Water." On this note, they set sail for Timor.

I therefore after examining what our real Stock of provisions was and recommending this as a sacred promise forever to their memory, bore away across a Sea where the Navigation is dangerous and but little known, and in a Small Boat 23 feet long from Stem to Stern, deep loaded with 18 Souls, without a Single Map, and nothing but my own recollection and general knowledge of the situation of places assisted by an old Book of latitudes and longitude to guide me. . . .

The boat bore away under a reefed lug foresail. The crew was divided into two watches, and then, wrote Bligh, "We returned God thanks for our miraculous preservation, and fully confident of his gracious support, I had a mind more at ease than I had before felt."

10

THROUGH THE BARRIER REEF
May 3–May 28, 1789

The next morning (May 3) found Bligh and his men at sea running before a severe gale. In the troughs of the waves the boat was becalmed and the sail slack, but each time the hull lifted to a wave crest, the wind overburdened even the small, reefed foresail. But the sail had to be kept flying to give the boat steerageway in the overtaking seas, which continuously broke over the stern. The men were kept constantly bailing the overloaded boat—"with all our might," said Bligh, and "a situation equally horrible perhaps was never experienced.

Our bread was in Bags and getting Wet, to be Starved to death was therefore inevitable if it could not be prevented. I therefore began to examine What cloaths there were in the Boat and what other things could possibly be spared, and having determined for only two Suits to be kept for each person, the rest was thrown overboard, which with some Rope and Spare Sails lightened the Boat considerable and We had more Room to bail the Water out. Fortunately the Carpenter had a good Chest in the Boat. I therefore fixed on it to put the Bread in the first favorable Moment. His Tool chest also was cleared and the Tools stowed in the Bottom of the Boat, so that this became a second convenience.

I now served a tea spoonfull of Rum to each person (for we were very wet and cold) with a quarter of a Breadfruit which was scarce eatable for dinner, but our engagement was now fully to be carried in Execution, and I was sacredly determined with my life to make what provisions I had to last Eight Weeks, let the daily proportion be ever so small.

Monday, May 4: Imagine a boat barely long enough for three men to stretch out lengthwise, one man to lie across its width.

Those were the living dimensions of the *Bounty*'s launch. Bligh described the misery of its 18 occupants at sea in a storm:

> This day the weather was very Severe, it blew a Storm from N.E. to E.S.E. The Sea run higher than Yesterday and the fatigue of bailing to keep the Boat from filling was exceedingly great. We could do nothing more than Keep before the Sea, in the course of which the Boat performed so wonderfully well that I no longer dreaded any danger in that respect, but among the hardships we were to undergo that being constantly Wet was not the least. The Nights were very cold, and at daylight our limbs so benumbed that we could scarce find the use of them. At this time I served a tea spoonfull of Rum to each person which every one agreed did him a great deal of good.

Here is the quintessential William Bligh, master seaman who is so confident in both his sailing ability and the seaworthiness of his boat that he can dismiss " . . . any danger in that respect." And then, as the boat runs helpless before the seas with the waves breaking over the low gunwales and the men bailing, a small island is sighted. It is not enough to pass it; Bligh must chart it:

> It was with great difficulty I could Observe, I however got a good latitude & found my situation to be in 18° 58′ S. 182° 16′ E.,[31] having made a N 72 W Course dist. 95 Miles from Yesterday Noon.

And then he added:

> I now divided five Small Cocoa Nutts for our dinners and every one was satisfied.

It is doubtful that every one "was satisfied." No one had eaten anything approaching a full meal for six days. But five coconuts among 18 men was at least enough to sustain life for another day. Another day that would carry Bligh closer to the objectives of his resolute mind: Timor and justice for the men who, by their actions, had deprived him of his ship and placed this boat with its miserable occupants in this hazardous situation.

The island they had sighted was Yangasu Levu in the Lau Group, in the Fijian archipelago. For the next few days they sailed through the islands, which offered the tantalizing prospect of food, water, and rest. But Bligh and the men, remembering Tofua and the death of Norton, knew they could not land because they had no defense against the island inhabitants. (As it turned out,

their caution was well advised; the Fijians were fierce warriors, and their rituals extended to eating the flesh of their victims.) Bligh gave each island a rough fix as he passed, and he drew a chart of his passage through the channel between the two main Fijian islands of Viti Levu and Vanua Levu.

Bligh was concerned about the distances the boat was running each day. He could determine his latitude from noon observations of the sun using the sextant or the less-preferred quadrant, but without an accurate timepiece (there was only a pocket watch aboard) he could not determine longitude by astronomical means. The alternative was to keep an hourly run of speed and courses steered, adjusting as necessary for current and leeway, and use these to estimate the distance and course made good in each 24-hour period from the process of deduced or dead reckoning. The result could be converted to a change in longitude given the distance represented by one degree of longitude in the average latitude of the day's run. Bligh had in the launch the requisite tables for the calculations, but so far he had only been able to make rough estimates of the boat's speed. To improve the accuracy of his navigation, he marked off a log line and then had the crew practice counting the seconds. With this improvised log, he was able to record the day's run more accurately. To keep an account of the boat's run, he wrote, " . . . is of itself laborious, being constantly Wet with the Sea breaking Over us, but as we advanced towards the land the sea became smoother, and I was enable to form a sketch of the Island which will serve to give a General Knowledge of their Extent."

That sketch has been preserved by the Mitchell Library in Sydney, Australia. A. B. Brewster, in his book *The Hill Tribes of Fiji,* wrote: " . . . Bligh's boat almost touched the islets of Nananu, just off the extreme point of Viti Levu. . . . The chart is a perfect sketch of that particular spot, and corresponds accurately with the ordnance map . . . [which was made] when there was every facility for making the survey. How different from the conditions under which Bligh laboured, cramped up in a 23-foot boat, drenched with spray and starved. It shows what a resolute and observant officer he was, and that under the most adverse circumstances he could . . . produce a delineation easily recognisable at the present day." Bligh charted the islands so well that they were known as Bligh's Islands for nearly 80 years.

Tuesday, May 5: In the evening of this day the gale moderated, and the sea was calm enough during the night for the men to rest without bailing. In the morning much of the bread was found to be damaged by seawater and some of it had rotted. Nevertheless, it was all carefully stored in the carpenter's tool chest for future use. Dinner consisted of some of the rotten bread and a gill (or jill, a quarter pint) of water. A fish was hooked, but it was lost before it could be boated. Wrote Bligh:

> Our wants are now beginning to have a dreadfull aspect which nothing but a firm and determined resolution can fight against, a situation peculiarly miserable on a Commander.

Thursday, May 7: It may readily be supposed that our Lodgings are very miserable and confined and I have it only in my power to remedy the last defect by putting ourselves at Watch and Watch so that one half is sitting up while the other has no other Bed than the Bottom of the Boat or upon a Chest, and nothing to cover us but the Heavens. Our Limbs are dreadfully Cramped for we cannot Strech them out, and the Nights are so cold and being generally very wet, we can scarce move ourselves after a few hours Sleep.

Being very Cold I served a teaspoonfull of Rum and a Morsel of Bread for Breakfast.

A current set the boat toward an island shore, and in the late morning two large sailing canoes were observed pursuing the boat. The crew began rowing, and by mid-afternoon the canoes gave up the chase as a rainstorm swept in across the sea. By catching the rain, every man's thirst was quenched and all the water containers were filled. As grateful as they were for the rain, its "attendant consequence," said Bligh, "made us pass the Night very miserably, for being very Wet and no dry things to shift or Cover us, we experienced Cold and Shiverings scarce to be conceived."

The weather moderated on Saturday, May 9. In the afternoon all hands were employed in cleaning the boat and drying clothes. The few rations passed out to the crew had been roughly measured by guess so that each man would get his fair and precious share of the food. Bligh was able to improve the accuracy of the system by making a simple balance scale with two coconut shells and some pistol balls found in the boat, 24 of which weighed 16 ounces. The weight of one pistol ball (272 grains) was adopted as the weight of bread to be issued each man.

The log for this day reflects the compassionate concern of a commander for his men. Realizing that something could happen to him, Bligh described as best he could the location of Timor, and by drawing a map explained to his crew how they might find their way there without him. Dinner that night was a sip of water and a half-ounce of moldy bread—so rotten, commented Bligh, that it was "only eatable by such distressed people." With that, "[we] Sung a Song and Went to Sleep."

"Our wants are now beginning to have a dreadfull aspect...."

By May 10, Bligh estimated the boat had traveled 596 miles since Tofua. The Fiji Islands were astern as he held to a west-by-north course (281°) that he hoped would carry them north of the New Hebrides (known to Bligh only through the record of Cook's second voyage, which had touched there in 1774).

The fair weather continued into the afternoon of May 10, which gave the crew additional time to work on the boat. Rope shrouds were attached to each mast, and by means of these supports, a canvas weather guard was stretched along the boat. It provided an additional eight inches of bulwark height, substantially reducing the amount of spray and broken water that came aboard.

That night a severe thunderstorm dropped drenching rain on the crew. Twenty gallons of water were caught and saved. At midnight, when all hands were "miserable Wet and Cold," a teaspoon of rum was served. The awful night dragged on "without sleep but such as could be got in the Midst of the Rain." The only relief brought by the dawn was its light, which showed "The Sea . . . constantly breaking over us and kept two persons bailing, and we had no Choice how to Steer for we were obliged to keep before the Waves to avoid filling the Boat." For dinner, each man received a half-ounce of pork—"a mouthful for any moderate person," said Bligh, which "was divided into three and four."

Monday, May 11: Strong Gales and very Squally Wr with a high breaking Sea, so that we are miserable Wet and suffer great cold in the Night. Our Limbs being so crampt as scarce to feel the use of them. Our situation was now highly dangerous, the Sea frequently running over our Stern which kept us bailing with all our Strength. . . . Served a tea Spoonfull of Rum and a Morsel of Bread for Breakfast.

After another night of gales, rain, and breaking seas, the dawn, wrote Bligh, "showed to me a poor Miserable set of Beings full of Wants but nothing to releive them. Some complained of a great pain in their Bowels and all of having but little use of their Limbs. I served my tea spoonful of Rum at day dawn as usual, and ¼₄ of a lb. of Bread. . . . Saw fish but cannot catch any. . . . Our cloaths will not dry."

Floating vegetation and birds were sighted on May 13, raising hopes that land was close by. The weather remained the same—dark, cloudy, and squally. The boat constantly shipped water, and the crew was "miserably Wet and Cold." The men found they could stay warmer by rinsing their clothes in the warmer-than-air seawater. That morning Bligh did not issue the regular allowance of rum, as the supply was growing critically short.

The first of the New Hebrides islands were sighted on May 14, by Bligh's estimate 969 miles west of Tofua. The closeness of land, offering as it did rest and nourishment, only increased the misery of the boat's occupants. "We are," commented Bligh, "now but little better than Starving with plenty in View, Yet the risk was so great to get that releif, that prolonging of life even in the midst of misery is preferable While we have hopes of surmounting all our hardships." The islands they sighted, at the northern end of the New Hebrides archipelago, were named collectively by Bligh the Banks Group in honor of his patron.

Hope. It is the fundamental ingredient of survival. It can sustain life in otherwise untenable conditions. Bligh kept his men alive not with their daily "1/24 lb. of Bread and a Jill of Water," but with the small rituals performed in the task of weighing out the meager food, in songs sung in cracked notes, in the keeping of watches, and in the daily recording of observations and progress. As long as there was something that every man could do, would do, there was hope. A gallon of water bailed out of the boat or a leg stretched in the crowded press of bodies was an act of hope.

Even in storm, hope could make wind and rain an ally. The following wind and sea pushed the boat rapidly to the west with runs averaging more than 100 miles a day. And rain, miserable and cold as it was, provided the water that sustained life.

Bligh dispensed hope to his men from the bottomless well of his own determination. To him, the awful weather was "a providential blessing" because, he wrote, "Hot weather would have caused us to have died raving Mad with thirst, yet now altho we Sleep covered with Rain or Sea we suffer not that dreadful Calamity."

Rain and sea continued to cover them on May 16 as the boat ran before a southeasterly gale through a night "dark and dismal" without a "Star to be seen to Steer by and the Sea breaking constantly over us." For dinner, each man was served the luxury of an

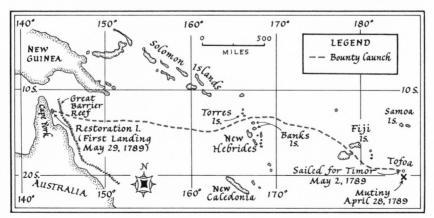

ounce of pork. Bligh's noon sight placed the launch at 13°33'S, and he reckoned their longitude at 165°52'E.

For 17 days and 1,200 miles the launch had been at sea. In all that time, the best weather they had encountered, wrote Bligh, was like "a Winters day in England."

Worse was to come.

Sunday, May 17: Strong Breezes and dark Gloomy Wr with Storms of thunder Lightning and Rain added to our distresses this day, and the Night was truly horrible. . . . Two persons constantly bailing and so dark scarce able to see each other. . . . Always Wet and suffering extreme Cold in the Night without the least Shelter from the Weather. Constantly bailing to keep the Boat from filling is perhaps not an evil to us as it gives exercise. . . . The little Rum I have is of great avail to us, when our Nights are peculiarly distressing. I issue a teaspoonfull to each person, which is always joyfull tidings when they hear of my intentions.

In the morning a waterspout passed them close aboard. The sky was "dreadfully black all around," and no noon sight was possible.

Monday, 18 May: No stars. Steering as the Sea directs us. . . . Every person now complained of violent pain in their Bones. I am only surprized that I have no One yet laid up.

Bligh was aware that with the islands now clear astern, the coast of New Guinea had become another lee shore, much bigger and more difficult to dodge.

I find it necessary to act as much as possible against these Southerly Winds lest I be drove too near New Guinea, for in general we are drove so much before the Sea [that] unless at moderate intervals I was to keep my course up more to the Southward to prevent my falling in with that Coast, we should inevitably from a continuance of the Gales be thrown in sight of it, in which case most probably an End to our Voyage would soon be the consequence.

On this day, Bligh decided that he must get to the south of Endeavour Straits (the direct route to Timor)[32] and search for a break in the Barrier Reef that would get him to the coast of Australia, where he could rest and resupply his food stores.

On the next day, the wind veered from southeast to northeast, which put the boat on a heading that would intersect the Barrier Reef. More like a string of islands awash, the Barrier Reef rises as a great undersea rampart off the northeastern coast of Australia. Along the 1,200-mile eastward edge of the reef break the constant swells of the Coral Sea. In midocean, it suddenly appears as a line of boiling shoal water crossing the horizon. In some places 45 miles wide, the reef is occasionally broken by intricate channels that trend east and west and lead to the more sheltered waters of the Australian coast.

Survival for Bligh and his men lay on the sheltered side of the barrier—but only if they could make it through safely. In their present position, possible disaster confronted the boat as the wind blew it westward toward a lee shore nightmare of coral and breaking seas. The tactical problem confronting Bligh was that his boat was not capable of sailing off a lee shore, and his crew was too weak to row off if they encountered the barrier at an impassable place. In addition, Bligh was in doubt as to where he would come upon the barrier because the location of its outer edge was unknown to him.

Experience at sea is best defined as the ability to anticipate a problem and then work out a solution to avoid that problem. Bligh had already worked out his strategy: "I must keep my Situation so as to make a Southerly Wind a fair One and to range along the Reefs untill I can find an Opening. . . ."

For the moment, the northeast wind suited his plan, which was to sail well south, positioning himself to then turn northward and sail parallel to the reef as he looked for a channel through the barrier. The direction of the wind was favorable, but the weather carried with it was awful. Once again a noon sight proved impossible.

Tuesday, May 19: We past this day miserably Wet and Cold. Covered with Rain and Sea, which we could only act against at intervals by pulling of [off] our Cloaths and wringing them through the Sea Water. In the Night we had severe Lightning but otherwise so dark we could scarce see each other. The Morning produced to me many complaints on the Severity of the Weather, and I would gladly have issued my allowance of Rum if it had not appeared to me that we were to suffer much more, and that it was necessary to preserve the little I had to give releif at a time when less able to bear such hardships, but to make up, I issued about an half ounce of Pork to each person with the allowance of ¼₄ lb. of Bread and a Jill of Water for Dinner . . . which was thought a Feast. All Night and day bailing without intermission.

If Bligh's open boat voyage had been a fictional creation, the writer would have found it difficult and unnecessary to invent ad-

ditional scenes of human misery. But the trials of Bligh and his men continued through another five days of storm, rain, wind, and desperation. Bligh's log, somehow written as he sat cramped and cold in the stern of the boat—his eye constantly on the boat's course, the run of the waves, the set of the sail, and the condition of his men—records the agony:

Wednesday, May 20: Constant heavy Rain and at times a deluge. Always Bailing. At Dawn of day some of my People half dead. Our appearances were horrible. . . . Extreme hunger is now evident, but thirst no one suffers or have we an Inclination to drink, that desire being satisfied through our Skin. What little Sleep we get is in the midst of Water, and we wake with Severe Cramps and Pains in the Bones.

Thursday, May 21: Our Distresses are now extremely great. We are covered with Rain and Sea that we can scarce see or make use of our Eyes. Sleep, altho we long for it, is horrible, for my part I seem to live without it. We suffer extreme cold and every one dreads the approach of Night. About 2 O'Clock in the Morning we experienced a most extreme deluge of Rain, it fell so heavy that we were afraid of a dangerous tendency to the Boat and were obliged to bail with all our might. . . . Our Compass no use to us by Night and we are obliged to steer as the Wind and Sea direct us. . . . Many Sharks, Dolphins and other Fish but we cannot catch any . . . the Sea every five Minutes breaking over us, so that we never can omitt bailing.

On the 22nd, the wind backed more to the southeast, stronger, but without rain. Sail had to be carried to give the boat steerage, but Bligh wrote that he trembled every minute in fear of "losing my Mast." Several seas broke over the boat and almost filled it, and as the day wore on Bligh was forced to a course slightly north of west.

Our Situation to day [is] highly perilous. If ever Men experienced the power of goodness of Divine providence we do at this instant in a most emminent degree, and I presume to say our present situation would make the boldest Seaman tremble that ever lived. We are obliged to take the Course of the Sea, running right before it and breaking all over us. Watching with the utmost Care, as the least Error in the Helm would in a Moment be our destruction.

Despite all this, Bligh, with foam and sea "running over our Stern and quarters . . . got prop[p]ed up" and dutifully made his observations: Latitude 14° 17′ S; course N 85° and W, distance (run) 130 miles; longitude made 155° 42′E.

Saturday, May 23: The misery of this day has exceeded the preceeding. The Night was dreadful. The Sea flew over us with great force and kept us bailing with horror and anxiety. At Dawn of day I found every one in a most distressed Situation, and I now began to fear that another such Night would produce the End of several who were no longer able to bear it. Everyone complained of Severe Bone Achs which was cured in some Measure by about two Spoonfulls of Rum, and having wrung our Cloaths and taken our breakfast of Bread and Water we became a little refreshed.

Finally, on the evening of May 24, after 15 days of storm, the sun came out for the first time, and with it some warmth. Bligh estimated the distance sailed to be 2,040 miles.

Some commanders might have celebrated this break in the weather by serving an extra ration of food. For Bligh, the situation called for the opposite—a reduction in the daily food allowance. He estimated that his bread supply would last 29 days. Bligh believed that he could reach Timor in that amount of time, but not knowing what he would find there, he considered it possible that he might have to sail farther, to Java. To do that, he estimated that he would need a six-week supply of bread. The only way to extend the supply was by a reduction in the daily allowance, a decision that "appeared like robbing them of life. . . ."

In the men's starved condition, this reduction of an already minuscule bread allowance could have presented Bligh with a second mutiny. It was a gamble he was willing to take. By stretching the bread supply, he was able to buy time—another two weeks, if needed, of sailing.

The men caught a noddy "the size of a small pigeon" that flew close to the boat. It was divided into 18 portions. The tiny bits of flesh and bone were distributed by the "Who shall have this?" method (described in Chapter 4).

The men caught more birds during the next two days. Then, on May 27, the weather turned hot, and with the heat came the condition that Bligh feared: " . . . a languor and faintness which gives an indifference to life."

The breakers of the Great Barrier Reef were suddenly heard, then sighted a quarter of a mile ahead at 1 A.M., May 28. Quickly, the boat was put about and sailed clear. The next morning, the men saw the ocean breaking furiously across the north-south line of the horizon. Slowly, Bligh worked the boat back toward the reef. The wind suddenly came down on the boat from the east, and the reef loomed ahead as a dreaded lee shore. Bligh recorded the desperate moment:

I now found that we were embayed, and I could not lie clear with my Sails, such a heavy Sea Setting in and the Wind having backed against us, so that our Situation now became dangerous. I expected but little from the Oars because we had no Strength to pull them, and it was becoming every minute more and more probable that I should be obliged to take the Reef in case we could not pull off.

By good luck, a passage through the reef was discovered about a mile ahead. The launch entered the break, and a strong westward moving current carried it through to the protected waters of the reef's lee.* "All our past hardships already seemed to be forgot," wrote Bligh, adding, "We now returned God thanks for his gracious protection and with much content took our miserable allowance of 1/24 of Bread and a Jill of Water for Dinner."

Once inside the reef, the launch landed on an island and the crew stepped ashore. Behind them was the ordeal of 2,488 miles and 26 days and nights in the boat; in all that time, no man had eaten a full meal, been sheltered, or enjoyed a night's sleep, and only a few had moved their bowels. That every man survived was remarkable. That Bligh's navigation had been so accurate was equally remarkable. Had he possessed all modern navigation aids, he could not have sailed a more direct route to the landfall he set as his objective. His course intersected the Great Barrier Reef exactly where he planned, south of Cape York, so that he could range along the reef in search of an opening across it, then sail the sheltered inside waters in search of food.

William Bligh stands with James Cook as one of the greatest navigators of all times. Was Bligh, captain of a lifeboat, a different man from the Bligh who commanded the *Bounty*? Here, on this difficult voyage—as in his contest with Cape Horn—Bligh was able to summon the true qualities of leadership: skill, decisive action, and compassion for those he commanded. In the most difficult and adverse conditions, his authority was mandated by the demands of wind and sea, and he rose to his magnificent best. Authority backed by curses and the threat of punishment might have been appropriate for the quarterdeck of a King's ship. For a starving, wet, and cold crew, constantly exposed to the punishment of the open sea, a commander's threat of additional punishment would have been meaningless. Bligh's role in the voyage of the open boat was not to threaten, but to encourage, and to stand for his men against their common adversary, the cruel and inhospitable open sea; his role was not to inflict pain, but to accept it. And perhaps most difficult, to accept it without complaint.

*The opening is still on the charts as Bligh Passage, at 12°53′S, 143°55′E.

11

TO TIMOR
May 29–June 15, 1789

Low, rocky, and nearly barren, the island off the northeastern coast of Australia where the *Bounty*'s launch landed was nothing like the Tahitian paradise the men had left behind nearly two months before. Yet probably no human being ever touched land with more relief and gratitude than did the 18 men who stumbled ashore late in the afternoon of Friday, May 29 on this speck of land. Its very desolation was safety; since it was uninhabited, the men were able to devote what energy they had not to defense, but to the gathering of food.

Bligh named their landfall Restoration Island, "This being the Day of the Restoration of King Charles the Second, and the name being not inapplicable to my present situation (for it has restored us to fresh life and Strength). . . ."

The crew searched the island and found a few oysters. Bligh started a fire with a magnifying glass, and the oysters, cooked with some bread and pork in a copper pot, made a stew that "was eatable by People of more delicate appetites of which each person received a full pint."

Everyone was very weak. The general complaints were dizziness, weakness of the joints, and "violent Tenesmus [a painfully urgent but ineffectual attempt to defecate], most of us having had no evacuation since we left the ship." But none of the complaints were serious. "On the contrary," he observed, "every one retained marks of Strength that with a mind possessed of any fortitude could bear more fatigue than I hoped we had to undergo in my route to Timor."

A work party dug a well and refilled the boat's water kegs. Another party cleaned the boat and in doing so, discovered that one of the rudder pintles had fallen out. It was a shocking discovery. Had it happened at sea, wrote Bligh, it "would probably have been the Cause of our perishing, as the Management of the Boat would have been lost."

In preparing a second stew, Bligh withheld the bread ration. Fryer, the master, and Purcell, the carpenter, protested, which tended, Bligh wrote, "to create disorder among those if any were weak enough to listen. . . ." More trouble followed when Bligh ordered a few men to gather oysters for sea stores. They complained and Bligh, furious as always when one of his orders was questioned, wrote: "Our full Bellies made us forget the Necessity and I had an Opposition to such a plan Alledging they were too Weak. . . . I [saw] that these unthankfull people were no sooner saved from perishing with want and fatigue than they had forgot the mercies they had received."

Some of the men wanted to stay longer on the island; some wanted to leave immediately. They were employed gathering as much food and water as could be found. Bligh read prayers on the afternoon of Sunday, May 31, and immediately thereafter natives were seen on the mainland shore. They were armed with spears and made motions for the boat crew to row toward them. Bligh ordered an immediate departure from the island.

All night the launch sailed northward, Bligh piloting the boat according to what he remembered of Cook's 1770 survey of the northeastern Australian coast. Daybreak revealed "the appearance of the Country all changed, as if in the Course of the Night I had been transported to another part of the World, for I had now a miserable low Sandy Coast in view with very little Verdure or anything to indicate it was at all habitable to a human being. . . ." Other small groups of natives were seen, their gestures and behavior ambiguous, but no canoes gave chase.

At 8 A.M. on Sunday morning (Monday in civil time) the boat again landed on a small island. Bligh immediately ordered two parties to search for food. For the second time, his authority was challenged. The men he assigned to gather food "declared that they would rather go without their Dinner than go out."

Then Purcell, wrote Bligh, "began to be insolent to a high degree, and at last told me with a mutinous aspect he was as good a Man as I was. I did not just now see where this was to end, I therefore determined to strike a final blow at it, and either to preserve my Command or die in the attempt, and taking hold of a Cutlass I ordered the Rascal to take hold of another and defend himself, when he called out that I was going to kill him and began to make concessions."

Fryer then called on Cole (the boatswain) to put Bligh under arrest. Bligh threatened to kill Fryer "if he interfered when I was in the execution of my duty to preserve Order and regularity. . . ."

His threat nipped the incipient revolt, but Bligh was reminded that he could not command without power, "for some had forgot every degree of obedience." The only weapon he carried was his cutlass, and he "determined never to have it from under my Seat, or out of my Reach, as providence had seemed pleased to give me sufficient Strength to make use of it."

In Fryer's version of the altercation, three groups of men had gone off to gather shellfish, the agreement being (because some men were less able or willing to forage than others) that each group could keep what they found. According to Fryer, Bligh reneged by trying to appropriate Purcell's oysters for consumption by all of them, which Purcell refused. Bligh seized a cutlass, Pur-

"I determined to strike a final blow at it. . . ."

cell declined to take up arms against his commander, and Fryer then intervened, ordering that both men be placed under arrest. Fryer would have us believe that Bligh's exercise of authority here was arbitrary and shrill, his use of force improper. But the suggestion that Bligh be arrested was an extreme and ridiculous challenge, a sullen proposition from a man only too anxious to undermine his leader. Fryer cannot have had the success of their desperate voyage or the safety of his fellows squarely in view.

The rebellion put down, Bligh again ordered the men to collect food and water while he walked to the highest point on the island to survey the waters ahead. He was looking for an island on which they could spend the night, believing the one they were on too vulnerable to attack by natives. The food gathering party was unsuccessful; the oysters they had hoped to gather were too hard to pry from the rocks, and clams were scarce.

That afternoon, after another meal of oyster stew, the men left the island and headed north, toward an island Bligh had spotted. They reached it just at dark and found it ringed by a reef that Bligh did not want to cross at night. They anchored the boat offshore and slept aboard.

Food sources were as bleak on this island as they had been on the one just left behind. Turtle tracks were seen, but no turtles. The island marked a low spot in the morale, discipline, and health of the crew. A severe case of sunstroke afflicted Nelson, leaving him unable to walk. Purcell and Cole were also ill, and nearly all the men were "shockingly distressed with the Tenesmus," wrote Bligh, "so that I had but few who were not complaining." Most of the stomach troubles were caused because the men had gorged themselves on wild beans and berries despite Bligh's warnings to be cautious about eating unknown foods. Bligh's noon sight with the Ramsden sextant placed them at 11°47′S. Fryer was finally permitted to discharge his professional duty by taking a confirming sight with the quadrant. His result was 11°50′S.

A strong wind prevented their sailing that afternoon, and Bligh decided to lay over another night. He told the men to keep the evening fire as small as possible to avoid detection by natives. Fryer, more and more a problem, started his own fire. It quickly got out of control, burned a large grassy area, and became a beacon inviting attack. The natives, feared Bligh, "now being assured that we were on this Key it only rested with them to come after us and we must inevitable fallen a sacrifice, for even when all were in health I had only 12 Men that had either Spirit or resolution to Combat any difficulty."

That evening several men went out to search for turtles and birds. The bird hunters returned about midnight with only a dozen noddies. Others might have been caught had it not been for Robert Lamb, able-bodied seaman, who separated from the hunting group and frightened off the birds. (He later admitted to catching nine of the birds and eating them raw.)

"Thus all my Plans were totally defeated," wrote the disappointed Bligh, who had hoped that the coastal islands would provide him with a food reserve for the difficult voyage ahead.

Another disappointment befell Bligh this day: the stoppage of his timepiece. Regretfully, he wrote, "The Gunner when he left the Ship brought his Watch with him and had regulated our time untill to day when unfortunately I found it Stopt, so that at Noon, Sun Rise and Set are the only parts of the 24 Hours I can speak to particularly as to time."

At dawn on June 2 (June 3 civil time), the launch put to sea on a course to clear Cape York. Almost immediately the boat moved out of the shelter of the Barrier Reef and was surrounded by heavy seas. Bligh was now following the track laid down by Cook in his exploratory passage through Endeavour Straits in 1770. Since the strait provided a critical link between the Coral and Arafura seas, Bligh, always the surveyor and cartographer, did the best he could to provide additional charting information. Sailing westward before half a gale, his crew weakened by starvation, his only timepiece no longer working, and still 1,500 miles from a port of refuge, Bligh apologized in his log for being unable to sound the channel in one critical section of the strait. He wrote: "I am sorry it is not in my power to speak of the depth of Water." He had hoped to make a more complete survey of the waters around Cape York itself, but circumstances did not allow it: "In the deplorable Situation I was in I would have endeavored to determine this point if I had any fire Arms, but any encrease of trouble or fatigue I feared would have been of too dangerous a tendency. . . ."

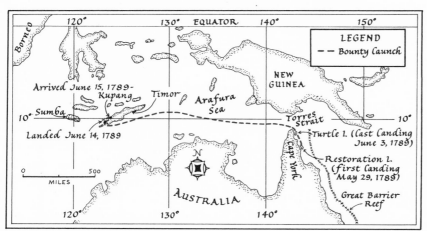

In the afternoon of June 3, the cape drew abeam, and in the early evening they anchored for a windy night off Turtle Island, six miles from the mainland and several miles south of Mt. Adolphus Island. They sailed again at dawn. Bligh mistook Endeavour Strait for a deep embayment which he dared not enter for fear of being trapped on a lee shore, and by noon they were entering the Prince of Wales Channel to the north. After negotiating the channel the boat was put on a course for Timor, across the open Arafura Sea. By the following evening all land was astern, and, reported Bligh, "I was once again launched into the midst of an Open Ocean, miserable as we were in every respect."

It could have been a time of deep despair as the men were again forced to huddle cramped in the boat, their rations once more a pitiful morsel of bread and a jill of water. But in some sense they had returned to their element. As the launch sailed westward before a fresh gale, Bligh wrote:

On reflexion I was surprized to see it [the departure] did not appear to effect anyone as a melancholy matter of necessity; on the contrary it seemed as if every one had only embarked with me to proceed to Timor, and were in a Vessel equally calculated for their Safety and convenience. So much confidence gave me great pleasure, & I may assert that owing to it we may attribute their being so well as they are, for whoever had despaired would have been dead before I got to New Holland. I now gave everyone hopes that eight or ten days might restore us to a land of Safety, and after praying to God for a continuance of his most gracious protection I served an Allowance of Water for Supper and kept my Course to the W.S.W. to counteract a Gale from the Southward in case it should overblow.

Reviewing the six days the launch had spent in the sheltered waters inside the Barrier Reef, Bligh felt that the food and rest obtained had prolonged the men's lives. Without that, he wrote:

It would have been about this time that human Nature would have no longer been able to defend itself against hunger and extreme fatigue, several would have given up Struggling with life that only insured wretchedness and misery, and those possessed of more bodily Strength would on such a Sight soon have followed their miserable and unfortunate companions. Even in our present situation we are reduced beings horrible to behold. Yet while any fortitude and Spirit remain we drag on, and I hope that the Idea of the End of our Misery being so near at hand will yet enable me to land every one safe at Timor.

Bligh himself, driven by his determination to reach Timor, seemed impervious to the hardships of the voyage. "I feel no extreme hunger or thirst," he wrote. "My allowance satisfied me, knowing I can have no more."

As he contemplated each day the hollow-eyed countenances of 17 starving men, the possibility of cannibalism crossed his mind. Feeling no great hunger himself, he admitted that perhaps he was not "a proper judge . . . of miserable people like us being at last drove to the necessity of destroying one another for food. . . . I say I do not believe that among us such a thing could happen, but death through famine would be received as from any violent disease."

It would take 12 days for the *Bounty*'s launch to cross from Cape York to Coupang (now Kupang), the Dutch colony on the southwest tip of Timor. At Cape York the voyage had already lasted a month and covered a distance of 2,642 miles. Constant exposure to the weather, the lack of food, and the cramped living conditions aboard the boat had left the crew with nothing to draw on for the journey ahead except Bligh's determination to reach Timor.

Saturday, June 6: Constantly Shipping Water and bailing. In the Evening a few Boobies came about us, one of which I caught with my hand, the blood was divided among three who were most in Want, but the Bird I ordered to be Kept for dinner. . . . In the Course of the Night we suffered much Cold and Shiverings.

"Amongst most of the others I observe more than a common inclination to Sleep. . . ."

On June 7, the bread supply was inventoried and Bligh felt there was enough so that it could again be issued three times a day at ¹⁄₂₄ pound per serving. The gale continued, the sea high and frequently breaking over the launch. The voyage this day passed the 3,000-mile mark.

The men were slowly slipping toward death—two of them, Ledward the surgeon and Lebogue the sailmaker, rapidly failing. Bligh had held a small amount of rum in reserve for just such a crisis; the two men were given a teaspoon each. The rest of the crew was not much better off.

"Amongst most of the others," noted Bligh, "I observe more than a common inclination to Sleep, a Symptom of Nature being almost reduced to its last effort."

Another 106 miles were reeled off before strong east winds and a high running sea.

A small dolphin was caught on June 9. Each person was served four ounces of the fish at midday; the rest was put aside for a one-ounce dinner serving. At daylight, observed Bligh, "I . . . heard and felt every miserable complaint." Bligh knew he was in a race with death. All he could offer the two sick men was the hope that in a few days they would be in Timor. Although the continuous northeast gale brought misery and kept the men constantly bailing, it was his only ally. "Shipping much Water and bailing," he wrote, "but it is a blessing that we are going on so rapidly." By noon on June 9, another 109 miles had been put astern.

But how much farther? Bligh did not know. He did not know where or *if* he could find the Dutch outpost. In his own mind, he was prepared–if necessary—to sail farther west to Batavia on Java. He had hoarded his bread supplies for the possibility of such an extended passage. But how many would arrive with him at whatever port of refuge they found? Not many if the voyage lasted much longer.

Wednesday, June 10: Fresh Gales and fair Wr but a continuance of much Sea which by breaking almost constantly over us, we are miserable Wet and suffer much Cold in the Night.

. . . In the Morning after a miserable Night I began to see an Alteration for the Worse with more than half my people, whose looks rather indicated an approaching end to their distresses.

In solemn, almost liturgical language, he wrote: "They received of Bread and Water for Breakfast and Dinner."

On the long voyage across the Coral Sea, Bligh had been able to sustain the spirits of his men by the rituals of watch keeping and carefully weighing out food rations, by stories told, and by nightly singing. Now the men were beyond caring. The only life-sustaining events of the day were three morsels of bread and Bligh's noon observation, which recorded their progress across an empty, gale-lashed sea.

This is the log entry on the last day of a voyage without hope. That it sailed one more day, and in so doing, reached the island of Timor, was because one man had willed that he, in defiance of all adversity, would reach this destination.

Thursday, June 11: Birds and Rock Weed show us we are not far from Land, but I know such signs must be here, as a long String of Islands stretch to the Eastward from Timor towards New Guinea. I however hope to fall in with Timor every hour, or else I have scarce a hope but I shall lose some of my People. An extreme Weakness, Swelled legs, Hollow and Ghastly countenances, great melancholy proofs of an approaching disolution.

The Surgeon and an Old hard Seaman Lawce. Lebogue are indeed miserable Objects. I issue to them a few tea spoonfulls of Wine out of the little I have preserved for this dreadfull Stage, and it seems to help and may secure their existence a little longer. For my own part a great share of spirits and no doubt of being able to accomplish the Voyage seems to be my principal Support; but the Boatswain when I was rallying him to day, very innocently told me that he realy thought I looked Worse than any one in the Boat [Bligh had been poisoned by eating the dolphin's stomach parts]. The simplicity however with which he uttered such an Opinion diverted me, and I had good humour enough to return him with a better Compliment.

Incredibly, after sailing a distance of 3,419 miles without charts or an accurate time-keeper, during which his observations had been made from a wildly dancing boat as men supported him upright, he projected his position as being only "33 leagues" (ninety-nine miles) from the eastern end of Timor. At sundown, Friday, June 12, a lookout was posted in the bow to watch for the landfall. At three the next morning, Timor was sighted, just 10 miles short of Bligh's expected landfall. The log entry reads:

It is not possible for me to describe the joy that the blessing of seeing the Land diffused among us, indeed it is scarce within the scope of beleif that in 41 days I could be on the Coast of Timor in which time we have run by our Log 3623 Miles which on a Medium is 90 Miles a Day.

It was Timor, but not yet the Dutch colony. The launch sailed to within two miles of the coast and then continued running on a westerly course along the southeast shore as Bligh searched for the settlement. He dared not land for fear of natives, and not knowing how far he would yet have to sail, he kept the men on the same small ration of bread three times a day. "Voraciousness," he later wrote, "had I been incapable of acting, would have carried the Boat on shore as soon as I made the Island, without considering or knowing that landing among the Malays might be as bad as among any other Indians."

That evening the boat hove to for the night so the settlement would not be passed in the dark. They got underway again Sunday morning with fresh gales. Bligh stood out from shore to clear what he thought at first was the southern end of Timor, but turned out to be a small, off-lying island. When the mistake was clear they stood back inshore in testing seas; Fryer claimed in his journal that he tried without success to keep Bligh from the error, which Bligh then tried to blame on him. With the boat close inshore, Fryer and Purcell, "[who had] been troublesome," reported Bligh, "and asserted I kept them from getting Supplies," were given leave to quit the Boat. No other men wanted to follow, and the two remained aboard.

Sunday, June 14: At 2 O'Clock this Afternoon after having run through a very dangerous Sea . . . We discovered a Spacious Bay or Sound with a fair Entrance about 2 or 3 Miles Wide. I now conceived Hopes that my Voyage was nearly at an End, as no place could Appear more eligible for Shipping and of Course likely to be the Dutch Settlement. I therefore bore up and Came to a Grapnel [anchor] on the East side of the Entrance in a small sandy Bay where we Saw a Hut, a Dog and some Cattle, and I immediately sent the Boatswain and Gunner away to the Hut in Order to discover the Inhabitants.

"A signal of distress. . ."

The two crewmen brought back some Malaysians, one of whom agreed to guide the boat to Coupang. That night the wind died and the boat was forced to anchor again. Now, for the first time, Bligh "issued a double Allowance of Bread and a little Wine to each person."

"At one O'Clock in the Morning," he continued, "After the most happy & sweetest Sleep that ever Men had, I weighed and continued to keep the East shore on board in very Smooth Water. . . ."

All through the dark morning the crew rowed, fortified by a double allowance of bread and wine. At 4 A.M., they were off the settlement. And then Bligh, always a King's officer, showed that although he had lost his ship, he had not lost his manners as a gentleman.

During the long voyage he had sewn together strips of old signal flags into a small Union Jack. This pathetic patchwork of rags he hoisted in the mizzen shrouds as, he wrote, "a Signal of distress, for I did not for very evident reasons chuse to land without leave."

Bligh landed first, was officially welcomed, and then asked that his men be allowed to land. He described the scene:

> The abilities of the most eminent Artists perhaps could never have more brilliantly shone than in a delineation of two Groups of Figures that at this time presented themselves, and where one might be so much at a loss to know which most to admire, whether the Eyes of Famine sparkling at immediate releif, or their Preserver horror Struck at the Spectres of Men. For anyone to Conceive the picture of such poor Miserable Beings, let him fancy that in his House he is in the moment of giving releif to Eighteen Men whose ghastly countenances, but from the known Cause, would be equally liable to affright as demand pity; let him view their limbs full of Sores and their Bodies nothing but Skin and Bones habited in Rags, and at last let him Conceive he sees the Tears of Joy and gratitude flowing O'er their Cheeks at their Benefactors. With the mixture of horror, surprize and pity that his Mind will be then agitated, were the People of Timor on giving us releif.

12

RETURN TO ENGLAND
June 15, 1789–March 14, 1790

B ligh and his men spent more than a month in Coupang recuperating from their terrible ordeal. The Dutch governor of the colony provided them with a house, furniture, servants and, of course, all the food the wretched men could eat. Recovery was slow.

Every man was still suffering from the "excruciating torture" of tenesmus, in addition to extreme weakness, vomiting, swollen legs, and open sores. The resident doctor prescribed moderate eating, frequent baths, and moderate exercise.

Bligh was sick with a fever and could eat very little. Many of the crew, however, were suffering from gorging themselves, particularly on fruit. Confined to his bed, Bligh reflected on "the suffering I had gone through, of the failure of my expedition" and thanked God "who had given me power to support and bear such heavy calamities, and to enable me at last to be the means of Saving 18 Lives which would never otherwise have been thought of."

Bligh wrote that the difficult part of the voyage, for him, was that daily he " . . . had to oblige every one to drag on a lingering life with a miserable allowance of support . . ." and daily he had to say no to the crew's " . . . melancholy request of 'Give us more Bread. . . .'"

Summing up the ordeal of the long voyage in his June 14 log entry, he wrote,

When I reflect how providentially our lives were saved at Tofua by the Indians delaying their Attack, and that with scarce anything for forty Eight Days to support life we have crossed a Sea of more than 1200 leagues without shelter from the inclemency or protection from the Evils of the Climates; When I reflect how natural it was to be expected that disease might have taken most of us off, besides the great probability of foundering at Sea . . . it calls up a distracted mind of astonishment, and most humble gratitude and reverence to Almighty God. Through such blessing only could I bear with the failure of an expedition on which I had so much set my mind, had completed so far with such extraordinary Success. . . .

Within hours of his landing, Bligh prepared letters and reports that would eventually reach both England and India to initiate the search for what was now the pirate ship *Bounty*. In a letter to his wife, Betsy, Bligh wrote:

My Dear, Dear Betsy,
I am now in a part of the world that I never expected; it is, however, a place that has afforded me relief and saved my life, and I have the happiness to assure you I am now in perfect health. . . . What an emotion does my heart and soul feel that I have once more an opportunity of writing to you and my little angels [Bligh's daughters], and particularly as you have all been so near losing the best of friends, when you would have had no person to have regarded you as I do, and you must have spent the remainder of your days without knowing what was become of me, or what would have been still worse, to have known I had been starved to death at sea or destroyed by Indians—all these dreadful circumstances I have combated with success, and in the most extraordinary manner that ever happened, never despairing from the first moment of my disaster that I should overcome all my difficulties.[33]

Bligh overstated the condition of his own health, but in spite of his fever and weakness, he began to make preparations for leaving Coupang. Batavia (now Djakarta), on the island of Java, was the headquarters of the Dutch East India Company. There Bligh knew he could find a ship that would return him to England. The climate of Batavia, however, was known to be particularly unhealthy for Europeans. The worst months of the year for malaria and dysentery were the monsoon months of November, December, and January.

He made an unsuccessful attempt to charter a vessel to transport the men to Batavia. Finally he purchased a small schooner, which he named *Resource*. It measured 34 feet 7 inches long, with a beam of 10 feet 7 inches. (Bligh was able to purchase this vessel, outfit it, and pay for his crew's keep at Timor by writing drafts on the Royal Navy account, which the governor of Timor honored.) The carpenter, the boatswain, and the sailmaker began working with Chinese laborors to ready the boat for sea.

By the early part of July, the general health of most of the crew had improved. Some, however, remained stricken with fevers, including Nelson, the botanist, who was seriously ill.

On July 20, wrote Bligh, "Mr. David Nelson departed this life. The Fever was inflamatary." He was buried without a tombstone "behind the Chappel in the Ground appropriated to the Europeans of the Town." Bligh was greatly saddened by the loss of Nelson, a man who, he wrote, "had accomplished through great care and diligence the object he was sent for, always forwarding every plan I had for the good of the Service we were on."

The journal entry for July 31 provides a rare glimpse of Bligh's own state of mind during what must have been a time of physical weakness and emotional regret:

The Mango Trees are now in blossom and some of the Jambolang, and the Bushes in general indicate the advance of Spring. All these circumstances recalls to me the loss of Mr. Nelson and the object of my Voyage, which at times almost bear me down, but for the impropriety to let so much Weakness get the better of me.

By mid August, work on the schooner was nearly completed, and it was stocked with food, water, and firewood. The governor of Timor loaned Bligh muskets, ammunition, and four swivel cannons as protection against possible pirate attacks. On August 20, with the *Bounty*'s launch in tow, Bligh and his 16 loyal crewmembers set sail in the schooner for the voyage west through the Savu Sea, the Straits of Mangaryn (west of Flores Island), and the Java Sea to Batavia.

Bligh kept a second journal, titled *Voyage in the Resource*,[34] which followed his voyage from Coupang to Batavia and his journey from there to England by way of the Cape of Good Hope in the Dutch East India merchant ship *Vlydte*.

Ill health, grumbling, and frayed tempers marked the schooner's slow passage in light winds through the sultry, hazy weather of the Savu Sea. Intermittent views of the islands revealed high volcanic peaks set back from green, jungle-clad valleys. Strong currents at times took charge of the boat's course as Bligh attempted to follow an inaccurate chart through the islands of the Indonesian archipelago.

Three weeks and 1,125 miles out of Coupang, the schooner came to anchor in Surabaja on the island of Java, where supplies were taken on. As the schooner was about to sail, Bligh's old nemeses, Fryer and Purcell, brought about an ugly uprising. "The carpenter became the spokesman," wrote Bligh, and said " . . . 'we are used damned Ill, nor have we any right to be used so.'" For Bligh, this was not only an insubordinate act but one which publicly humiliated him as a naval officer. He called for the Dutch authorities to investigate the accusations because, as he wrote, "I now no longer found my Honor or Person safe among these people." He ordered the arrest of the two men.

The authorities ordered a court hearing, and Cole, Hallett and Ledward were brought before it for questioning. All apologized and were excused. Bligh, however, had had enough of Fryer and Purcell for the time. Two local sailing craft were assigned to guide the *Resource* to Batavia, and in one of these Fryer and Purcell sailed in chains. It was a sad and ignoble conclusion to the remarkable and courageous open boat voyage from Tofua to Timor. Those men who owed so much to Bligh (and he to them) he now referred to as "The Mutinous pack of people about me."

On October 1, after a voyage of 1,576 miles from Coupang, the *Resource* anchored at Batavia. Bligh immediately came down with a fever so severe he feared "after all my distresses that I was finally to close my Carreer of life in this sad place. . . ." Two other men were also down with fever (malaria). One of them, Thomas Hall, died from it.

Though desperately ill himself, Bligh arranged to sell the schooner and the *Bounty*'s launch at public auction and began making inquiries for passage home. He was able to arrange almost immediate passage on the *Vlydte,* along with his clerk, John Samuel, and seaman John Smith. The rest of the crew were to take passage on the next available ship. Bligh made arrangements for the crew's lodging at Batavia, and on October 16 he set sail for the Cape of Good Hope.

Those left behind were:

           John Fryer, Master
           Wm. Cole, Boatswain
           Wm. Peckover, Gunner
           Wm. Elphinstone, Master's Mate
           Thos. Hayward, Midshipman
           John Hallett, Midshipman
           Wm. Purcell, Carpenter
           Thos. Ledward, Surgeon
           Geo. Simpson, Quartermaster's Mate
           Lawrence Lebogue, Sailmaker
           Peter Linkletter, Quartermaster
           Robt. Tinkler, Able-Bodied Seaman
           Robt. Lamb, Able-Bodied Seaman

Bligh was not long aboard the *Vlydte* before his journal remarks turned to criticism of Dutch seamanship. "The men," he observed, "are stinking and dirty with long beards, and their Bedding a nuisance, as may be conceived when they have not washed Hammocks since they have been from Europe. The Capt. in his person and bedding equally dirty. Some of the people [have] not a second shift of Cloaths. Cookery so bad I cannot make a Meal: such nasty beasts."

Continually, he thought the ship undersailed. "Jogging along in a Slavenly way" is how he described the long run across the Indian Ocean to the Cape of Good Hope. Bligh took his own sights at noon, which he then compared with the Dutch officer's observations. Often, the positions of the two observations were miles apart, Bligh, of course—and with justification—assuming his to be the more accurate.

Owen Rutter, who edited the journal Bligh kept while a guest aboard the *Vlydte,* excuses Bligh's impatience this way:

"He had been Cook's navigator; he was a naval officer accustomed to a severe discipline, and to naval standards of smartness and cleanliness; and, finally, he was impatient to get home and bring retribution to the mutineers of the *Bounty.*"

Bligh's journals, Rutter says, "thus display many of Bligh's characteristics which remained constant throughout his career: his detestation of inefficiency, his insistence upon discipline, his accuracy as a navigator, his determination in the face of danger, [and] his irascibility. . . ."[35]

On December 17, 61 days out from Batavia, the *Vlydte* arrived at Cape Town. Immediately Bligh went ashore to make his report to the Dutch governor. Bligh's health had greatly improved, and he decided not to await the arrival of the men who had been left in Batavia but to continue on to England in the *Vlydte.*

On January 2, 1790, Bligh headed out into the Atlantic Ocean on the homeward leg of the voyage he had begun two years earlier. It was an uneventful passage, with Bligh frequently chafing at the slow progress of the ship. ("If I had the Command of this Vessel I could run 1 ½ Knot per Hour more than this Man.")

On Sunday, March 14, 70 days out from the Cape of Good Hope, Bligh landed at Portsmouth. Within a few months, he was famous throughout England.

Back in London, he wrote a book about the voyage of the *Bounty* and the mutiny. It made Bligh something of a hero when it was published under the sweeping title of *A Narrative of the Mutiny on board His Majesty's Ship Bounty; and the Subsequent Voyage of a Part of the Crew in the Ship's Boat, From Tofoa, one of the Friendly Islands, to Timor, a Dutch Settlement in the East Indies.*

The book, of course, was Bligh's view of the events, and the story was slanted in his favor. He was absolved of all blame for the loss of his ship and promoted to post-captain. Within 18 months he was given command of another ship, the *Providence,* and in her he returned to Tahiti to complete the breadfruit mission, thus at last discharging the responsibility he had assumed with command of the *Bounty* five years before.

RETURN
TO
ENGLAND

13

THE MUTINEERS
April 28–September 23, 1789

Twenty-five men were left aboard the *Bounty* after the mutiny. Some had been active participants in the uprising; others found themselves left aboard not by preference but by circumstance. A few men had been restrained from joining Bligh, and several more were unable to go with Bligh because there was no room in the dangerously overloaded launch. Thus, Christian's command began with divided loyalties; it would end a few years later in violence and death.

With the *Bounty*'s launch disappearing from sight, Christian called the men together, and all agreed to return to Tahiti. He divided the men into two watches, taking charge of one watch himself and placing the other under the command of Midshipman George Stewart. Morrison was placed in charge of stores and was appointed boatswain. His journal provides our only account of the dark, turbulent weeks that unfolded.

For the next month, the *Bounty* sailed eastward. During this time, says Morrison, he and a few other men (of whom only Coleman is named) laid plans to retake the ship after she anchored at Tahiti, at which time resistance might be weakened by extra rations of grog, and those most feared (certainly including Christian and Churchill, and probably Quintal and McCoy) could be put ashore. Christian, however, got word of the plot and armed his most loyal supporters, so Morrison's plan was never carried out. From then on, Christian himself was always armed, and, wrote Morrison, " . . . a sharp look out was kept by his party one of which took care to make a third when they saw any two in Conversation."

One can only speculate on the thoughts and fears that might have crossed Christian's mind as the *Bounty* retraced its track to Tahiti. If Bligh and his companions were lost at sea, he, Christian, would be guilty of murder. On the other hand, if Bligh were to return to England, then Christian and his men would be declared outlaws and the object of a search. Either way, all knew that they faced a future of self-imposed exile. But where?

On May 28 the *Bounty* closed with the island of Tubuai, some 300 miles south of Tahiti. Cook had charted the island on his third voyage, and Christian was aware of an opening in the reef, described by Cook, that made it possible for a ship to anchor there. A boat was put out to sound the opening, but its crew was immediately attacked by the island natives. Ignoring this hostile reception, Christian continued to work his way through the reef and brought the *Bounty* to anchor in the lagoon.

Canoes surrounded the ship. No further attack occurred, but the natives could not be coaxed aboard to trade. The next day more canoes appeared, one of them carrying a group of 18 women who, wrote Morrison, were " . . . neatly dressed and their heads & necks decorated with flowers & Pearl shells. . . . They were all young and handsome having fine long hair which reached their Waists in waving ringlets."

The women and six men boarded the ship. Immediately, wrote Morrison, the men began to " . . . steal evry thing they Could lay hands on, one of them took the Card off the Compass, the Glass being broke, but being observed by Mr. Christian while he was secreting it, he took it from Him, but not before it was torn, as he refused to part with it and being a stout fellow a Scuffel ensued; however he was worsted & Mr. Christian gave him two or three smart stripes with a ropes end and sent Him into the Canoe, the others who had not been Idle followed Him as did the Weomen which we did not think prudent to detain."

The islanders in the waiting canoes brandished weapons. Christian ordered a gun loaded with grapeshot to be fired, and the natives hastily retreated to the shore. Some of the *Bounty* crew gave chase in the ship's boat, and in the ensuing battle—cannons and muskets against stones and spears—12 natives were killed. The mutineers had committed the first of the many acts of violent bloodshed that were to mark their passage through the islands of the South Seas. In what would prove to be a grim omen of events to come, Christian named the lagoon at Tubuai "Bloody Bay."

Despite the hostile attitude of the islanders, Christian "formed a resolution of settling on the Island, determined to return again as soon as he could procure sufficient stock of Hogs Goats & Poultry of which we Saw None on the Island."

Tubuai, 18 miles in circumference, appeared to offer what Christian was looking for: a safe hideout from the long arm of the Royal Navy, where, wrote Morrison, " . . . He would be permitted to live . . . in peace, which was all he Now desired knowing that he had taken such steps as had for ever debar'd him from returning to England or any Civilized Place, & dream't of nothing but Settling at Toobouai."

On May 31 the *Bounty* sailed out of Bloody Bay and once more charted a course for Tahiti, there to procure the necessary livestock for a permanent settlement. As fugitives from the law, Christian and his crew were now prisoners of their crime and their mutual distrust. If, while they were at Tahiti, word got out that Tubuai was to be their refuge, discovery and recapture by a King's ship would be only a matter of time. Christian threatened to punish severely any man who mentioned the name of the island. Any man who deserted would be hunted down and shot. A divided crew sailed the *Bounty* back to Tahiti: Christian's loyalists, always armed and on guard and suspicious of the second group—the fate-trapped men whose lives and futures had forever been changed by mutiny.

The ship anchored again in Matavai Bay on June 6, amid the usual boisterous Tahitian reception. "They were glad to see us," wrote Morrison, "and Enquired where the rest were, and what had brought us back so soon, where we had left the Plants as they knew our stay had been too Short to have reached home from the account we had formerly given them of the distance."

Christian had a ready story. He told the curious islanders that the *Bounty* had met Captain Cook at sea. The plants were transferred to Cook's ship, along with Bligh and some of the crew. The *Bounty* had returned to Tahiti, he told the natives, to get hogs and goats for a new settlement ordered by King George to be founded in Australia.

The familiar round of trading and social calls back and forth between the ship and the village resumed. The foundry was set up on shore, where the armourer (blacksmith) forged tools for trade. Other men were sent out to buy hogs and goats. Christian entertained the visiting chiefs on board, " . . . plying them with Wine and Arrack," wrote Morrison, "of which they became very fond."

On June 16 the ship departed with 460 hogs, 50 goats, a number of chickens, a few dogs and cats, a bull, and a cow. Nine Tahitian men, eight boys, one girl, and ten women had joined their fate to that of the *Bounty*. The voyage back to Bloody Bay was rough. The animals trampled each other on the crowded deck, and the bull, unable to stand, was thrown about so much that it died during the passage.

The Tubuaians appeared more friendly when the *Bounty* again anchored in Bloody Bay. "They appeared," wrote Morrison, "a different people, coming on board in a peaceable manner without Weapons or Conch Shells, or the least appearance of Hostility;

which induced Mr. Christian to land the Cow and two Hundred hogs on the Island."

When these creatures—animals never seen on Tubuai—were let loose, the natives were terrified. But though 12 of their people had been killed by the white men and half-wild animals had been let loose to destroy gardens, the friendly and innocent Tubuaians bestowed all honors on Christian. Morrison described the ceremony:

"The Chief [Tummotoa] first made a long speech presenting him [Christian] with a young Plantain tree (which here is the Emblem of Peace) and a root of the Yava Saluting him by the Name of Tummotoa, it being the Custom to exchange Names on making friends; his relations came next in rotation, each performing the like Ceremony, but with this difference, that each of them presented him with a piece of Cloth besides the plantain & Yava— after them Came the landed men each attended by a Man (to the Number of 50) loaded with two basketts of Provisions, and a piece of Cloth . . . all which were placed before him, the Weomen of the Chiefs family Came Next followed in like Manner, and when all was finish'd the Men took the Cloth, Provisions & Yava and Carried them to the Boats, the Chief coming on board with Mr. Christian Where he remained all night most part of which he spent in prayer at Mr. Christian's bedside."

Christian apparently did not understand or honor the concept of friendship made sacred by this ceremony. He insulted Tummotoa by deciding to start his colony on a distant part of the island controlled by Tummotoa's enemy, Chief Taroatchoa. Christian then went through the name-exchanging ceremony with Taroatchoa. Tummotoa, furious at this breach of friendship, allied himself with a third island chief (Tinnarow), and together they established a boycott of all trade with the men of the *Bounty*. Christian's colony was doomed before it began.

Taroatchoa's district was small and its food supplies insufficient to take on the added burden of feeding the *Bounty*'s crew. In spite of these obstacles, Christian ordered his men to begin construction of a fort on land given to him by Taroatchoa. The *Bounty* was warped along the inside of the shallow lagoon. At one point, the ship had to be lightened in order to proceed through the shallow waters. Booms and spars were thrown overboard and lost, but, Morrison wrote, " . . . Mr. Christian thought it no great loss as he never intended to Sea any More."

The crew worked hard to get the *Bounty* to what they thought would be its final resting place in the lagoon of Tubuai. Then, according to Morrison, John Sumner and Matthew Quintal went ashore without first getting permission from Christian. When the

two men returned, Christian demanded an explanation for their absence and was told that "the Ship is Moord and we are now our own Masters."

"I'll let you know who is Master," Christian replied, and the two men were arrested and placed in leg irons.

Christian needed to hold on to his authority in order to build the fort he believed essential for their collective safety. His organization and planning for the project would have pleased Bligh himself. William Brown, assisted by a Tahitian man, was to prepare a garden. Christian assigned Joseph Coleman and William McCoy to the forge to make spades, hoes, and mattocks. Henry Hillbrant was appointed cook. Michael Byrne was to take care of the boats, along with Thomas Ellison and a few Tahitian boys. The rest of the crew, armed against a possible attack by the natives, began construction of the fort.

British history does not honor either the day or the event, but on the morning of June 18, Fletcher Christian and the men of the *Bounty* hoisted the Union Jack on a staff, quaffed a double allowance of grog, and began work on Fort George, the first English colony attempted in the South Pacific. Just three days earlier, on June 15, 4,000 miles distant, William Bligh raised his ragged Union Jack as he and his crew approached Coupang in Timor.

Christian knew he would soon be a hunted man, and he planned his fort for defense against both natives and armed men of his own nation. His plan called for a four-sided structure with walls 100 yards long surrounded by a moat 20 feet deep from the top of the walls. The walls at the base were to be 18 feet wide, narrowing to 12 feet at the top. At each corner a cannon was to be mounted, and smaller swivel guns were to be placed so that they could aim in any direction.

"Evrything being settled," wrote Morrison, "we proceeded to Work tho not a man knew any thing of Fortification; some Cut stakes others made Battins some cut Sods & brought to hand, some built and others Wrought in the ditch, the Carpenters made barrows & Cut timber for the Gates & Drawbridge, & the work began to rise apace. Nor was Mr. Christian an Idle Spectator for He always took a part in the Most laborious part of the Work, and half a Pint of Porter was served twice a day extra."

Peace, both external and internal, settled on the fledgling colony. Daily the working men were visited by natives who brought with them food. Thieving was no longer a problem as the natives did not seem to value the iron implements and tools the crew worked with. But then on August 25, islanders attacked a group of Tahitian men and boys, one of whom was nearly killed. Christian ordered an armed party to retaliate; in the ensuing scuffle, one Tubuaian was shot and killed.

A few days later some of the crewmembers were, as Morrison put it, "decoy'd by the Weomen of Tinnarow's district where they were Strip'd." All managed to escape except Alexander Smith, who was held prisoner. Again an armed party set out to "punish the Offenders." They burned a house and returned with Smith and two carved idols. Christian, knowing that the idols were of great value to the natives, kept them in the belief that they could be traded for peace.

Work resumed on the fort, and by September 1 the gate posts were in place and three-quarters of the wall was built. The next day Chief Tinnarow appeared, accompanied by a number of attendants bearing baskets of provisions, which were presented to Christian as a peace offering. The chief begged Christian for the return of the idols. Christian agreed to release them if the chief promised to desist in any further attacks against the crewmen. Tinnarow agreed and asked Christian to partake in a symbolic drink of yava. Christian refused, having been warned that the attendants were secretly armed. The chief became enraged, but retreated, without the idols, under the menacing arms of crewmen who quickly took up stations along the wall of the fort.

This apparent victory gave Christian a false sense of security. He decided that Fort George would be their permanent home; to support that decision, he began to make plans for taking the masts out of the *Bounty* and dismantling the ship.

Hearing this, Morrison, along with George Stewart and Peter Heywood, began to make plans to escape from the island in the cutter, which, they felt, could be safely sailed to Tahiti in five or six days.[36]

The other men were not yet ready to accept the exile that the destruction of the *Bounty* would mean. In addition, each of them wanted a woman, and when they demanded of Christian that they be allowed to take a native woman by force, he refused them. All work on the fort stopped, and for three days they drank and argued the issue. When Christian refused to issue more grog, his loyalists broke into the stores and drank their fill. Christian called the men together and asked what should be done. All agreed that Fort George should be abandoned and the search continued for another island hideout. But first they wanted to return to Tahiti, knowing, wrote Morrison, "that there they could get Weomen without force." The men also decided that those who chose could leave the ship to live ashore on Tahiti where they would be given their share of arms and other necessary supplies. Christian and his

An orgy of bloodshed

135

followers were to have the ship in the proper condition ready for sea and the continuation of their search for a home.

An orgy of bloodshed preceded the mutineers' departure from Tubuai. Natives frequently attacked as the men made forays around the island to round up their stock of hogs and goats. Again musket fire repelled the natives' spears and stones. A few mutineers were wounded, none seriously. Sixty native men and six women were left dead in the wake of the *Bounty*'s departure from Tubuai. Christian carried away with him the Tubuaian idols.

By September 22 the ship was anchored again at Tahiti. Bligh, at this time, was thousands of miles to the west and again in command of a vessel, the *Resource*, which was slowly approaching Batavia.

At Tahiti, Christian ordered supplies to be divided according to the agreement, and the following men left the *Bounty* to live ashore on the island:

> Charles Churchill
> George Stewart
> Peter Heywood
> James Morrison
> John Millward
> Charles Norman
> Thomas McIntosh
> William Muspratt
> Matthew Thompson
> Richard Skinner
> Thomas Ellison
> Thomas Burkett
> John Sumner
> Michael Byrne
> Joseph Coleman
> Henry Hillbrant

The crew of the *Bounty* was down to nine. In addition to Christian, they were:

> John Mills
> Isaac Martin
> William Brown
> Edward Young
> William McCoy
> John Williams
> Matthew Quintal
> Alexander Smith

The shore party lost no time in removing their possessions and supplies from the ship. These things included blacksmith and carpentry tools, a pig of iron for an anvil, a grindstone, bar iron, pots, arms, ammunition, two spyglasses, a compass, canvas, a few old sails, and three gallons of wine per man. The Tahitians, wrote Morrison, " . . . received us with evry Mark of Friendship and hospitality; amongst us we found the whole of them striving to outdoe each Other in civility towards us and we found our Old friends ready to receive us with open Arms and all were glad when We informed them that we intended to Stay with them."

The *Bounty*'s third visit to Tahiti was brief. It was late before all the shore supplies were unloaded. Christian then stated that he planned to stay a few days while he resupplied the ship with water. After that, wrote Morrison, ". . . he intended to Cruize for some Uninhabited Island where he would land his Stock and set fire to the Ship, and where he hoped to live the remainder of His days without seeing the face of a European but those already with him."

Under cover of darkness, the *Bounty* sailed. "We were all much surprised," said Morrison, and " . . . suppose that He either was affraid of a Surprize or had done it to prevent His Companions from Changing their mind."

Christian must have been uneasy. With so many men now in close contact with the islanders, the true story of how he had assumed command of the *Bounty* in Bligh's place would soon come out. It must also have occurred to him that many in the shore group now realized they faced the possibility of a long and perhaps dangerous exile. As a last desperate act, they could—if allied with enough natives—retake the ship.

Morrison provides this last description of the *Bounty* on September 23, 1789, as it sailed away, carrying with it nine mutineers and 26 Tahitian men and women.

"In the Night we found the Ship under way, standing out of the Bay, but it proving Calm in the Morning She was not out of Sight till Noon during which She stood to the Northward on a wind."

On October 1, seven days after the *Bounty* departed from Tahiti, Bligh brought the schooner *Resource* into Batavia. He was well on his way toward achieving his goal, the driving force that had carried him across 5,000 miles of sea: "to be able to recount to my King and Country my misfortune."

14

A SHIP IS BUILT

September 23, 1789–March 23, 1791

Framing the Resolution

The 16 men left on Tahiti soon separated into small groups, some taking up residence in Oparre (Pare), while others remained at Matavai Bay. By November each man had settled in, some with wives, some with families, and others with native friends. There were a few arguments, many misunderstandings, and a few skirmishes between the Europeans and the Tahitians, but all in all, the Europeans were left alone, and they, in turn, did not overly upset the established patterns of island life.

Morrison, however, wanted to escape. Along with two other men (McIntosh and Millward), he began to make plans to build a vessel in which, wrote Morrison, "I had hopes of reaching Batavia & from thence to England."[37] He kept his real motive for building the vessel a secret but enlisted other men in its construction by telling them that it would be used for "Pleasuring about the island." Morrison was given permission by the island chiefs to cut what timber he wanted.

It is nearly impossible to comprehend the immensity of the challenge Morrison confronted. With few and inadequate resources he built a vessel of sound construction and pleasing performance, whose seaworthiness was ultimately demonstrated beyond doubt. Most men could not even contemplate such a staggering task. To this remarkable man goes the credit for the first English-built ship in the South Pacific, the *Resolution*, so named for Cook's ship.

The keel was laid on November 12 for a schooner-rigged vessel of these dimensions: length of keel, 30 feet; length on deck, 35 feet; beam, 9 feet 6 inches; depth of hold, 5 feet. It was an undertaking that called for ingenuity and dedication. The tools at hand were barely sufficient. The island trees were of poor quality for shipbuilding, and rope and canvas were in short supply.

Molds were set up and the stem and stern posts were cut from a tree called *purau*. Several men began splitting breadfruit trees for planking. It required a week's work to cut a single plank. Frames and knees straightened as they dried; once dry, each piece had to be removed, reworked, and then replaced. Finding suitable trees for the structural timbers of the boat required long trips into the hills. By January the backbone was in place, held together by wooden pins cut from a hardwood tree called *amai*.

"The business of searching for timber," wrote Morrison, "always took up a whole day, having Several Miles to go before any Could be found to answer our purpose, and when we found them we frequently had the misfortune to breake them by tumbling them down the precipices, which we could not avoid, it being impossible to Carry them along the Steep Cliffs, and what we Cut in one day would keep McIntosh and Myself employd for three or four. . . .

"Nor was the making of Plank less troublesome, having no Saws (except handsaws) the largest tree would afford no more than two thicknesses of Plank, Some of the trees Cut for that purpose measuring six feet round which took a deal of Labour to reduce into plank of Inch & a quarter with axes and adzes."

The work stopped on numerous occasions because various island celebrations required the attendance of the men. Thieving was also a continuous problem as curious islanders visited the construction site. Added to these problems were the frequent clashes that arose between some of the men of the *Bounty* and their island hosts, which had to be settled before the work on the ship could resume.

Yet, by March 15, 1790, the ship's framing was completed, and the planking of the hull began. Various bowsprit and rudder parts had to be fashioned out of iron; to supply these, a makeshift bellows was made from bits of canvas and the iron handle of a saucepan. A piece of iron ballast from the *Bounty* served as an anvil. Hanging the first six planks took two weeks of work.

Then, as a result of a complicated feud, Matthew Thompson shot and killed Charles Churchill and was in turn killed by the natives to revenge the murder. Morrison was called away from the shipbuilding site to settle this outbreak of violence. When he returned, he found the boat nearly planked.

It now needed caulking and rigging, and again ingenuity made it possible to make do with what was available. Boiled gum from breadfruit trees was mixed with hog fat as a substitute for pitch. Planks were caulked with oakum made from old ropes from the *Bounty*.

The schooner was fully decked by June 1. Casks for storing food and water were made with a wood that resembled white oak.

Another tree produced timber for masts and booms, and small strips of it were bent to form mast hoops. Hardwood trees provided material for blocks. A sheet of copper made the barrel for a pump. Rope was woven from the bark of the *purau* tree. A shortage of iron for fastenings had been a problem during the construction of the ship. Now, ready to launch, all the augers used to bore holes were driven through the ship's timbers and clinched to add strength to the frame and keel members. The ship was completed on July 5. Morrison then asked permission to launch it.

"We applied to Poeno Who told me that the Priest must perform His prayers over Her, and then He would have her Carried to the Sea.—the Priest being sent for and a Young Pig & a Plantain given Him When he began Walking round and round the Vessel, stopping at the Stem & Stern, and Muttering short sentences in an unknown dialect; and having a Bundle of Young Plantain trees brought to him by Poenos Order, he now and then tossd one in on Her deck. He kept at this all day and night and was hardly finished by sunrise on the 6th. When Poeno . . . Came with Three or four Hundred Men . . . He then ran fore & aft, and exorted them to exert themselves, and on a Signal being given they closed in, and those who Could not reach by hand got long Poles, A Song being given they all Joind in Chorus & She soon began to Move and in Half an hour she reachd the Beach, where She was launched & Calld the *Resolution*."

With the schooner at anchor, the various tasks of outfitting for sea began. Kettles of seawater were boiled night and day to produce salt, necessary for preserving a store of pork. The salt water, wrote Morrison, "proved so weak owing to the fresh water river which emptys itself at the Point, that we could not make more than one pound per Day." The woven bark rope made shrouds, stays, and an anchor cable.

Morrison, meanwhile, directed his efforts to the repair of his watch and the manufacture of other instruments that would be needed to navigate the ship to Timor. With a screwdriver made from a nail, he took the watch apart and " . . . found about two inches of the inner part of the Main Spring broke of [off], to remidie this I softened the broken part of the Spring and cut a new hole for the ketch, and having put the work together found that she went very well.

"We also prepared a Log reel and line and by Cutting a Glass Phial in halves with a Flint and fixing a leaded Center Cast . . . made a tolerable good half Minute Glass, counting the Seconds by the Musquet ball slung to a thread, between which and the Watch we made it tolerable correct.

"The Box of the Azimuth Compass being too large to be conveniently kept, we got a small gourd which answerd to the size of the glass, and made a Compass box of it, slinging it in Jymbals [gimbals] in the Binnacle where it was intended to remain for the purpose of Steering only—and the spare Glass answered to fix in the Binnacle to keep the Wet out, and a lamp made to burn oil over the Compass, which answer very well, we also made some Candles of Goats fat which we had saved for the purpose.

"Evry thing seemd to be had without trouble or Dificulty except sails, and how to procure them we Could not tell, Matting being scarce and at the Best very unserviisable, and tho we had Cut up our Cloaths, we had not sufficient Canvas amongst us to make her one Sail which would be fit to set at sea.

"However we Continued at Work preparing such things as were in our power, and trusting in Providence for the rest—Salting Pork Boiling Salt & making Casks, and getting ready evry thing that we Could think we might want."

On September 12, Morrison and his men were able to rout an attack by natives from another district, and as the price for defending their host chief, Morrison demanded and received enough mats for sails. With the mats, the schooner was fitted with a mainsail, foresail, and jib. On September 26 the *Resolution* departed on its maiden voyage to nearby Oparre. It arrived the next day in a calm and was towed into the harbor by a string of forty canoes with the paddlers decked out in feathered headdresses and keeping time to the rhythms of flutes and drums. More feasting took place as the native chiefs of Oparre welcomed the crew of the *Resolution*. The next stage of the voyage took the schooner to Matavai, but on this passage the foremast broke and was carried away. It was replaced with a more durable hardwood tree and the ship rerigged.

Crossing over to Moorea, an island offshore of Tahiti, the *Resolution* encountered strong gale winds and high seas. The vessel hove to and proved to be exceptionally seaworthy. The wind, however, nearly destroyed the mat sails. By December, the *Resolution* was back at Oparre. The ship was hauled up on the beach for safekeeping during the impending wet season. The short voyage proved to Morrison that the schooner was seaworthy, but Coleman, said Morrison, would "not have any thing to do with the Schooner, and our finding that our hopes of reaching Batavia or any other place without sails, and finding that even Matts could not be had, we dropd any further attempts that way. . . ."

Morrison and his crew of the *Resolution* spent the wet months entertaining visitors as they settled into the routine of island life. Then an island chief proposed a scheme to Morrison to use the schooner for a raid on a nearby district. It was launched,

equipped, and sailed on March 21, with Morrison, Norman, Ellison, Byrne, Millward, and Hillbrant on board. Coming to anchor the next day, the *Resolution* was met by Burkett, Sumner, Brown, and Muspratt. All the men were having breakfast on shore the following morning when a runner arrived with word that a ship had dropped anchor in Matavai Bay and that manned boats had been sent out to look for the *Bounty* mutineers.

"No time was now to be lost in fixing on the best plan," wrote Morrison, "and it was agreed to avoid seeing the Boats: and for this reason we got on board leaving Brown & Byrne on shore, and Got under way stood out with a fresh Breeze. . . . We hoped by keeping out of sight of the Boats to reach the Ship and go on board of our own accord, hoping thereby to have better treatment then if we stayed to be made prisoners."

The ship at anchor in Matavai was H.M.S. *Pandora,* under the command of Captain Edward Edwards. His orders were to search the Pacific for the *Bounty* mutineers.

15

PANDORA'S VOYAGE AND ITS AFTERMATH
November 7, 1790–June 19, 1792

Bligh's courageous voyage had achieved its purpose. By the summer of 1790 he was experiencing a brief heyday as a national hero, having eloquently made his appeal to his King and Country. National prestige and the integrity of the Royal Navy demanded that the mutineers be found and brought to trial. That assignment fell to Captain Edward Edwards, 49, who was given command of the 24-gun frigate *Pandora*. Basil Thomson, in his introduction to the *Voyage of H.M.S. Pandora*, writes:

"Captain Edward Edwards . . . had a high reputation as a seaman and a disciplinarian, and from the point of view of the Admiralty, who intended the cruise simply as a police mission without any scientific object, no better choice could have been made. . . .

"Edwards belonged to that useful class of public servant that lives upon instructions. With a roving commission in an ocean studded with undiscovered islands the possibilities of scientific discovery were immense, but he faced them like a blinkered horse that has his eyes fixed on the narrow track before him, and all the pleasant byways of the road shut out."[38]

He was, concluded Thomson, "a cold, hard man, devoid of sympathy and imagination, of every interest beyond the straitened limits of his profession. . . ."

Edwards was ordered to proceed first to Tahiti. If the mutineers were not there, he was to look for them in the other islands of the Society and Friendly groups. Upon finding the mutineers, he was to keep them " . . . as closely confined as may preclude all possibility of their escaping, having, however, proper regard to the preservation of their lives, that they may be brought home to undergo the punishment due to their demerits."

Among the complement of 120 men assigned to the *Pandora* were two newly appointed lieutenants, Thomas Hayward and

John Hallett. Both had served Bligh as midshipmen aboard the *Bounty,* had made the open boat voyage to Timor, and now were assigned to the *Pandora's* mission because of their knowledge of both the South Sea islands and the mutineers. The *Pandora's* surgeon, George Hamilton, must also be mentioned because of the journal he kept of the voyage, which provides information not included in Edwards's journal of the fateful voyage. (As has been mentioned already, Thomson's edition joins Edwards's account with that of Hamilton.)

On November 7, 1790, just eight months after Bligh's return to England, the *Pandora* sailed from Portsmouth for Cape Horn. Hamilton recorded the departure:

"As the white cliffs of Albion receded from our view alternate hopes and fears took possession of our minds, wafting the last kind adieu to our native soil." Nearly a third of the crew would never see England again.

Pandora made a quick run downwind to Tenerife, where the ship was resupplied with water, wine, fruit, and vegetables. From there, Edwards sped across the Atlantic and anchored off Rio de Janeiro on the last day of 1790. So different is Edwards's terse narrative from the detailed journal kept by Bligh. Two brief paragraphs record *Pandora's* passage from Portsmouth to Rio de Janeiro. Fortunately, Hamilton filled in some of the details of the voyage that Edwards left out:

"We pursued our voyage with a favorable breeze; but *Pandora* now seemed inclined to shed her baneful influence among us, and a malignant fever threatened much havoc, as in a few days thirty-five men were confined to their beds. . . . What rendered our situation still more distressing, was the crowded state of the ship being filled to the hatchways with stores and provision, for, like weevils, we had to eat a hole in our bread, before we had a place to lay down in; every officer's cabin, the Captain's not excepted, being filled with provisions and stores."

A single paragraph of the Edwards log describes the voyage of *Pandora* south, around Cape Horn and to Tahiti:

"I sailed from that port [Rio de Janeiro] on the 8th of January, 1791, ran along the coast of America, Tierra Del Fuego, Hatin Land [Staten Island], round Cape Horn and proceeded directly to Otaheite, and arrived at Matavy Bay in that Island on the 23rd March without having touched in any other place in my passage thither."

He added that the "ship's company arrived in Otaheite in perfect health, except for a few debilited constitutions no climate, provisions or medicine could much improve."

Rounding Cape Horn, Edwards had turned north to follow the

well-established sailing track, which crossed the Pacific to the north of the prevailing westerly winds of the high latitudes. By chance his course led him to the discovery of Ducie Island, his second landfall west of Cape Horn. What Edwards did not know—could not have known—was that the mutineers he was seeking were hiding out on Pitcairn Island, just 300 miles to the west. His orders were to sail directly to Tahiti, and that he did, arriving there the day Morrison and nine other *Bounty* men were breakfasting aboard the schooner *Resolution* at Papara, a few miles south of Matavai Bay. Four men—Stewart, Heywood, Coleman, and Skinner—had remained behind in Matavai Bay; they were the first to sight the arriving *Pandora*.

Even before the *Pandora*'s anchor was down, the first man surrendered, when Coleman stepped aboard the ship. Stewart and Heywood came aboard next, and by evening Skinner joined these three. All four had hoped that their immediate surrender would be taken as evidence of their innocence of any participation in the mutiny. Instead, they were declared "piratical villains," arrested, and clapped in irons. From these four, Edwards learned that the *Bounty* had departed from Tahiti eighteen months previously with nine mutineers aboard, and that 10 other men were with the schooner *Resolution* at Papara.

Edwards immediately dispatched Lieutenant Hayward with two armed boat crews and a native guide to capture the schooner. Morrison and the men on the *Resolution,* having been told of the *Pandora*'s arrival, decided that their best course of action would be to surrender themselves aboard the *Pandora* before they were captured. At some point in the ensuing action, six of the men (Burkett, Sumner, Muspratt, Hillbrant, McIntosh, and Millward) decided to try to escape to the mountains. Morrison, Norman, and Ellison remained with the schooner, and Brown and the nearly blind Byrne walked back to Matavai. It was all over quickly. Their attempt to reach the *Pandora* having been derailed by circumstance, Morrison, Norman, and Ellison walked into the camp of one of the *Pandora*'s boat crews and were immediately arrested and bound. The next day the six men who had tried to hide out in the mountains were captured while they slept in a native hut.

With the entire Tahiti contingent arrested, wrote Edwards, "I put the pirates in the round house which I had built at the first part of the Quarter deck for their more effectual security, airy and healthy situation, and to separate them from, and to prevent their having any communications with, or to crowd and incommode the ship's company."

The "round house" of Edwards's description became known as "Pandora's Box." For the 14 men imprisoned there in leg irons and

handcuffs, it was a place of horror. Morrison described it in his journal:

"This place we stiled Pandora's Box, the entrance being a scuttle on the top, of 18 or 20 inches square, secured by a bolt on the top thro' the coamings; two scuttles of nine inches square in the bulkhead for air, with iron grates and the stern ports barrd inside and out with iron. The centrys were placed on the top, while the midshipman walked across the bulkhead. The length of this box of 11 feet upon deck, and 18 wide at the bulkhead. No person was suffered to speak to us but the master-at-arms, and his orders were not to speak to us on any score but that of our provisions. The Heat of the place when it was calm was so intense that the Sweat frequently ran in Streams to the Scuppers, and produced Maggots in a short time; the Hammocks being dirty when we got them, we found stored with Vermin of another kind, which we had no Method of erradicating but by lying on the Plank; and tho our Friends would have supplied us with plenty of Cloth they were not permitted to do it, and our only remedy was to lay Naked,—these troublesome Neighbours and the two necessary tubbs [toilets] which were Constantly kept in the place helpd to render our situation truely disagreeable."

The *Pandora* lay anchored for six weeks in Matavai Bay while the crew overhauled the ship and loaded it with fresh water, fruit, and livestock. Daily, grief-stricken women and wives of the prisoners gathered with their children around the ship to mourn the imprisonment of their men. Morrison describes how these women cut their heads "till the Blood discolloured the water about them. . . ." On the day the *Pandora* left Tahiti, he added, these mourning rites "were sufficient to evince the truth of their Grief & melt the most obdurate Heart."

The schooner *Resolution* was commissioned as an escort vessel to the *Pandora*, with a crew of nine aboard. Together, the two vessels cleared Matavai Bay on May 8. Somewhere in the vast and largely unexplored waters of the southwestern Pacific Ocean, Edwards hoped to find the speck of land that sheltered the missing men of the *Bounty*.

Edwards must have realized that he had very little chance of finding the mutineers still at large. Christian had revealed no plan to the men he left behind on Tahiti, except for his declared intention of settling somewhere on an uninhabited island.

"This information," Edwards wrote, "was too vague to be followed in an immense ocean strewed with an almost innumerable number of known and unknown islands." Even so, he made a diligent search, the best that could be expected of one man in one ship in a largely uncharted corner of the world's largest ocean. Every mile of the search led him farther from his quarry and their hideout on lonely and remote Pitcairn Island, far to the east of the *Pandora*'s search track.

From Tahiti, the *Pandora* and the *Resolution* made a circle of the Society Islands, Bora-Bora, Huahine, and Maururoa. From there the two vessels headed west to Aitutaki and Palmerston Island.

At Palmerston Island, a shore party discovered a piece of a yard from the *Bounty*. Boat crews were sent out to make a thorough search of the island group. One of the boats was caught in a squall and driven out to sea with four men. For five days the area was searched for the boat, but it was never found.

Sailing northwestward, the *Pandora* reached Atafu in the Union (Tokelau) Islands on June 6, and from there Edwards directed the two vessels south to Samoa. On the evening of June 22, while the *Pandora* and the *Resolution* were lying off Upolu (the present island location of Apia, capital of Samoa), a sudden rainstorm hit the two ships. When it cleared, the *Resolution* had disappeared.

For the next 18 days, Edwards searched in vain for the missing schooner. For the prisoners in "Pandora's Box," it was a time of misery. The men were constantly wet, and in their helpless, chained condition in the prison box, they were rolled and thrown against each other. By chance, one of the islands visited was Tofua, where Bligh first landed after Christian and the mutineers took command of the *Bounty*. Lieutenant Hayward recognized some of the natives as the same men who had killed John Norton, the *Bounty*'s quartermaster, in the attack on Bligh and his men as they left Tofua.

On July 11 Edwards gave up hope of finding the schooner, and on August 2, he abandoned his search for the *Bounty*. For 86 days he had combed the South Pacific islands in vain. He had found nothing, had lost a ship's boat and his escort vessel, and had charted a number of previously undiscovered islands. From the Tonga islands he steered northward to Wallis Island; from there he set a course due west toward the dangerous waters of Endeavour Straits.

The ship's lookout first sighted the Great Barrier Reef on August 25. Carefully Edwards worked the *Pandora* south as he sought an open passage westward through the wall of coral. Each possible opening proved false as the ship ranged farther south along the eastern edge of the reef. On the afternoon of August 28, a promising lead was sighted at 11° 22' S, 144° 03' E, and the yawlboat was sent out to sound the channel. The officer in the boat signaled

for the *Pandora* to follow. Darkness fell before the *Pandora* got underway, and the ship followed signals made from the yawlboat with torches and pistol fire. No bottom was found at 110 fathoms.

Shortly after 7 P.M., the ship closed with the boat as the leadsman found bottom at 50 fathoms. Sails were dropped, but before the ship lost headway, it struck a reef. Immediately an effort was made to lay out an anchor, but while this was being accomplished the ship struck again. Within five minutes, the hold had flooded to a depth of four feet. Breaking seas carried the ship over the reef, and she anchored, crippled, in 15 fathoms of water. The water in the hold rose to eight feet. Frantic efforts were made to pump out the ship and rig a temporary patch over the bottom, but the *Pandora* was doomed. Hamilton offers a vivid record of the last hours of the stricken ship:

"The hands were immediately turned to the pumps, and to bale

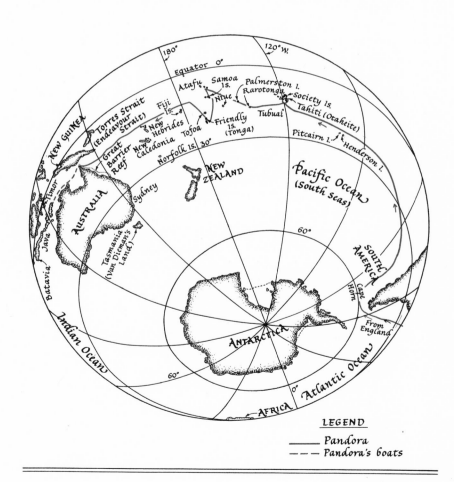

LEGEND

———— *Pandora*
– – – *Pandora's boats*

at the different hatchways. Some of the prisoners were let out of irons, and turned to the pumps. At this dreadful crisis, it blew very violently; and she beat so hard upon the rocks, that we expected her, every minute, to go to pieces. It was an exceeding dark, stormy night; and the gloomy horrors of death presented us all round, being every where encompassed with rocks, shoals, and broken water. About ten she beat over the reef; and we let go the anchor in fifteen fathom water.

"The guns were ordered to be thrown overboard; and what hands could be spared from the pumps, were employed thrumbing a topsail to haul under her bottom, to endeavour to fodder her. To add to our distress, at this juncture one of the chain-pumps gave way; and she gained fast upon us. The scheme of the topsail was now laid aside, and every soul fell to bailing and pumping. All the boats, excepting one, were obliged to keep a long distance off on account of the broken water, and the very high surf that was running near us. We baled between life and death; for had she gone down before day-light, every soul must have perished. She now took a heel, and some of the guns they were endeavouring to throw over board run down to leeward, which crushed one man to death; about the same time, a spare topmast came down from the booms, and killed another man.

"About half an hour before day-break, a council of war was held amongst the officers; and as she was then settling fast down in the water, it was their unanimous opinion, that nothing further could be done for the preservation of his Majesty's ship; and it was their next care to save the lives of the crew. To effect which, booms, hencoops, and every thing buoyant was cut loose, that when she went down, they might chance to get hold of something. The prisoners were ordered to be let out of irons. The water was now coming faster in at the gunports than the pumps could discharge; and to this minute the men never swerved from their duty. She now took a very heavy heel, so much that she lay quite down on one side.

"At that instant she took her last heel; and, while every one were scrambling to windward, she sunk in an instant. The crew had just enough time to leap overboard, accompanying it with a most dreadful yell. The cries of the men drowning in the water was at first awful in the extreme; but as they sunk, and became faint, it died away by degrees. The boats, who were at some considerable distance in the drift of the tide, in about half an hour, or little better, picked up the remainder of our wretched crew."

On the deck of the *Pandora* the scene had been one of pandemonium; in the prisoners' box it was one of black terror. The prisoners knew that the ship was sinking, but only three of them were released from their chains to assist at the pumps. Morrison re-

called the superhuman struggle of the men to break free from
their chains:

"Seeing the Ship in this situation we judged she would not hold
long together, and as we were in danger at every stroke of killing
each other with our Irons, we broke them that we might be ready
to assist ourselves and keep from killing each other, and Informed
the Officers what we had done. . . .

"As soon as Captain Edwards was informd that we had broke
our Irons he ordered us to be handcuffd and leg Irond again with
all the Irons that could be Mustered, tho we beggd for Mercy and
desired leave to go to the pump. . . . The Master at Arms and Cor-

The prisoners knew that the ship was sinking

poral were now armd with each a Brace of Pistols and placed as additional Centinals over us, with Orders to fire amongst us if we made any Motion; and the Master of Arms told us that the Captain had said he would either shoot or hang to the Yard Arms those who should make any further attempt to break the Irons."

Only at the last minute did Edwards order the prisoners to be released. For four of them, the release order came too late. Stewart, Sumner, Skinner, and Hillbrant went down with the ship. In irons. Thirty-one members of the *Pandora* crew were lost in the wreck.

A scene of utter desolation greeted the dawn. The *Pandora* was gone, and the 99 survivors, loaded into four ship's boats, slowly rowed to the only visible land in the broken seas inside the Barrier Reef. It was a tiny sandy key, barely 50 paces long. Now they confronted the agonies of survival: heat and thirst. Supplies consisted of a small barrel of water, some wine, biscuits, a few muskets, and some ammunition.

"The heat of the sun," wrote Hamilton, "and the reflection from the sand, was now excruciating; and our stomachs being filled with salt water, from the great length of time we were swimming before we were picked up, rendered our thirst most intolerable; and no water was allowed to be served out the first day."

The suffering of the prisoners was even worse. Tents made out of sails protected the *Pandora* crew from the sun, but by the command of Edwards, as pitiless as ever, the 10 prisoners lay on the hot, sandy beach without any kind of shelter. Morrison described their suffering:

" . . . The sun took such an effect on us, who had been Cooped up for these five Months, that we had our skin flea'd off, from head to foot, tho we kept our Selves Covered in the Sand during the heat of the Day, this being all the Shelter that the Island affoards. . . ."

During the night, a copper kettle was filled with salt water and set to boil. The steam produced only a cup of water. One seaman became hysterical during the night, and it was believed he had stolen wine and gotten drunk. In the morning it was discovered that he had drunk salt water. He went mad and later died.

The next day some of the men set out in a boat to gather whatever might have survived the wreck. They returned with the ship's cat, a piece of mast, and a length of copper chain. The links of the chain were made into nails, which the men used to nail canvas dodgers around the gunwales of the boat as a protection against breaking waves. During the evening each man was issued a spoonful of tea.

On August 31 the survivors of the *Pandora* departed from the tiny sandbank that Edwards had named Wreck Island. Oars placed across the thwarts provided a platform, thereby double-decking the boats, with some men sitting on the oars while others sat below them in the bilge. The survivors distributed themselves in the four boats as follows:

Pinnace: Captain Edwards, 21 men, and three prisoners.
Red Yawl: Lieutenant Larkin, 18 men, and three prisoners.
Launch: Lieutenant Corner, 27 men, and two prisoners.
Blue Yawl: George Passmore, master, 19 men, and three prisoners.

Each officer in charge of a boat was given the latitude and longitude of Timor, 1,100 miles to the west. For Lieutenants Thomas Hayward and John Hallett, the situation was painfully ironic. Now they were forced to duplicate the long voyage across the Arafura Sea that they had so recently made with Bligh in the *Bounty*'s launch.

A scene of utter desolation

For defense and because one boat held most of the stores, Edwards ordered the boats to stay close together and to be linked at night by connecting lines. On September 1 two of the boats landed on the northern coast of Australia, but their crews obtained only a very small supply of water before inhospitable natives drove them back to the sea. Farther down the coast, all four boats landed safely. A well was dug, and it provided enough water to fill the few containers available for storage—including, wrote Morrison, "the carpenter's boots . . . [which] was first served out, on account of leakage."

The laconic Captain Edwards devoted one brief paragraph to the ordeal of the voyage from Cape York to Timor:

"It is unnecessary to retell our particular sufferings in the boats during our run to Timor and it is sufficient to observe that we suffered more from heat and thirst than from hunger, and that our strength was greatly decreased. We fortunately had good weather, and the sea was generally not very rough, and the boats were more buoyant and lively in the water than we reasonably could have expected considering the weight and numbers we had in them."

And with that brief description of a voyage to rival Bligh's open boat journey, Edwards concluded his remarks by writing, "At seven o'clock in the morning of the 13th of September we saw the island of Timor bearing N.W."

Fortunately for history, both Hamilton and Morrison recorded the more significant details of the two-week voyage, a voyage that began with a water supply of only 200 gallons for the 99 men.

"As soon as we cleared the land," wrote Hamilton, "we found a very heavy swell running, which threatened destruction to our little fleet; for should we have separated, we must inevitably perish for want of water, as we had not utensils to divide our slender stock. For our mutual preservation, we took each other in tow again; but the sea was so rough, and the swell running so high, we towed very hard, and broke a new tow-line. This put us in the utmost confusion, being afraid of dashing to pieces upon each other, as it was a very dark night. We again made fast to each other; but the tow-line breaking a second time, we were obliged to trust ourselves to the mercy of the waves.

"On the night between the 5th and 6th, the sea running very cross and high, the tow-line broke several times; the boats strained, and made much water; and we were obliged to leave off towing the rest of the voyage, or it would have dragged the boats asunder."

So acute was their thirst that few of the men could eat the tiny morsel of bread that was rationed out each day. "As their suffer-

ings continued," added Hamilton, "they became very cross and savage in their temper."

For Morrison and the other two prisoners in the pinnace with Edwards, the last few days of the voyage were unrelieved torture. Something Morrison did or said prompted Edwards to a rage. He ordered all three prisoners bound to the bottom of the boat.

"I attempted to reason and enquire what I had now done to be thus Cruelly treated," wrote Morrison, "but received for answer 'Silence, you Murdering Villain, are you not a Prisoner? You Piratical Dog what better treatment do you expect?' I then told him that it was a disgrace to the Captain of a British Man of War to treat a prisoner in such an inhuman Manner, upon which he started up in a Violent Rage & snatching a Pistol which lay in the Stern sheets, threatened to shoot me. I still attempted to speak, when he Swore 'by God if you speak another Word I'll heave the log with You' and finding that he would hear no reason & my mouth being Parchd so that I could not move my tongue, I was forced to be silent & submit; and was tyed down so that I could not move. In this Miserable Situation Ellison & I remained for the rest of the passage. . . ."

Timor was sighted on September 13, but with land and desperately needed water so close, the wind dropped. The boats separated, and the survivors rowed toward the land in a hot, dead calm. The next day the red yawl, bearing Hamilton, closed with the shoreline of Timor. A huge surf kept the boat from landing, but two men jumped overboard and swam to the island with bottles tied around their necks. They returned to the boat with their water bottles full, which gave temporary relief to the thirsty men. Hamilton's narrative continues:

"We now gained fresh spirits, and hazarded every thing in gaining our so much wished for haven. It is but justice here to acknowledge how much we were indebted to the intrepidity, courage, and seaman-like behavior of Mr. Reynolds the master's mate, who fairly beat her all over the reefs, and brought us safe on shore. The crew of the blue yawl, who had been two or three hours landed, assisted in landing our party. A fine spring of water near to the creek afforded us immediate relief. As soon as we had filled our belly, a guard was placed over the prisoners, and we went to sleep for a few hours on the grass."

By September 19, all four boats had safely reached Coupang. Governor Timotheus Wanjon, the same man who had welcomed Bligh after his arrival in Coupang in the *Bounty* launch, greeted Edwards and his men. The crew of the *Pandora* were housed in the church, and a house was made available for the officers. Morrison and the other prisoners were confined in stocks in the castle, where, wrote Morrison, "we were forced to ease nature where we lay. . . .

"We had laid 6 Days in this situation when the Dutch Officer Commanding the Fort, being informed of our distress, came to visit us & taking Compassion on us, ordered Irons to be procured, and linked us two & two; giving us liberty to walk about the Cell."

In that same prison were eight other English men and a woman and her two children, who had all escaped by boat from the British penal colony in Australia's Botany Bay. This is another remarkable story of small boat navigators—a journey of ten weeks and 3,250 miles—and it deserves to be placed alongside the small boat voyages of Bligh and Edwards.

One of its central characters was the woman, Mary Bryant. Sentenced to seven years' deportation for stealing a coat, she was part of the first group of convicts to be sent to the penal colony. On the voyage to Botany Bay she gave birth to her first child, a girl. Soon after arriving in the colony, she married William Bryant, a Cornish fisherman who had been deported on a charge of smuggling. He fathered her second child, a boy named Emanuel.

Bryant procured a compass, muskets, and a chart from a visiting East Indies trader. Then, with a crew of seven men, his wife, and the two children, he managed to steal a boat and escape the colony.

Slowly the boat sailed north along the eastern coast of Australia. For five weeks its crewmembers suffered constant rain and cold. Then a storm blew them off the coast, and for three weeks they lived on uncooked rice. Finally, half dead from exposure and starvation, they were blown ashore on one of the islands of the Barrier Reef. They killed a number of turtles and smoked the meat to provide a food supply for the long crossing of the Arafura Sea.

Arriving in Timor, the convicts claimed they were the survivors of an English ship that had been wrecked on the Australian coast. Their true identity was soon discovered, however, and the governor of Timor held them in detention, where they were joined by the *Bounty* prisoners.

As an interesting aside, Mary Bryant's ordeal captured public interest, and in England she became known as "the Girl from Botany Bay." James Boswell, the English essayist and author of *Boswell's London Journal* and the biography of Samuel Johnson, took an interest in her case, petitioned for her pardon—which was granted—and gave her a lifetime income of 10 pounds a year.

On October 6, 1791, the survivors of the *Pandora*, the 10 men from the *Bounty*, and the eight convicts, along with Mary Bryant and her two children, departed on a Dutch East India Company ship for Batavia. On October 12, wrote Hamilton, a storm nearly destroyed the ship:

"In passing the island of Flores, a most tremendous storm arose. In a few minutes every sail of the ship was shivered to pieces; the pumps all choaked, and useless; the leak gaining fast upon us; and she was driving down, with all the impetuosity imaginable, on a savage shore, about seven miles under our lee. This storm was attended with the most dreadful thunder and lightning we had ever experienced. The Dutch seamen were struck with horror, and went below; and the ship was preserved from destruction by the manly exertion of our English tars, whose souls seemed to catch redoubled ardour from the tempest's rage. Indeed it is only in these trying moments of distress, when the abyss of destruction is yawning to receive them, that the transcendent worth of a British seaman is most conspicuous."

Even Morrison—badly treated as he had been by Edwards— attested to his seamanship during the storm:

"The ship was badly found and Worse Managed and if Captain Edwards had not taken the Command and set his Men to work she would never have reached Batavia."

At Semarang, on the island of Java, another surprise greeted Edwards. The schooner *Resolution* and its crew, whom he had given up for lost, were there to welcome him. Hamilton wrote:

"Never was social affection more eminently pourtrayed than in the meeting of these poor fellows; and from excess of joy, and a recital of their mutual sufferings, from pestilence, famine, and shipwreck, a flood of tears filled every man's breast."

The men had endured frequent native attacks (including an attack on Tofua, where Norton had met his death), terrible suffering from lack of food and water, and one death during the long ordeal of sailing from Anamooka (Nomuka) Island and through Endeavour Straits to a landing at a Dutch outpost colony. There they were mistaken for *Bounty* mutineers and were sent under Dutch escort to Semarang, where they were identified by Edwards.

On November 7, one year to the day after the voyage of the *Pandora* had begun, the Dutch ship and the schooner arrived in Batavia. Immediately Edwards made arrangements for the transport of all his people to the Cape of Good Hope. The *Pandora* crewmembers, the *Bounty* crew, and the Botany Bay convicts were all housed temporarily on an anchored Dutch ship to avoid the sickness and fevers which made this port a deathtrap for Europeans. Morrison called Batavia a "golgotha of Europe, which buries the whole settlement every five years."

Dead bodies were dumped in the many canals, and these bodies, wrote Morrison, "floating down the canal struck our boat, which had a very disagreeable effect on the minds of our brave fellows." Morrison complained that the bay "teems with such filth that the Road where the large Ships lye is little better than a Stagnate Pool; during the Night the Dew falls very heavy and the Morning is generally darkened by a thick Stinking fog which continues till it is exhaled by the Heat of the Sun." Dutch ships, he added, "were forced to send to Holland for hands to Navigate them and even now they were not half Mannd, tho the crews of the outward bound ships were put on board as fast as they came to Anchor. It was said that 2500 Officers & Seamen had been carried off this season exclusive of the Inhabitants."

Edwards was fortunate. Only two people died while he was in Batavia, the convict William Bryant, husband of Mary Bryant, and their infant son, Emanuel.

Edwards sold the schooner *Resolution* in Batavia and divided the profits among the survivors of the *Pandora* crew. Owen Rutter notes in his edition of the Morrison journal: "The schooner, which had been built in such difficult conditions, had a fine turn of speed; she was afterwards employed in the sea-otter trade and made one of the quickest passages ever known from China to the Sandwich Islands. Later she was used in surveying the coast of China and saved the lives of the crew of H.M.S. *Providence* when that ship was wrecked off Formosa in 1797."[39]

On November 25, the 10 mutineers, Edwards, and 23 officers and men from the *Pandora* departed in the Dutch ship *Vreedenburg* for the Cape of Good Hope. Two other Dutch ships carried the balance of the *Pandora* officers and crew and the Botany Bay convicts. Aboard the *Vreedenburg*, the *Bounty* prisoners were kept below decks for most of the passage. The deck above them leaked, and, wrote Morrison, "We were continually wet, being alternately drenched with Salt water, the Urine of the Hogs or the Rain which happened to fall."

Three and one-half months later, on March 18, 1792, the *Vreedenburg* arrived at the cape and anchored in Table Bay, where, according to Morrison, "to our inexpressable Joy we found an English Man of war was riding which we were soon informed was His Majestys Ship *Gorgon* . . . and on the 19th we were sent on Board her, where our treatment became less rigorous and ⅔ Allowance of Provisions was now thought Feasting."

On April 5 the *Gorgon* weighed anchor for England, and on June 19 the ship arrived at Spithead. The *Bounty* men were im-

mediately transferred to H.M.S. *Hector*, where they remained until standing trial on charges of mutiny in Portsmouth, beginning August 12, 1792.

Edwards closed his account of the *Pandora*'s voyage with this paragraph:

"Although I have not had the good fortune to fully accomplish the object of my voyage, and that it has in other respects been strongly marked with great misfortunes, I hope it will be thought that the first is not for want of perseverence, or the latter for want of the care and attention of myself and those under my command, but that the disappointment and misfortune arose from the difficulties and peculiar circumstances of the service we were upon; that those of my orders I have been able to fulfill, with the discoveries that have been made will be some compensation for the disappointment and misfortunes that have attended us, and should their Lordships upon the whole think that the voyage will be profitable to our country it will be a great consolation to, Your most humble and obedient servant, Edw. Edwards."

He was acquitted by the Lords of the Admiralty for the loss of the *Pandora* and continued his naval career, eventually attaining the rank of rear admiral.

16

THE TRIAL
August 12, 1792–December 3, 1794

Bligh was again on his way to Tahiti when the 10 *Bounty* crewmen returned to England. Sir Joseph Banks had successfully obtained royal support for another breadfruit expedition, and Bligh was placed in charge of this second attempt. His new ship was H.M.S. *Providence,* and his escort vessel was the brig *Assistant.* He had sailed on August 3, 1791—just as *Pandora* was giving up the search for the missing mutineers and setting a course for home—and on this voyage he had the support of a marine guard. He left, vindicated of any responsibility for the *Bounty* mutiny, and took no part in the proceedings of the court-martial.

The court-martial opened on August 12, 1792, aboard H.M.S. *Duke* in Portsmouth Harbour. Lord Hood, vice admiral of the Royal Navy, was the presiding officer. He sat with 11 other naval officers. The detailed proceedings were published in May 1794.

The 10 men on trial were Joseph Coleman, Charles Norman, Thomas McIntosh, Peter Heywood, James Morrison, John Millward, William Muspratt, Thomas Burkett, Thomas Ellison, and Michael Byrne. These men were charged with a "Mutiny on the 28th of April, 1789, on board His Majesty's ship *Bounty,* for running away with the ship and deserting His Majesty's Service."

The question to be resolved was whether these men who had remained aboard the *Bounty* on the day of the mutiny had been participants in the mutiny or innocent victims of the event.

Public interest in the trial centered on Peter Heywood. His family had influential connections, which his mother and sister, Nessy, used to full advantage. One of the court-martial judges, Captain Albermarle Bertie, was related by marriage to the Heywood family.

The proceedings opened with a reading of Bligh's report, which he had written while still in Coupang. The report carried the full

details of the mutiny, the open boat trip, Bligh's purchase of the *Resource,* and the subsequent voyage to Batavia. Testimony was then taken from the witnesses who had sailed in the launch with Bligh. After each testimony, the prisoners had the opportunity to question the statements.

John Fryer, master of the *Bounty,* was the first witness called. He summarized the events of the mutiny and spoke in Morrison's defense by stating, "I saw Morrison fixing a tackle to the launch's stern. I said, 'Morrison, I hope you have no hand in this business.' He said, 'No, sir; I do not know a word about it.'"

Fryer also declared that McIntosh, Norman, and Byrne were not members of the mutineering group. He stated that he had observed Burkett and Millward "under arms as sentinels over Captain Bligh. . . ."

William Cole was the second witness. He recalled seeing Peter Heywood go below deck and he then "saw no more of him." He, too, declared that McIntosh and Norman were left behind on the *Bounty* against their will, and he added Coleman's name to that list. Cole stated his belief that Peter Heywood also had wanted to join Bligh in the launch, but that he was detained against his will. He also spoke on Morrison's behalf, but remembered seeing Millward, Muspratt, Burkett, and Ellison bearing arms. Ellison (only 16 years old at the time of the mutiny) questioned Cole, asking, "Are you certain it was me? I was only a boy and scarcely able to lift a musket at that time." Cole reaffirmed that he remembered seeing Ellison standing next to Bligh with a musket and a fixed bayonet.

The testimony of Peckover, the *Bounty*'s gunner, also absolved Coleman, Norman, and McIntosh as active participants.

William Purcell, carpenter in the *Bounty,* stated that he, too, had observed Ellison, Millward, and Burkett bearing arms. He was asked by the court how he viewed Peter Heywood. Purcell's response: "I looked upon him as a person confused." He was then asked if Heywood gave the impression of assisting in the mutiny; he replied, "No."

Thomas Hayward, midshipman in the *Bounty* and later a lieutenant in the *Pandora,* accused Ellison of publicly insulting Bligh on the morning of the mutiny. He also testified that he had heard Millward call out to the departing launch, "Go and see if you can live upon a quarter of a pound of yams per day." He stated that he did not see Heywood armed, and that Coleman, Norman, McIntosh, and Byrne were nonparticipants. Burkett, Millward, and Muspratt, he stated, were armed and active members of the mutiny group. Hayward was vague in his remarks about Heywood, suggesting that Heywood's failure to join the launch was evidence of support for Christian, but adding that "must be only stated as an opinion, as he was not employed during the acting part of it [the mutiny]."

Three other witnesses gave similar testimony. John Hallett and John Smith, from the launch, were followed by Lieutenant Larkin of the *Pandora*, who described how some of the *Bounty* crew came aboard the *Pandora* voluntarily (Coleman, Heywood, Norman, Ellison, and Morrison) and how others (McIntosh, Muspratt, Millward, and Burkett) were captured.

On the fifth day of the hearing, August 16, the 10 prisoners were brought before the court to hear its decision.

Coleman, Norman, McIntosh, and Byrne were acquitted. Heywood, Morrison, Muspratt, Millward, Burkett, and Ellison were found guilty and sentenced to death by hanging. But the court at the same time informed Heywood and Morrison that it would recommend them to the king for mercy. The court could only reach a verdict of guilty or not guilty. Though the evidence presented convinced the court that Heywood and Morrison had not taken an active part in the mutiny, their passiveness in staying aboard the *Bounty* was, technically, tantamount to aiding and abetting the mutiny. The only conclusion the court could render was a verdict of guilty with a recommendation for pardon.

Muspratt, though judged guilty, was excused on a legal technicality. During the trial the court had refused to allow the testimony, on Muspratt's behalf, of his fellow crewman Norman. The court later decided that such evidence should have been received. Through this tiny loophole Muspratt escaped with his life.

The conclusion of the court-martial began a period of agonized waiting for Heywood and Morrison. Millward, Burkett, and Ellison also waited, but not to learn their fate; for them the court's decision meant a noose at the end of a yardarm.

The execution was carried out on October 29 aboard H.M.S. *Brunswick* in Portsmouth Harbor. Officers and men crowded the ship, while around it circled the boats of the assembled fleet.

The printed record of the court-martial carries Millward's parting remarks. Standing on the forecastle of the *Brunswick*, he addressed the assembled men with these words:

"Brother Seamen, you see before you three lusty young fellows about to suffer a shameful death for the dreadful crime of mutiny and desertion. Take warning by our example never to desert your officers, and should they behave ill to you, remember it is not their cause; it is the cause of your country you are bound to support."

The well-educated siblings, Peter and Nessy Heywood, began a passionate correspondence with each other and with influential people. To a friend Peter wrote: "I have not been found guilty of the slightest act connected with that detestable crime of mutiny, but am doomed to die for not being active in my endeavours to suppress it. . . .

"Why should I be sorry to leave a world in which I have met with nothing but misfortunes and all their concomitant evils? I shall on the contrary endeavour to prepare my soul for its reception into the bosom of its Redeemer. For though the very strong recommendation I have had to his Majesty's mercy by all the members of the Court may meet with his approbation, yet that is but the balance of a straw, a mere uncertainty, upon which no hope can be built."

The prisoners were brought before the court

His next letter was to Nessy:

"Though I have indeed fallen an early victim to the rigid rules of the service, and though the jaws of death are once more opened upon me, yet do I not now nor ever will bow to the tyranny of base-born fear.

"Oh! my sister, my heart yearns when I picture to myself the indescribable affliction which this melancholy intelligence [the news of his conviction] must have caused in the mind of my much honoured mother. But let it be your peculiar endeavour to watch over her grief and mitigate her pain."

Daily the letters between sister and brother went back and forth, she indulging in hope, he preparing her for the worst with resignation while attesting to his innocence and integrity. He spent his days, yet a prisoner, compiling one of the first dictionaries of the Tahitian language.

To the Earl of Chatham, first Lord of the Admiralty, Nessy wrote:

"When I assure you, my lord, that he is dearer and more precious to me than any object on earth, I am persuaded you not wonder, nor be offended, that I am thus bold in conjuring your lordship will thus consider, with your usual candour and benevolence, the 'Observations' I now offer you." She then refuted point by point the arguments that had condemned her brother.

A few weeks after the trial, the king's pardon was granted for both Heywood and Morrison. Upon hearing the good news, Nessy immediately wrote her mother:

"Oh, blessed hour!—little did I think, my beloved friends, when I closed my letter this morning, that before night I should be out of my senses with joy!—this moment, this ecstatic moment, brought the enclosed [the king's pardon]. I cannot speak my happiness; let it be sufficient to say, that in a very few hours our angel Peter will be Free! . . . I shall be—oh, heaven! what shall I be? I am already transported, even to pain: then how shall I bear to clasp him to the bosom of your happy, ah! how very happy, and affectionate Nessy Heywood."

Sweet, adoring Nessy did not live long after her brother's freedom. Less than a year after his pardon she died of consumption.

For William Bligh the case did not end with the court-martial verdict. It was then his turn to stand accused—not by a court of the Admiralty, but by Edward Christian, brother of Fletcher. Though Bligh had been exonerated on all charges, testimony during the court-martial had brought evidence of his domineering character, his temper, and his abuse of his officers. Fletcher Christian, meanwhile—a man of good birth and education—was perceived in some quarters as a victim of cruel circumstances. Edward Christian, a celebrated barrister, moved quickly to restore the good name of his family by indicting Bligh as the real culprit in the *Bounty* mutiny.

Bligh returned home after a successful second voyage to Tahiti only to confront Edward Christian's assertions, which were carried as an appendix to the court-martial proceedings. With his astute legal mind, Christian stayed away from any comments that might have been read as an attempt to vindicate " . . . the crime which has been committed. Justice, as well as policy," he wrote, "requires that mutiny, from whatever causes produced or with whatever circumstances accompanied, should be punished with inexorable rigour."

His purpose, he wrote, was to bring out the "true causes and circumstances which have hitherto been concealed or misrepresented."

The appendix was based on interviews Christian claimed to have conducted, before witnesses, with nine of the former members of the *Bounty* crew. These included men who had accompanied Bligh in the open boat and others who had stayed in the *Bounty* but whom the court judged innocent: Fryer, Hayward, Peckover, Purcell, Smith, Coleman, McIntosh, and two of Bligh's favorites, the old sailmaker Lebogue and Michael Byrne, the blind fiddler. Their information, he stated, was not forthcoming in the trial because the court had confined its line of questioning to the narrow issue of "Who was actually engaged in the mutiny?" Mutiny, being a crime without legal justification of any sort, would not admit to the hearing of "the relation of previous circumstances . . . yet what passed at the time of the mutiny was . . . immediately connected with what had happened previously in the ship. . . ."

In their interviews, stated Christian, the nine men alleged that "Captain Bligh used to call his officers 'scoundrels, damned rascals, hounds, hell-hounds, beasts and infamous wretches'; that he frequently threatened them, that when the ship arrived at Endeavour Straits, 'he would kill one half of the people, make the officers jump overboard, and would make them eat grass like cows'; and that Christian and Stewart [later drowned in the wreck of the *Pandora*] . . . were as much afraid of Endeavour Straits as any child is of a rod.

"Captain Bligh was accustomed to abuse Christian much more frequently and roughly than the rest of the officers, or as one of the persons expressed it, 'whatever fault was found, Mr. Christian was sure to bear the brunt of the captain's anger.' In speaking to him in this violent manner, Captain Bligh frequently shook his fist in Christian's face."

It was the incident of the coconuts (when Bligh accused Christian of stealing his private stock) that broke Fletcher Christian, his brother stated. It drove him to tears and to the statement, "I would rather die ten thousand deaths than bear this treatment."

The appendix describes how Christian planned to make a solitary escape from the *Bounty* when it passed closed to an island, how his plan failed, and that though he first proposed the mutiny, he would never have done so had it not been for Midshipman Stewart, who said to him, "When you go, Christian, we are ripe for anything."

"The mutiny," Edward Christian stated, "is ascribed by all who remained in the ship to this unfortunate expression, which probably proceeded rather from a regard for Christian than from a mutinous disposition."

Skillfully, Edward Christian drew a background to the mutiny that explained and justified his brother's passionate statement made to Bligh at the time of the mutiny: "I have been in hell for weeks past."

Christian concluded his defense of his brother by writing, "The crime itself in this instance may afford an awful lesson to the navy, and to mankind, that there is a degree of pressure beyond which the best formed and principled mind must either break or recoil. And though public justice and the public safety can allow no vindication of any species of mutiny, yet reason and humanity will distinguish the sudden unpremeditated act of desperation and frenzy from the foul, deliberate contempt of every religious duty and honourable sentiment; and will deplore the uncertainty of human prospects when they reflect that a young man is condemned to perpetual infamy, who, if he had served on board any other ship, or had perhaps been absent from the *Bounty* a single day, or one ill-fated hour, might still have been an honour to his country and a glory and comfort to his friends."

It was an eloquent defense. Bligh, of course, had to respond to Edward Christian's assertions.

He did so with "An Answer to Certain Assertions contained in the Appendix to a Pamphlet entitled Minutes of the proceedings on the Court-Martial held at Portsmouth, 12th August 1792, on Ten Persons charged with Mutiny on Board his Majesty's Ship the *Bounty*." His elaborate self-defense, supported by letters and affidavits from former crewmembers, was dated December 3, 1794.

His task was a difficult one; he was trying to prove that he was not a tyrant. He began his reply by stating: "It is with no small degree of regret that I find myself under the necessity of obtruding my private concerns on the public."

Bligh stated that he would not defend his character by his own

protestations, but would draw on the record—the testimony of others and his record of the written orders he issued in the course of the *Bounty*'s voyage. He then introduced his "List of Proofs": his orders upon his arrival at Tahiti, orders that dealt with desertions, the Dutch governor's testimony at Batavia, and various other documents and extracts.

The appendix was written, he pointed out, by "Edward Christian, the brother of Fletcher Christian, who headed the mutineers of the *Bounty*, written apparently for the purpose of vindicating his brother's conduct at my expense."

Bligh then attempted to discredit Christian's case with this statement:

> The mixing together the names of men, whose assertions merit very different degrees of credit, and blending their evidence into one mass, is liable to two objections: 1st, the impossibility of tracing the author of any particular assertion; and 2dly, the danger, which to a reader is unavoidable, of supposing that the statement made by those who were actually accomplices in the Mutiny, came from men of respectable character. . . .

As was so often the case with Bligh, his reasoning was sound but his propensity for extravagant positions was evident. None of the nine men Edward Christian claimed to have interviewed had been an accomplice to the mutiny; they included six who had been with Bligh in the launch, and three—Coleman, McIntosh, and Byrne—whose innocence Bligh himself had noted at the time. More to the point were the statements Bligh gathered, including those from Coleman and Lebogue. In his affidavits, Coleman asserted that "I never heard Captain Bligh say, he would make his officers jump over board, and eat grass like cows. . . . I never saw Captain Bligh shake his hand in Christian's face. . . ." Smith said, "I have known the Captain to be angry and damn the people, as is common; but the Captain immediately afterwards always behaved to the people as if nothing had happened. I never heard the Captain damn the officers, and call them names, and threaten to make them jump over board. . . . I never knew or hear that such a thing [the incident of the coconuts] could be the cause of the Mutiny. . . . I never told Mr. Edward Christian that his brother never kept a girl; for I remember he had a girl, and she was called Tittriano's girl, which was the name Christian went by."

Under oath, Lebogue said that "I have heard the Captain damn the people, like many other captains; but he was never angry with a man the next minute; and I have never heard of their disliking him. I said, Captain Bligh was not a person fond of flogging his men; and some of them deserved hanging, who had only a dozen [lashes]. . . . I remember that a heap of coco-nuts, which the Captain had ordered to be saved as a rarity until we got to sea . . . when we should enjoy them, was taken away; and that the Captain told the officers they had neglected their duty, and disobeyed his orders; and that all the cocoa-nuts, on that account, were brought upon deck; and the matter ended with their being divided.

"I said Captain Bligh was the best friend Christian ever had."

Stated Hallett: "I will by no means affirm, that I never heard Captain Bligh express himself in warm or hasty language, when the conduct of his officers or people has displeased him; but every seafaring gentleman must be convinced, that situations frequently occur in a ship when the most mild officer will be driven, by the circumstances of the moment, to utter expressions which the strict standard of politeness will not warrant: and I can safely assert, that I never remember to have heard Captain Bligh make use of such illiberal epithets and menaces as the Appendix attributes to him. . . . I remember a complaint of some cocoa-nuts having been stolen, but I did not hear that Captain Bligh accused any individual of the theft."

A final letter that Bligh submitted in his rebuttal of Edward Christian's statement came from one Edward Lamb, who had been chief mate aboard the *Britannia* with Bligh and Christian. Lamb wrote:

"When we got to sea [in the *Britannia*], and I saw your partiality for the young man [Christian], I gave him every advice and information in my power, though he went about every point of duty with a degree of indifference, that to me was truly unpleasant; but you were blind to his faults, and had him to dine and sup every other day in the cabin, and treated him like a brother, in giving him every information. In the Appendix it is said, that Mr. Fletcher Christian had no attachment amongst the women at Otaheite; if that was the case, he would have been much altered since he was with you in the *Britannia;* he was then one of the most foolish young men I ever knew in regard to sex."

Bligh concluded his statement by saying:

I submit these evidences to the judgement of the Public, without offering any comment. My only intention in this publication, is to clear my character from the effect of censures which I am conscious I have not merited: I have therefore avoided troubling the Public with more than what is necessary to that end; and have refrained from remark, lest I might have been led beyond my purpose, which I have wished to limit solely to defence.

Conspicuous by their absence from the affidavits Bligh gathered were Fryer and Purcell, his old nemeses, and it must be safe to assume that a great deal of the testimony Christian amassed had come from these two. It hardly mattered. Bligh may have had the law on his side, but the popular vote supported Edward's summation of the mutiny and his defense of his brother Fletcher. Thus was born the legend that ever since has made Bligh the villain and Christian his victim.

17

PITCAIRN ISLAND
September 22, 1789–December 4, 1825

There is no written record of the *Bounty* or its people after the ship sailed from Tahiti in the evening of September 22, 1789. A fairly reliable story of the *Bounty*'s last voyage was later told, however, by the Tahitian woman known as Jenny, who made this journey as *taio* (friend) to Isaac Martin.[40]

When the *Bounty* cleared Tahiti, it carried aboard nine Englishmen, six Tahitian men, and 11 native women. The ship was in good order and well supplied with food, stores, equipment, livestock, and fowl—many successful colonizing expeditions had set out with little more. But the *Bounty* was a hunted ship, its white crew outlaws and its native men and women little better than slaves. The fate of this biracial group was already cast by the unequal numbers of males and females. The couples were paired in this way, with the white men having the first choice of selection:

Bounty men	*Tahitian women*
William Brown	Teatuahitea
Fletcher Christian	Isabella
Isaac Martin	Jenny
William McCoy	Mary
John Mills	Vahineatua
Matthew Quintal	Sarah
John Adams*	Paurai
Edward Young	Susan
John Williams	Pashotu

The six Tahitian men, Menalee, Nehow, Ohoo, Talaloo, Tetaheite, and Timoa were to share two native women, Mareva and Tinafaneca.

---

*Formerly Alexander Smith, Adams had changed his name after the mutiny.

The trade winds blew westerly, and in that direction the *Bounty* sailed on a search for an island that all knew would be their last home. A map of the South Pacific shows the island jewels that lay before them: islands of wind-curved palms standing back from coral beaches, obsidian sands, and sparkling lagoons. Each island was a possible paradise—but not for the people of the *Bounty,* because each was also inhabited. Natives sometimes made long passages from island to island. They would certainly carry with them news of any European settlement, information that would eventually find its way back to England. Christian's mutiny had made him an outcast before the law, and security for him and his men would only be found at the outer reaches of an uninhabited world.

The ship stopped briefly at Rarotonga, the well-settled gem of the Cook Islands. A native was shot as he attempted to board the ship, and Christian ordered a quick departure. Island after island, the telescope showed, had canoes drawn up on the beaches and huts behind the screen of trees. Hope, then disappointment, followed the *Bounty* as it sailed on looking for a place no one else wanted. The search took the ship as far west as Tongatapu in the Tonga Islands, just a few miles from Tofua where, seven months earlier, Bligh and his men had been forced into the launch on the morning of the mutiny.

At Tongatapu, where the *Bounty* was resupplied with food and water, Christian gave up the western search for an island home. While studying Bligh's charts, he came across a copy of Hawkesworth's *Voyages* (at the time, the most complete history of British explorations in the South Pacific), and in that book he found the report of the 1767 voyage of Captain Philip Carteret, H.M.S. *Swallow,* and the reference to an obscure island he had discovered far to the east of Tahiti. Upon approaching the island, wrote Carteret, "It appeared like a great rock rising out of the sea; it was not more than five miles in circumference, and seemed to be uninhabited; it was, however, covered with trees . . . and we saw it at the distance of more than fifteen leagues, and it having been discovered by a young gentleman, son to Major Pitcairn of the marines, we called it Pitcairn's Island." The report also mentioned that because of a high surf, they could not land on the island.

Carteret's position of the island (nearly 200 miles in error) placed it almost 3,000 miles to the east of Tongatapu, upwind against the easterly trades. Getting there for the *Bounty* and her tired crew involved an arduous two-month voyage.

Christian's four-month search for an island home ended January 15, 1790, as the *Bounty* hove to off Pitcairn Island. What the people aboard the ship saw was an isolated volcanic rock, one mile wide by two miles long, which rose out of the sea as black and broken crags and cliffs over a thousand feet high. There was no offshore shelf or reef, no gap in the continuous surf that lashed the unbroken rock shore. There was no sign of life except the wheeling, crying birds that skimmed the cliff faces and summits. The mutineers had escaped the Admiralty's wrath, but the cost was a self-imposed life imprisonment on an isolated island.

For three days of stormy weather, the ship stood off Pitcairn Island, the surf too high to attempt a landing. When the seas calmed, Christian and six armed men aboard the cutter made a landing on a tiny, shelf-like indentation of the shore.

Cautiously—there remained the possibility of unseen natives lying in ambush—yet eager to inspect their new island home, the men climbed from the landing to level ground 300 feet above the

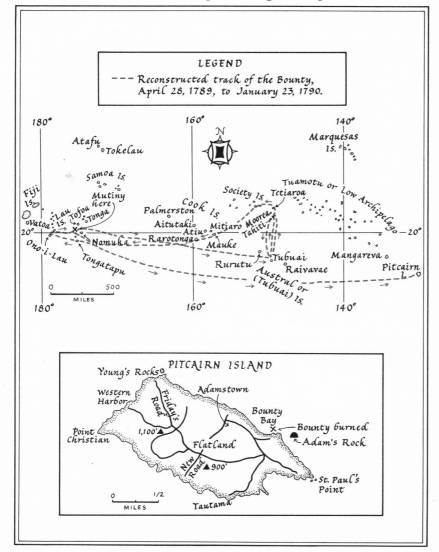

LEGEND
--- Reconstructed track of the Bounty,
April 28, 1789, to January 23, 1790.

PITCAIRN ISLAND

beach. As they moved inland, the trees screened out the roar of the surf and the cries of disturbed birds. The only sound was the wind blowing through the trees of an island long abandoned by its human population.

Who these people had been, why they left, and where they went has never been determined. The relics they left behind—including flat-nosed stone idols similar to the statue gods of Easter Island—showed their connection with the Polynesian culture of the Pacific. The mutineers cared not why they had left, only that they had gone; the island was theirs to occupy. Its soil supported a rich vegetation of plants and trees, water was adequate, the climate was tropical, and—most important—the island was far south of the sailing track of the ships that rounded Cape Horn for the voyage across the Pacific to Tahiti.

Returning to the ship, Christian ordered the *Bounty* to be brought close to the shore, where it was anchored for the unloading of its valuable stores and equipment. Everyone worked at a furious pace to strip the ship before a storm could blow it out to sea or onto the rocks below the cliffs. Hatch covers were made into rafts, which were loaded with goats, pigs, chickens, tools, the *Bounty*'s heavy forge, and other vital supplies. These were then pulled by ropes back and forth between ship and shore. The masts of the ship were cut down and were floated, along with the sails and rigging, to the tiny landing on the beach. Railings, coamings, cabin roofs, and all other parts of the ship that could be torn apart to furnish lumber and nails were sent ashore. All knew that building the new colony with the material of the *Bounty* destroyed their last connection with the outside world. There was no other choice. The ship could not last long at anchor. There was no other place for them to go. And yet it must have been a sad affair, this dismantling of the *Bounty*, the final act that closed and locked the prison door behind them.

Reduced to a hulk, the *Bounty* was burned to the waterline, then sank, giving its name to its final resting place—Bounty Bay.

As the 18th century drew to a close, the *Bounty* affair was far removed from the concerns of the Royal Navy. England was at war with France. A more significant mutiny occupied national attention: the great uprising at Nore, where navy crews demanded, and received, better pay and working conditions. British interests in the South Pacific centered on Australia and the establishment of the penal colonies at Botany Bay. The war with France put a severe strain on the resources of the navy, and the assignment of another ship and crew to continue a search for nine mutineers lost somewhere in the Pacific was not even considered.

The great battle of Nelson and his death at Trafalgar in 1805 and the American War of 1812 ushered in the large events of the new century, and the long-ago incident of the *Bounty* was forgotten history.

In 1808 the American ship *Topaz,* a sealer out of Boston commanded by Captain Mayhew Folger, rounded Cape Horn and headed west across the Pacific on a track considerably south of the normal sailing route. The course of the *Topaz* brought it to Pitcairn Island. In need of fresh water and food, Folger brought his ship to anchor off the island as soon as the weather permitted.

No ship had visited the island since the mutineers' arrival. A generation of mixed English-Polynesian blood had been born and grown up. One of these, a dark, slender, 18-year-old boy, was among the crew of a canoe that put out from the island to greet the strange ship. Coming aboard the *Topaz,* he surprised Folger by introducing himself in English. His name was Thursday October Christian.

The name meant nothing to Folger until Thursday Christian explained who his father had been and how he had come to be born on Pitcairn Island. Folger went ashore and walked through a community of women and children and was then introduced to the only adult male living on the island, John Adams (formerly Alexander Smith), able seaman of the *Bounty.* Whether as a gift or as proof of his story, Adams gave Folger Bligh's chronometer to take with him on the *Topaz.*

Folger sailed from Pitcairn Island to continue his sealing voyage, but on his return voyage, he stopped at Valparaiso, Chile, to give a full report to a British naval officer. The report eventually reached England, now in a desperate struggle with France. No action was taken.

Back in the United States on the eve of his country's second war with England, Folger sent the Admiralty a full report. Because of the war, the dispatch did not reach London until 1813. Again no action was taken; England had more pressing problems than the arrest of an old mutineer living on a rock thousands of miles away.

Among the Admiralty's problems with the pesky new American nation was the United States ship *Essex,* which had been harassing British whalers off the west coast of South America. Two Royal Navy ships, the *Briton,* commanded by Captain Staines, and the *Tagus,* commanded by Captain Pipon, were sent to sink or capture the *Essex.* The two ships rounded the Cape of Good Hope and were sailing eastward across the Pacific toward South America, hunting for the *Essex,* when they sighted Pitcairn Island.

The year was 1814. For 25 years John Adams had been hiding. Now, before him, two Royal Navy ships came to anchor. Sons of mutineers went out to greet them. What were old Adams's feelings: fear at being discovered or joy to see at last his own countrymen?

Staines and Pipon landed on the island and looked around: one old man, tribes of children, and a harem of women. What had this to do with a crime committed a quarter of a century ago? To arrest him, they later wrote, would have been an act of cruelty. The last of the mutineers was left in peace.

The full story, however, had yet to be reported. The reports brought back by Folger, Staines, and Pipon after their discovery of the mutineers' hideout carried few details about the history of the colony. That history had to wait until 1831 to be told. In that year was published the *Narrative of a Voyage to the Pacific and Beering's Strait, Performed in His Majesty's Ship Blossom Under the Command of Captain F. W. Beechey, R. N.*

Here, the *Bounty*'s story intersects another and equally great story in British maritime history: the search for the Northwest Passage.

Sir John Franklin was the leading figure in the obsessive 19th century English quest for a passage from the Atlantic to the Pacific along the frigid coast of arctic Canada. His credentials were those of a surveyor, and his appointment to lead the search for the passage had come with the support of Bligh's aging patron, Sir Joseph Banks. Franklin eventually gave his life to the quest, but added a colorful chapter to the history of geographical exploration in North America.

On his second expedition, Franklin was supported by Captain Beechey, in command of the *Blossom*. Beechey was instructed to make his way to the Bering Sea by way of Cape Horn and there, at a designated location, await the arrival of Franklin at the conclusion of his exploratory journey. Since the voyage took the *Blossom* through Pacific waters still largely unexplored, Beechey was also ordered to perform all the survey work possible during the time available to him before his rendezvous in the Bering Sea. He was specifically instructed to make an accurate survey of Pitcairn Island and its surrounding waters.

The *Blossom* cleared England on May 19, 1825, ran down the Atlantic to Rio de Janeiro, made an easy rounding of Cape Horn, sailed northward along the Chilean coast, and then headed west across the Pacific. On December 4, the lookout sighted Pitcairn Island.

At this point, I yield my writing to the superb narrative skills of Captain Beechey:

"The interest which was excited by the announcement of Pitcairn Island from the mast-head brought every person upon deck, and produced a train of reflections that momentarily increased our anxiety to communicate with its inhabitants; to see and partake of the pleasures of their little domestic circle; and to learn from them the particulars of every transaction connected with the fate of the Bounty."

The ship was met by a boat and a crew of men that included John Adams.

"Before they ventured to take hold of the ship, they inquired if they might come on board, and upon permission being granted, they sprang up the side and shook every officer by the hand with undisguised feelings of gratification.

"The activity of the young men outstripped that of old Adams who was consequently almost the last to greet us. He was in his sixty-fifth year, and unusually strong and active for his age, notwithstanding the inconvenience of considerable corpulency. He was dressed in a sailor's shirt and trousers and a low-crowned hat, which he instinctively held in his hand until I desired him to put it on. He still retained his sailor's gait, doffing his hat and smoothing down his bald forehead whenever he was addressed by the officers.

"It was the first time he had been on board a ship of war since the mutiny, and his mind naturally reverted to scenes that could not fail to produce a temporary embarrassment, heightened, perhaps, by the familiarity with which he found himself addressed by persons of a class with those whom he had been accustomed to obey."

Beechey set up an observatory on Pitcairn for his survey work and spent over two weeks on the island. During that time he was able to record Adams's version of the mutiny (previously reported in Chapter 7) and the story of the colony's founding. It is a tragic, bloody story, dominated by the complicated elements of racism, sex, and liquor.

After the *Bounty* was stripped of all that could be floated ashore, most of the mutineers wanted to run the ship up on the shore, where its planks and timbers could be saved. Matthew Quintal (by all records a vicious and often drunk and violent man) left the group discussion on the disposal of the *Bounty*, went below, and set fire to the ship.

To the men of the *Bounty*, Pitcairn was their island, their community, their refuge, and their home. This feeling was reflected in the division of land and in their attitude toward the Tahitian men. Beechey records Adams's recollection of the flawed beginning of the island settlement:

"A suitable spot of ground for a village was fixed upon with the

exception of which the island was divided into equal portions, but to the exclusion of the poor blacks, who being only friends of seamen, were not considered as entitled to the same privileges. Obliged to lend their assistance to others in order to procure a subsistence, they thus, from being their friends, in the course of time became their slaves."

For the first two years, the men and women worked in a harmonious relationship. They built houses, planted gardens, and, remembered Adams, the community was "supplied with all the necessaries of life, and some of its luxuries, [and] they felt their condition comfortable even beyond their most sanguine expectation."

John Williams caused the beginning of the tragic series of events that overshadowed the settlement. He had made himself valuable as the community's blacksmith. Shortly after the arrival at Pitcairn, his "wife," Pashotu, fell from a cliff while gathering eggs and died. For two years, Williams lived alone, but then, tired of his celibate existence, he demanded that he be given another woman. If not, he threatened, he would steal the *Bounty*'s boat and leave the island.

Adams described the dilemma of Williams's demand and its outcome: "Williams, actuated by selfish considerations alone, persisted in his threat, and the Europeans not willing to part with him, on account of his usefulness as an armourer, constrained one of the blacks to bestow his wife upon the applicant. The blacks, outrageous at this second act of flagrant injustice, made common cause with their companion, and matured a plan of revenge upon their aggressors, which, had it succeeded, would have proved fatal to all the Europeans. Fortunately, the secret was imparted to the women, who ingeniously communicated it to the white men in a song, of which the words were 'Why does black man sharpen axe? to kill white man'."

Christian went in search of the Tahitian men to tell them their plot had been discovered. He encountered two of them—Talaloo, who had been forced to give his wife to Williams, and Ohoo. These two men fled when Christian fired a blank shot at them. The remaining natives bought a truce at a terrible price: They murdered Ohoo and Talaloo.

The peace that was restored lasted but two years. The oppression and mistreatment of the natives by the *Bounty* men, particularly by Quintal and William McCoy, again drove the Polynesian men to revolt. They acquired arms and killed first Williams and then Christian, John Mills, William Brown, and Isaac Martin.

And then there were four: Edward Young, Quintal, McCoy, and

Adams. "It was," reported Adams, "a day of emancipation to the blacks, who were now masters of the island, and of humiliation and retribution to the whites."

Adams, who had been wounded in the uprising, and Edward Young were spared. McCoy and Quintal escaped to the hills.

Dissension then erupted among the four remaining native men (Timoa, Nehow, Menalee, and Tetaheite) as to the disposition of the wives of the murdered men. In the ensuing quarrel, Menalee shot and killed Timoa and then attacked Tetaheite. Tetaheite fled, joining Quintal and McCoy in the hills. These three, now an armed and dominating force, demanded the death of Menalee as the price of peace. Menalee was shot.

Adams told Beechey: "It was not long before the widows of the white men so deeply deplored their loss, that they determined to revenge their death, and concerted a plan to murder the only two remaining men of colour." The plan resulted in Edward Young shooting Nehow. His wife, Susan, killed Tetaheite with an ax.

Adams carried the news of the native deaths to Quintal and McCoy, but these two, unconvinced that it was safe for them to return to the village, demanded the hands and heads of the dead men as proof. Adams delivered them on October 3, 1793. Of the 27 people who had landed on Pitcairn Island with so much hope less than four years prior to this gruesome day, there now remained but four *Bounty* men (Adams, Young, McCoy, and Quintal) and 10 women.

Adams gave Beechey the journal that Edward Young had begun to write, which covered the events of the Pitcairn Island colony after the massacre. Women outnumbered the men more than two to one. For a while, wrote Young, the survivors lived in harmony, then the women, "who lived promiscuously with the men," became discontented.

"Since the massacre," wrote Young, "it has been the desire of the greater part of them to get some conveyance, to enable them to leave the island." The men began to build them a boat, but it quickly upset as soon as it was launched. It was a great disappointment to the women who, added Young, "continued much dissatisfied with their condition; probably not without some reason, as they were kept in great subordination, and were frequently beaten by McCoy and Quintal."

The women formed a plan to kill the white men while they slept, but the plot was discovered by its intended victims. Though the women were pardoned, wrote Young, "We did not forget their conduct; and it was agreed among us, that the first female who misbehaved should be put to death."

Threats moved back and forth between the male and female groups, each party living in fear and suspicion of the other—the men more fearful, perhaps, because of the numerical superiority of the women.

The first ship in nearly five years was sighted on December 27, 1795, but the weather was stormy and it passed from view. One page of Young's journal sufficed to cover all the events of 1796. A kind of truce had been declared that brought with it "a very domestic and tranquil state."

And then McCoy, who had once been employed in a distillery in Scotland, learned how to make a fiery liquor from a native plant. He and Quintal set up an island distillery. Both were thereafter frequently drunk. In such a state, McCoy fell from a cliff and died.

Young did not continue his journal beyond that event, but Beechey recorded Adams's concluding narrative:

"In 1799, Quintal's wife was also killed in a fall from the cliffs where she had been gathering bird eggs. He demanded that either Young or Adams relinquish their wife. Neither agreed to Quintal's demand and he made an attempt to kill them. Adams and Young agreed that their own lives were not safe as long as Quintal lived. Together, they felt justified in killing him with an axe."

Beechey's own comments concluded his interviews with Adams:

"Adams and Young were now the sole survivors out of the fifteen males that landed on the island. They were both, and more particularly Young, of a serious turn of mind; and it would have been wonderful, after the many dreadful scenes at which they had assisted, if the solitude and tranquillity that ensued had not disposed them to repentance. During Christian's lifetime they had only once read the church service, but since his decease this had been regularly done on every Sunday. They now, however, resolved to have morning and evening family prayers, to add afternoon service to the duty of the Sabbath, and to raise up their own children, and those of their late unfortunate companions, in piety and virtue.

"In the execution of this resolution, Young's education enabled him to be of the greatest assistance; but he was not long suffered to survive his repentance; An asthmatic complaint, under which he had for some time laboured, terminated his existence about a year after the death of Quintal, and Adams was left the sole survivor of the misguided and unfortunate mutineers of the Bounty."

AFTERWORD

I can close the books now, all of them: The journals of Bligh, Morrison, Edwards, Hamilton, and Beechey. Out of these journals of men, ships, and the sea, has come this book. I hope I have done their authors credit.

As to the other men of the *Bounty*, those who left no journals, I let their obituaries stand as their judgments:

JOHN NORTON, quartermaster: killed by natives as the *Bounty* launch escaped from Tofua.

DAVID NELSON, botanist: died in Coupang from the ordeal of the launch voyage.

THOMAS HALL, able-bodied seaman, WILLIAM ELPHINSTONE, master's mate, PETER LINKLETTER, quartermaster, and ROBERT LAMB, able-bodied seaman: died as a result of fevers contracted in Coupang and Batavia.

THOMAS LEDWARD, surgeon's mate: lost at sea aboard the Dutch ship *Welfare* on the voyage from Cape of Good Hope to Europe.

CHARLES CHURCHILL, master-at-arms: murdered by Matthew Thompson on Tahiti.

MATTHEW THOMPSON, able-bodied seaman: murdered by Tahitians in revenge for killing Churchill.

GEORGE STEWART, midshipman, HENRY HILLBRANT, RICHARD SKINNER, and JOHN SUMNER, all able-bodied seamen: drowned in irons in the wreck of the *Pandora* along with 31 members of the ship's crew.*

THOMAS BURKETT, THOMAS ELLISON, and JOHN MILLWARD, able-bodied seamen: convicted of mutiny by a court-martial and hanged October 29, 1792.

---

*Another crewmember later died from dehydration. Four other members of the *Pandora* crew disappeared in their boat at Palmerston Island.

FLETCHER CHRISTIAN, JOHN WILLIAMS, ISAAC MARTIN, JOHN MILLS, and WILLIAM BROWN: murdered by Tahitians on Pitcairn Island.

MATTHEW QUINTAL: killed by Edward Young and John Adams on Pitcairn Island.

WILLIAM MCCOY: died after a drunken fall from the cliffs of Pitcairn Island.

EDWARD YOUNG, midshipman: Died on Pitcairn Island.

JOHN ADAMS, the last surviving male member of the original Pitcairn Island community: died in 1829 at the age of 65. His grave is the only known burial site of those mutineers who died on the island.

Some went on to honor:

PETER HEYWOOD, after his pardon, rose to command in a number of distinguished actions during England's long war with France. He died an admiral in 1831 after a career of 42 years of service, 27 years of which was spent on active sea duty.

JAMES MORRISON also returned to active duty with the Royal Navy. He is presumed to have gone down with all hands in the disappearance of H. M. S. *Blenheim* in 1807.

After sailing in the *Pandora*, both THOMAS HAYWARD and JOHN HALLETT continued their naval careers. Both were later lost at sea while serving in other vessels.

LAWRENCE LEBOGUE and JOHN SMITH sailed with Bligh in the *Providence*, on the second breadfruit voyage. ROBERT TINKLER and JOHN FRYER both served, as did Bligh, at the battle of Copenhagen. Tinkler rose from able-bodied seaman in the *Bounty* to post-captain; Fryer served as a master until 1812, and died in 1817.[41]

And in a way, honor attended Bligh's later career:

Though his second breadfruit voyage in the *Providence* had been successful, it was 1795 before he was again given a command and ordered to the coastal blockade of the Dutch fleet in the North Sea. In 1801 he took an active part in the bombardment of Copenhagen and was commended for his action by Lord Nelson.

His last significant appointment was achieved through his old patron, Sir Joseph Banks. He was made governor of the penal colony in New South Wales. A stickler for law and order like Bligh was perhaps what the Admiralty felt the lawless convict colony of Botany Bay needed. And indeed it did, but law and order were not what the controlling military forces of this colony wanted.

Bligh ran headlong into the established monopoly of the New South Wales Corps, formed out of the dregs of the British army to administer the colony. They controlled the sale of rum, and rum, in this corrupt, drunken, and violent outpost, was the prevailing currency. It was a case of gangsters ruling convicts, and Bligh's accustomed authority as a naval officer meant nothing there.

In what was called the "Rum Rebellion," he confronted his last mutiny. The men of the Corps, led by their officers, surrounded Government House and arrested him. In defeat, Bligh returned to England in 1810, where once again he had to face a court-martial. The leader of the rebellion, Corps Commander George Johnston, was found guilty of mutiny and was dismissed from the army.

Bligh was promoted to rear admiral in 1811 and Vice-Admiral of the Blue in 1814. His wife, Betsy, always his loyal supporter, died in 1812. Five years later, Bligh of the *Bounty,* old "Breadfruit Bligh" as he was known, died at the age of 63.

Appendix 1

SHIPBOARD RANK AND DUTY

Bligh commanded as a lieutenant, the lowest commissioned rank in the British Navy. He was the captain of his ship, but not a post-captain in the navy list. His was a first lieutenant's pay.

Bligh made Christian his second in command with the promotion to "acting lieutenant," an advancement that later—had not Christian mutinied—would have to be (and in all probability would have been) confirmed by the Admiralty. Having put to sea from Spithead with the rank of master's mate, Christian did not have a commission.

Below the commissioned officers of a ship stood the warrant ratings, the men who exercised authority over specific areas of responsibility. These men were the professionals, and the best of them serving under less competent commissioned officers were the glue that held their ships together. Lacking the education and often the familial influence of the gentlemen who were appointed by commission from the Admiralty, the officers appointed by warrant from the Navy Board were trained to their specialties by hard experience at sea. They could be disrated but not flogged by a captain.

The master was the most senior of these. He performed the essential task of the ship's navigator and—in difficult waters—its pilot. On the *Bounty,* Bligh, a former master, frequently served as his own navigator, thereby causing friction between himself and John Fryer. The master also oversaw the boatswain's responsibilities, and was expected to undertake coastal pilotage, sound harbor entrances, correct and add detail to charts, and sometimes make new ones. (There is no indication that Fryer had any talent or inclination for drawing charts.) In the aggregate the master's many responsibilities overlapped those of the other officers; he would be forever signing documents related to aspects of shipboard management. He took his orders from the captain, but a successful captain-master dynamic resembled a partnership. "In the hierarchy of pay," says Beaglehole, "[a master] might, depending on the rating of his ship, get more than a lieutenant. . . . There was a tendency for masters to remain masters: who would wish to waste such a man by giving him a commission?" (*The Life of Captain James Cook*, p. 27) Sir Joseph Banks's intervention was responsible for Bligh's transition from master to lieutenant. It would become increasingly difficult in the 19th century for a master to enter the ranks of commissioned officers.

The master gave orders directly to the master's mates, who also held warrants and were, like the master, allowed to walk the quarterdeck. It was not unusual for a master's mate drawn from the ranks of the gentlemen to be promoted to lieutenant when a master was not; thus Bligh's promotion of Christian to acting lieutenant need not be viewed as a slight to Fryer.

The gunner was another warrant rating. As the title would imply, his responsibilities were for the care and use of his ship's guns and powder.

The boatswain was responsible for the care and maintenance of the ship's spars, sails, rigging, anchors, gear, and stores. He had to have enough education to keep the inventory accounts.

The carpenter also held warrant rank. His job required a high degree of skill in maintaining the hull, decks, masts, yards, and ship's boats.

Below the warrant ranks were other specialized skills and responsibilities that conferred on their possessors some status above the position of the common sailor. Within this group were the armourer, or blacksmith, who served as an assistant to the gunner; the sailmaker, who was responsible to the boatswain; the master-at-arms, who stood guard duties and—when necessary—exercised the men in small-arms drill; and the quartermaster, whose prime responsibility was steering the ship.

The midshipmen were petty officers apprenticing for future careers as masters and commissioned officers. They might do the duty of a seaman, but the distinction they had—which placed them a world apart from the seamen and lower-rated warrant officers—was the right to walk the quarterdeck. They were known as "young gentlemen," and some were indeed young and inexperienced. Peter Heywood was 16 at the time of the *Bounty* mutiny; John Hallett was 15. Thomas Hayward, on the other hand, was older, with several years' seagoing experience. It was not uncommon for well-connected teenagers to enter the navy as able-bodied

seamen, then receive appointments as midshipmen within a few months. The road from there to the coveted lieutenant's commission comprised six years of experience and an examination.

Uniform for the commissioned officers and midshipmen was introduced in 1748 at the senior officers' request, to emphasize their status relative to the warrant officers. The midshipmen wore uniforms as commissioned officers in training, and those who were so predisposed could feel thereby socially superior to the warrant officers even if inferior in experience and ability. This altered somewhat in 1787, the very year the *Bounty* was refitted for her breadfruit voyage, with the introduction of uniform for warrant officers. Uniform codes were not strictly observed far from British ports, and the standards were probably more or less informal on the *Bounty* after several months in the tropics.

Below all were the able-bodied and ordinary seamen, known variously as the men, the people, or the ship's company. The ordinary seaman had little or no experience; in times of war he might be dragged aboard by press gangs or tricked aboard in a drunken stupor, only to sober up with the ship already at sea. The able seaman had more experience—usually two years before the mast. The *Bounty*'s was a peacetime mission, and she carried no conscripts; her people were all able-bodied seamen.

Appendix 2

VICTUALS AND GROG

Food and wind powered a sailing ship. The British Admiralty could do nothing about the wind, but it went to great effort to provide for its men the best food possible. The problem of provisioning for extended sea voyages was food preservation. In Bligh's time, the connection between diet and good health was beginning to be understood, but because of the limitations of preservation technology, only certain foods could be carried on long sea voyages.

The Georgian navy's standard weekly ration for one man was as follows:

Bread	7 pounds	Peas	2 quarts
Beer	7 gallons	Oatmeal	3 pints
Beef	4 pounds	Butter	6 ounces
Pork	2 pounds	Cheese	12 ounces

In addition to the standard weekly ration, ships were supplied with flour, suet, raisins, vinegar, and dried fish. The diet was very plain and monotonous, but it provided sufficient caloric intake for hard physical labor and enough vitamins to ward off scurvy. By the culinary standards of the day, the seaman who had a hot meal and a gallon of beer each day, meat four times a week, and a fair supply of dried vegetables and grain was much better off than many of the shoreside workers.

Bread was supplied to the ships in a biscuit or hardtack form, flint hard but susceptible to maggots nonetheless. Beef and pork were either salted or pickled in casks, and cheese and butter were also carried in casks. All food was prepared by boiling in large copper pots set over a brick hearth.

Despite the sameness of their food, seamen objected to any changes in the fare. These changes sometimes became necessary on long voyages when foreign foods had to be substituted for their regular rations. Any departures from the usual allotments were expected to follow a table of equivalents. For example, two pounds of potatoes or yams could be substituted for one pound of bread, or one pint of oil could equal one pound of butter.

In his *Life of Captain James Cook* (page 170), Beaglehole notes the inherent conservatism of seamen, particularly evident when any changes in their diet were concerned. He quotes Cook's journals on the subject:

"The Sour Krout the Men at first would not eate untill I put in practice a Method I never once knew to fail with seamen, and this was to have some of it dress'd every Day for the Cabbin Table, and permitted all the Officers without exception to make use of it and left it to the option of the Men either to take as much as they pleased or none atall; but this practice was not continued above a week before I found it necessary to put every one on board to an Allowance, for such are the Tempers and disposissions of Seamen in general that whatever you give them out of the Common way, altho it be ever so much for their good yet it will not go down with them and you will hear nothing but murmurings gainest the man that first invented it; but the Moment they see their Superiors set a Value upon it, it becomes the finest stuff in the World and the inventer a damn'd honest fellow."

Cook's method of dealing with this seemingly mundane but potentially inflammatory problem stands in stark contrast to Bligh's verbal bluster whenever complaints about shipboard fare were aired.

In protracted periods of bad weather, cooking conditions were difficult, and crews were forced to a diet of little more than survival rations. With hatches battened down to keep out the sea, the galley fires created suffocating conditions of smoke below deck. On the *Bounty*'s month-long attempt to round stormy Cape Horn, the crew's breakfast consisted of boiled wheat and barley in the amount of one gallon of wheat and two pounds of barley for 46 men.

Alcoholism in 18-century England was a national disease, but in the navy, grog was the sailor's friend, a reward for work well done and sometimes the only sustenance possible in wet and dirty weather.

In the diary of James Morrison, the *Bounty*'s boatswain's mate, he mentioned that in the attempted Cape Horn passage, " . . . the people requested that their Rum might be served without water . . . and this indulgence was not lost on the Seamen whose Spirits seemed to have additional flow from it, they thought nothing of Hardship and Notwithstanding fatigue and increasing bad weather they Carried on their duty with alacrity and Cheerfulness."

In port, crews drank themselves into oblivion. At sea, drunkenness was rarely punished unless the condition prevented a man from fullfilling his duty. Then he could be flogged. Officers drank as much as their men. Cook lost promising officers to alcoholism. Bligh's surgeon drank himself to death aboard ship and was buried in Tahiti. At Santa Cruz, Bligh bought 863 gallons of wine, enough to supply each man in the crew with 19 gallons. Fresh water spoiled quickly in wooden casks, so wine and beer were the most feasible shipboard potables.

Because privately bartered hogs and their subsequent ownership became an issue aboard the *Bounty,* some explanation is required as to how and why certain crewmembers "owned" animals that Bligh was determined to confiscate. N. A. M. Rogers, in his book *The Wooden World, an Anatomy of the Georgian Navy* (page 71), provides this insight:

"Cattle were supplied by the Navy as part of the regular diet, but pigs, goats, hens and geese were usually bought by officers and men out of their own pockets. . . . Those who had the most money were naturally in the best position to buy livestock, but it is quite untrue to say that it was the prerogative of the captain and the wardroom officers. Any sensible captain would much rather see his men spend their money on food than on drink and women, which were the likely alternatives. No doubt a mess [a crew group eating together] which proposed to buy a pig or two would have been wise to ask the lieutenant's permission, but there was no reason why he should refuse, considering how much of a farmyard this ship was likely to be already."

In larger-rated ships there might be separate cooks for the captain, the lieutenants, and the ship's company. Aboard the *Bounty,* one cook served all.

Appendix 3

A *BOUNTY* CHRONOLOGY

1787
AUGUST 16: Bligh appointed to command of the *Bounty*.
DECEMBER 23: *Bounty* sails from Spithead.

1788
APRIL 22: Bligh gives up his attempt to round Cape Horn.
OCTOBER 26: *Bounty* comes to anchor in Matavai Bay, Tahiti.

1789
APRIL 5: *Bounty* departs Tahiti.
APRIL 28: Mutiny aboard the *Bounty*.
MAY 3: Bligh and his men attacked by natives on Tofua.
MAY 28: *Bounty*, under command of Christian, anchors in Bloody
    Bay, Tubuai.
JUNE 6: Christian and the *Bounty* return to Tahiti.
JUNE 14: The *Bounty*'s launch, Bligh, and 17 of his men arrive in
    Coupang, Timor.
JUNE 16: *Bounty* departs Tahiti for Tubuai.
AUGUST 20: Bligh and his men sail from Coupang aboard the
    Resource, bound for Batavia.
SEPTEMBER 23: *Bounty* again visits Tahiti, then immediately
    departs with nine of her crew, leaving 16 behind.
OCTOBER 16: Bligh sails from Batavia aboard the Dutch ship
    Vlydte, bound for Cape Town.

1790
JANUARY 2: Bligh sails from Cape Town.
JANUARY 15: *Bounty* arrives at Pitcairn Island.
MARCH 14: Bligh arrives at Portsmouth, England.
NOVEMBER 7: *Pandora* sails from Portsmouth for Tahiti.

1791

MARCH 22: *Pandora* arrives at Tahiti.

MAY 8: *Pandora* departs Tahiti to search for the missing *Bounty* mutineers.

AUGUST 28: *Pandora* wrecked on Great Barrier Reef.

SEPTEMBER 19: *Pandora* survivors arrive at Coupang.

1792

AUGUST 12: Trial of the mutineers begins.

OCTOBER 29: Three mutineers executed.

ALSO IN 1792: Three deaths, including two murders, on Pitcairn Island.

1793

Massacre on Pitcairn Island. By the end of the year only four *Bounty* men and 10 women remain alive. Three of the remaining men will die within the next seven years.

1825

DECEMBER 4: *Blossom* arrives at Pitcairn Island.

Appendix 4

EXCERPTS FROM THE
ARTICLES OF WAR

The following articles and orders were established from the 25th of December 1749; and are directed to be observed and put in execution, as well in time of peace as in time of war. [*Editor's note: Only those articles that would have applied equally in peace as in war are reprinted here.*]

Divine worship.

All commanders, captains, and officers, in or belonging to any of his Majesty's ships or vessels of war shall cause the public worship of Almighty God, according to the Liturgy of the Church of England established by law, to be solemnly, orderly, and reverently performed in their respective ships; and shall take care that prayers and preaching, by the chaplain in holy orders of the respective ships, be performed diligently; and that the Lord's day be observed according to law.

Swearing, Drunkenness, scandalous actions, &c.

II. All flag officers, and all persons in or belonging to his Majesty's ships or vessels of war, being guilty of profane oaths, cursings, execrations, drunkenness, uncleanness, or other scandalous actions, in derogation of God's honour, and corruption of good manners, shall incur such punishment as a court martial shall think fit to impose, and as the nature and degree of their offence shall deserve.

Delaying or discouraging any service.

XIV. If when action, or any service shall be commanded, any person in the fleet shall presume to delay or discourage the said action or service, upon pretence or arrears of wages, or upon any pretence whatsoever; every person so offending being convicted thereof by the sentence of the court martial, shall suffer death, or such other punishment, as from the nature and degree of the offence a court martial shall deem him to deserve.

Deserting to an enemy; running away with ships stores.

XV. Every person in or belonging to the fleet who shall desert to the enemy, pirate, or rebel; or run away with any of his Majesty's

192

ships or vessels of war, or any ordnance, ammunition, stores, or provision, belonging thereto, to the weakening of the service, or yield up the same cowardly or treacherously to the enemy, pirate, or rebel, being convicted of any such offence by the sentence of the court martial, shall suffer death.

XVI. Every person in or belonging to the fleet, who shall desert or entice others so to do, shall suffer death, or such other punishment as the circumstances of the offence shall deserve, and a court martial shall judge fit; and if any commanding officer of any of his Majesty's ships or vessels of war shall receive or entertain a deserter from any other of his Majesty's ships or vessels, after discovering him to be such deserter, and shall not with all convenient speed give notice to the captain of the ship or vessel to which such deserter belongs; or if the said ships or vessels are at any considerable distance from each other, to the secretary of the admiralty, or to the commander in chief, every person so offending, and being convicted thereof by the sentence of the court martial, shall be cashiered.

XVIII. If any captain, commander, or other officer of any of his Majesty's ships or vessels, shall receive on board, or permit to be received on board such ship or vessel, any goods or merchandizes whatsoever, other than for the sole use of the ship or vessel, except gold, silver, or jewels, and except the goods and merchandizes belonging to any merchant, or other ship or vessel which may be shipwrecked, or in imminent danger of being shipwrecked, either on the high seas, or in any port, creek, or harbour, in order to the preserving them for their proper owners, and except such goods or merchandizes as he shall at any time be ordered to take or receive on board by order of the lord high admiral of Great Britain, or the commissioners for executing the office of lord high admiral for the time being; every person so offending, being convicted thereof by the sentence of the court martial, shall be cashiered, and be for ever afterwards rendered incapable to serve in any place or office in the naval service of his Majesty, his heirs and successors.

XIX. If any person in or belonging to the fleet shall make, or endeavour to make, any mutinous assembly, upon any pretence whatsoever, every person offending herein, and being convicted thereof by the sentence of the court martial, shall suffer death. And if any person in or belonging to the fleet shall utter any words of sedition or mutiny, he shall suffer death, or such other punishment as a court martial shall deem him to deserve. And if any officer, mariner, or soldier, in or belonging to the fleet, shall behave himself with contempt to his superior officer, such superior

Desertion, and entertaining deserters.

Receiving goods and merchandize on board.

Mutinous assembly.

Uttering words of sedition and mutiny.

Contempt to superior officers.

officer being in the execution of his office, he shall be punished according to the nature of his offence, by the judgment of a court martial.

XX. If any person in the fleet shall conceal any traiterous or mutinous practice, or design, being convicted thereof by the sentence of a court martial, he shall suffer death, or such other punishment as a court martial shall think fit; and if any person, in or belonging to the fleet, shall conceal any traiterous or mutinous words, spoken by any, to the prejudice of his Majesty or government, or any words, practice, or design, tending to the hindrance of the service, and shall not forthwith reveal the same to the commanding officer; or being present at any mutiny or sedition, shall not use his utmost endeavours to suppress the same, he shall be punished, as a court martial shall think he deserves.

XXI. If any person in the fleet shall find cause of complaint of the unwholesomeness of the victual, or upon other just grounds, he shall quietly make the same known to his superior, or captain, or commander in chief, as the occasion may deserve, that such present remedy may be had, as the matter may require; and the said superior, captain, or commander in chief, shall, as far as he is able, cause the same to be presently remedied; and no person in the fleet, upon any such or other pretence, shall attempt to stir up any disturbance, upon pain of such punishment as a court martial shall think fit to inflict, according to the degree of the offence.

XXII. If any officer, mariner, soldier, or other person in the fleet, shall strike any of his superior officers, or draw, or offer to draw, or lift up any weapon against him, being in the execution of his office, on any pretence whatsoever, every such person being convicted of any such offence, by the sentence of a court martial, shall suffer death; and if any officer, mariner, soldier, or other person in the fleet, shall presume to quarrel with any of his superior officers, being in the execution of his office, or shall disobey any lawful command of any of his superior officers; every such person being convicted of any such offence by the sentence of a court martial, shall suffer death, or such other punishment as shall, according to the nature and degree of the offence, be inflicted upon him, by the sentence of a court marital.

XXIII. If any person in the fleet shall quarrel or fight with any other person in the fleet, or use reproachful or provoking speeches or gestures, tending to make any quarrel or disturbance, he shall, upon being convicted thereof, suffer such punishment as the offence shall deserve, and a court martial shall impose.

XXIV. There shall be no wasteful expence of any powder, shot, ammunition, or other stores in the fleet, nor any embezzlement thereof, but the stores and provisions shall be carefully preserved,

Concealing traiterous or mutinous designs, &c.

No person upon any pretence to attempt to stir up disturbance.

Striking a superior officer.

Quarrelling.
Disobedience.

Fighting.
Provoking speeches, &c.

Embezzlement of stores.

upon pain of such punishment to be inflicted upon the offenders, abettors, buyers, and receivers (being persons subject to naval discipline), as shall be by a court martial found just in that behalf.

XXV. Every person in the fleet, who shall unlawfully burn or set fire to any magazine or store of powder, or ship, boat, ketch, hoy, or vessel, or tackle, or furniture thereunto belonging, not then appertaining to an enemy, pirate, or rebel, being convicted of any such offence, by the sentence of a court martial, shall suffer death.

XXVI. Care shall be taken in the conducting and steering of any of his Majesty's ships, that through wilfulness, negligence, or other defaults, no ship be stranded, or run upon any rocks or sands, or split, or hazarded, upon pain, that such as shall be found guilty therein, be punished by death, or such other punishment as the offence by a court martial shall be judged to deserve.

XXVII. No person in or belonging to the fleet shall sleep upon his watch, or negligently perform the duty imposed on him, or forsake his station, upon pain of death, or such other punishment as a court martial shall think fit to impose, and as the circumstance of the case shall require.

XXVIII. All murders committed by any person in the fleet, shall be punished with death, by the sentence of a court martial.

XXIX. If any person in the fleet, shall commit the unnatural and detestable sin of buggery or sodomy, with man or beast, he shall be punished with death, by the sentence of a court martial.

XXX. All robbery committed by any person in the fleet, shall be punished with death, or otherwise, as a court martial upon consideration of circumstances shall find meet.

XXXI. Every officer or other person in the fleet, who shall knowingly make or sign a false muster or muster-book, or who shall command, counsel, or procure the making or signing thereof, or who shall aid or abet any other person in the making or signing thereof, shall, upon proof of any such offence being made before a court martial, be cashiered, and rendered incapable of further employment in his Majesty's naval service.

XXXII. No provost martial belonging to the fleet shall refuse to apprehend any criminal, whom he shall be authorized by legal warrant to apprehend; or to receive or keep any prisoner committed to his charge; or wilfully suffer him to escape, being once in his custody; or dismiss him without lawful order; upon pain of such punishment as a court martial shall deem him to deserve. And all captains, officers, and others in the fleet, shall do their endeavour to detect, apprehend, and bring to punishment all offenders, and shall assist the officers appointed for that purpose therein, upon pain of being proceeded against, and punished by a court martial, according to the nature and degree of the offence.

195

XXXIII. If any flag officer, captain, or commander, or lieutenant belonging to the fleet, shall be convicted before a court martial, of behaving in a scandalous, infamous, cruel, oppressive, or fraudulent manner, unbecoming the character of an officer, he shall be dismissed from his Majesty's service.

Mutiny, desertion,
disobedience when on
shore, in the king's
dominions.

XXXIV. Every person being in actual service, and full pay, and part of the crew in or belonging to any of his Majesty's ships or vessels of war, who shall be guilty of mutiny, desertion, or disobedience to any lawful command, in any part of his Majesty's dominions on shore, when in actual service, relative to the fleet, shall be liable to be tried by a court martial, and suffer the like punishment for every such offence, as if the same had been committed at sea, on board any of his Majesty's ships or vessels of war.

Crimes committed on
shore out of the king's
dominions.

XXXV. If any person who shall be in actual service, and full pay, in his majesty's ships and vessels of war, shall commit upon the shore, in any place or places out of his majesty's dominions, any of the crimes punishable by these articles and orders, the person so offending shall be liable to be tried and punished for the same, in like manner to all intents and purposes, as if the said crimes had been committed at sea, on board any of his Majesty's ships or vessels of war.

XXXVI. All other crimes, not capital, committed by any person or persons in the fleet, which are not mentioned in this act, or for which no punishment is hereby directed to be inflicted, shall be punished according to the laws and customs in such cases used at sea.

NOTES

1. Owen Rutter, from his introduction to Bligh's *Log of the Bounty*, p. 4. Bligh's official log is not to be confused with one he wrote after the mutiny and his return to England, entitled *A Narrative of the Mutiny on board His Majesty's Ship Bounty; and the subsequent voyage of a part of the crew in the ship's Boat, from Tofoa, one of the Friendly Islands, to Timor, a Dutch Settlement in the East Indies.* It was published in London in 1790. Though Bligh's book follows the essential outline of his official log, it is an altogether different account of the *Bounty* voyage and mutiny because it was written retrospectively—with Bligh looking backward at events. The perspective, by design and purpose, vindicates Bligh of any responsibility in the mutiny. Though an excellent story in itself, those events that did present some significant background to the mutiny are mostly absent from Bligh's later account.

2. Owen Rutter, from his introduction to *The Log of the Bounty*, p. 6.

3. J. C. Beaglehole, *The Life of Captain James Cook* (Stanford, California: Stanford University Press, 1974; first published by A & C Black Ltd., London, 1974), p. 498.

4. Bligh's verbal lashings of the men he commanded marred an honorable career and on three occasions were partly if indirectly responsible for bringing him to account before a court-martial hearing: as commander of the *Bounty,* as captain of the *Director* in 1799, and again in 1810 as the displaced governor of New South Wales, the colony in what is now Australia. In each instance he was exonerated.

5. The letter was included by Owen Rutter in his introduction to Bligh's *Log of the Bounty*, p. 1.

6. Quoted in *A Book of the Bounty and Selections from Bligh's Writings,* edited by George Mackaness. Everyman's Library Series (London: J. M. Dent and Sons, 1938), pp. 10–11.

7. N. A. M. Rogers, *The Wooden World, an Anatomy of the Georgian Navy* (Annapolis, Maryland: Naval Institute Press, 1986), p. 29.

8. *A Book of the Bounty and Selections from Bligh's Writings,* p. 290.

9. *A Book of the Bounty and Selections from Bligh's Writings*, p. 6.

10. *A Book of the Bounty and Selections from Bligh's Writings*, p. 7.

11. *A Book of the Bounty and Selections from Bligh's Writings*, p. 298.

12. *A Book of the Bounty and Selections from Bligh's Writings*, p. 300.

13. *A Book of the Bounty and Selections from Bligh's Writings*, p. 301.

14. N. A. M. Rogers, *The Wooden World, An Anatomy of the Georgian Navy*, pp. 207 and 219.

15. It is difficult to interpret what Morrison meant by "Pleasure and profit." Unlike the crew of a warship, who might have been rewarded with prize money for an enemy ship sunk, the men of the *Bounty* were on a fixed rate of pay. Pleasure could certainly be anticipated among the Tahitian women; the stories brought back to England from the voyages of Wallis and Cook would have seen to that. The men might look forward to trading on Tahiti, but what the Tahitians had to trade were fresh produce, coconuts, breadfruit, hogs, and the favors of the women, not items that could be sold for profit in England. There was interest among private collectors in England for artifacts and "curiosities" from Tahiti, but it seems unlikely the men could hope to participate in this market. Perhaps Morrison was simply expressing a general outlook of optimism for the success of the voyage, or a junior officer's hopes for career advancement.

16. This was an 18th century method of dividing unequal portions fairly. One man would turn his back. Another held up the portion behind his back, where the first man could not see it. The man holding the portion would ask, "Who shall have this?" The man whose back was turned would call out, "John Doe," or whoever. The meager rations in Bligh's open-boat passage were also divided by this method.

17. The 62nd degree of south latitude and 79th degree of longitude reported by Morrison placed the *Bounty* well to the west and south of Cape Horn, the position of which is 55° 59′ S, 67° 16′ W. Even from this position, however, the ship could not safely double the Horn without raising the western coast of South America as a dangerous lee shore. Anson, after his shattering confrontation with the Horn, had recommended working south to 61° or 62° in search of less violent weather and more favorable currents before attempting a westing. After a rounding in favorable conditions on his first Pacific voyage, Cook had modified and elaborated Anson's advice. Cook's log, quoted in J. C. Beaglehole's *Life of Captain James Cook* (p. 166) reasons that "it cannot be suppose'd any one will Stear South mearly to get into a high Latitude when at that time he can steer West, for it is not Southing but Westing thats wanting, but this way you cannot steer because the winds blow almost constantly from that quarter, so that you have no other choice but to stand to the Southward close upon a wind, and by keeping upon that Tack you not only make southing but westing also and sometimes not a little when the wind Varies to the northward of West, and the farther you advance to the Southrd the better chance you have of having the winds from that quarter or easterly and likewise of meeting with finer weather, both of which we ourselves experience'd. Prudence will direct every man when in these high Latitudes to make sure of Sufficient westing to double all the lands before he thinks of Standing to the

Northward." Cook was fortunate to round the Horn in January and early February, the height of the southern summer.

It is interesting that Morrison was privy to the ship's location, information not normally made available to the crew. Perhaps in these difficult conditions Bligh kept the crew informed of their westward progress, or perhaps Morrison got the information from Fryer or Christian.

18. *A Book of the Bounty and Selections from Bligh's Writings,* p. 303.

19. Bligh offers no explanation of the plantings, but sailing captains of the time often planted edible fruits and vegetables when they called at remote islands and ports to provide fresh food for later ship visits.

20. Sir John Barrow, *The Mutiny of the Bounty.* With an introduction and edited by Gavin Kennedy (Boston: David R. Godine, 1980), p. 65.

21. Under the strictest interpretation of naval regulations, Bligh as the only commissioned officer ought to have been the only man allowed private food stores. Probably this rule was bent more often than any other. See Appendix 2.

22. *A Book of the Bounty and Selections from Bligh's Writings:* "It may not be unworthy of remark that the whole distance which the ship had run by the log, in direct and contrary courses, from leaving England to our anchoring at Otaheite, was twenty-seven thousand and eighty-six miles, which on an average, is at the rate of a hundred and eight miles each twenty-four hours."

23. *A Book of the Bounty and Selections from Bligh's Writings,* p. 262.

24. *A Book of the Bounty and Selections from Bligh's Writings,* p. 271. This letter does not appear in Bligh's log. It was quoted by Bligh in his response to accusations later made against him by Fletcher Christian's brother, Edward.

25. Captain F. W. Beechey, *Voyage to the Pacific and Beering's Strait.* (Full citation in Bibliography.)

26. Bligh made this log entry on the beach at Tofua.

27. Whether or not Bligh carried a sextant with him on his open-boat voyage was long a question of scholarly debate, but the discovery and publication of the notebook Bligh used for daily log entries and navigational calculations in the launch has laid this to rest. The computations show that he did have a sextant, and his denial of it in the ship's log may have been a deliberate obfuscation designed to cast Christian in the worst possible light. The *Daily Assistant* to which Morrison refers was probably a comprehensive contemporary manual of navigation authored by John Hamilton Moore, which would have contained all the information necessary for Bligh's subsequent navigation. In his introduction to *The Bligh Notebook,* Bach concludes that the only navigational tools missing were a chronometer and nautical almanac for determination of longitude. The only timepiece in the launch was a watch.

28. N. A. M. Rogers, *The Wooden World, An Anatomy of the Georgian Navy.*

29. Sir John Barrow, *The Mutiny of the Bounty,* ed. Gavin Kennedy (Boston: David R. Godine, 1980), p. 194.

30. To follow the log, it should be noted that it was kept according to navy or nautical time rather than land or civil time. In this system, the day starts at noon and continues until noon the next day. Thus for example, the day that dawned June 1 would become June 2 at noon and remain June 2 throughout the afternoon, night, and following morning. The narrative stays with nautical time. Note that here Bligh is openly worried about the theft of his compass and quadrant, but does not mention a sextant.

31. A modern world map would not show Bligh's "183°" of east longitude, because longitude today is measured up to 180° either east or west of Greenwich, England. Logs of Bligh's period, however, often noted longitudes in excess of 180°, because it kept the arithmetic simpler. Often longitude was measured in degrees east up to 360°, but Cook on his first voyage measured longitudes in excess of 180° west—probably a simple expedient arising from the fact that his outward-bound track was westward.

32. Torres Strait, the 90-mile-wide, reef-choked channel that separates Cape York, on the northern tip of Australia, from New Guinea, was discovered by the Spanish navigator Luis Torres in 1606. It appeared on some charts of the region thereafter, but contradictory assertions cast doubt on its existence until 1770, when Cook, in H.M.S. *Endeavour*, traversed the southernmost passage of the labyrinthian strait, between Cape York and the off-lying Prince of Wales Island. Cook's route, which Bligh intended to follow, is still known as Endeavour Straits.

33. *A Book of the Bounty and Selections from Bligh's Writings*, p. 304.

34. William Bligh, *Voyage in the H.M.S. Resource*. Introduction and notes by Owen Rutter. London: Golden Cockerel Press, 1932.

35. Owen Rutter, in his notes to *Voyage in the H.M.S. Resource*.

36. This assertion of Morrison was meant to underscore his innocence and probably to vouch for Stewart and Heywood. While there is no way to verify the statement, it certainly seems plausible.

37. Morrison offered further proof of his innocence as a mutineer by recounting this remarkable effort to build a ship which, he claims, was to start him on the long voyage back to England.

38. *Voyage of H.M.S. Pandora, despatched to arrest the mutineers of the Bounty in the South Seas, 1790–91, being the narratives of Captain Edward Edwards RN, the commander, and George Hamilton, the surgeon*, with introduction and notes by Basil Thomson. London: Frances Edwards, 1915.

39. Cf. Gavin Kennedy's introduction to Sir John Barrow's *Mutiny of the Bounty*, p. 16. Kennedy reports evidence that Morrison's *Resolution* is here confused with another, larger *Resolution*.

40. H. E. Maude, *In Search of a Home: From the Mutiny to Pitcairn Island (1789–1790)* (Washington, D.C.: The Australian National University for the Smithsonian Institution, 1960). Writes Maude:
"Jenny was also in her way a remarkable character. Described as 'a good looking woman in her time,' she went with John Adams to Tubuai and was tattooed by him AS/1789 on her left arm. She landed on Pitcairn as Isaac

Martin's wife but was never reconciled to life there, possibly because she had no children of her own to compensate for the loss of her relatives and friends on Tahiti. After the death of her husband, Jenny led the abortive attempt of the women to leave Pitcairn in a boat, and finally succeeded in getting away by the whaler *Sultan* in 1817. On her return to Tahiti she gave two separate accounts of her experiences; one published in the *Sydney Gazette* for July 17, 1819, and the second in the *Bengal Hurkaru* for October 2, 1826. . . .

"Jenny's narratives are not only consistent with each other, but in all cases where they can be checked from other material they have proved to be reliable."

SELECTED BIBLIOGRAPHY

Allen, Kenneth S. *That Bounty Bastard*. New York: St. Martin's Press, 1976.

Bach, John. *The Bligh Notebook*. 2 vols. Canberra: National Library of Australia, 1987.

Ball, Ian M. *Pitcairn, Children of Mutiny*. Boston and Toronto: Little, Brown & Company, 1973.

Barrow, Sir John. *The Mutiny of the Bounty*. First published 1831 as *The Eventful History of the Mutiny and Piratical Seizure of HMS Bounty, its Cause and Consequences*. This edition edited by Gavin Kennedy. Boston: David R. Godine, 1980.

Bligh, Captain William. *An Answer to Certain Assertions Contained in the Appendix to a Pamphlet, Entitled Minutes of the Proceedings on the Court-Martial Held at Portsmouth, August 12th, 1972, on Ten Persons Charged with Mutiny on Board His Majesty's Ship the Bounty*. London: G. Nicol, 1794. Reproduced in Adelaide, Australia: Georgian House Pty. Ltd., 1952.

————. *Log of the Bounty*. Introduction and notes by Owen Rutter. London: Golden Cockerel Press, 1937.

————. *Voyage in the H.M.S. Resource*. Introduction and notes by Owen Rutter. London: Golden Cockerel Press, 1932.

Beaglehole, J. C. *The Journals of Captain Cook and His Voyages of Discovery*. Cambridge and London: The Hakluyt Society, 1955–1974.

————. *The Life of Captain James Cook*. Stanford, California: Stanford University Press, 1974. (First published in London: A & C Black, Ltd., 1974).

Beechey, Captain F. W. *Voyage to the Pacific and Beering's Strait*. London: Henry Colburn and Richard Bentley, 1831.

Burns, Sir Alan. *History of the British West Indies*. London: George Allen & Unwin Ltd., 1954

Cameron, Ian. *Lost Paradise, The Exploration of the Pacific*. Boston: Salem House, 1987.

Cobb, Hugh. *Cook's Voyages and Peoples of the Pacific*. London: British Museum Publications Ltd., 1979.

Dale, Paul W. *Seventy North to Fifty South: The Story of Captain Cook's Last Voyage*. Englewood Cliffs, New Jersey: Prentice-Hall, Inc., 1969.

Edwards, Edward and George Hamilton. *Voyage of HMS Pandora*. Introduction and notes by Basil Thomson. London: Francis Edwards, 1915.

Fryer, John. *The voyage of the Bounty launch*. Stephen Walters. Guildford, England: Genesis/Rigby, 1979.

Hughes, Robert. *The Fatal Shore*. New York: Alfred A. Knopf, 1987.

Mackaness, George (editor). *A Book of the Bounty and Selections from Bligh's Writings.* (Includes Bligh's *Narrative of the Mutiny on Board His Majesty's Ship Bounty; and the subsequent voyage of a part of the crew in the ship's boat, from Tofoa, one of the Friendly Islands, to Timor, a Dutch Settlement in the East Indies,* which he had published in London in 1790, shortly after his return. It also includes Stephen Barney's "Report of the Court-Martial of Ten Mutineers," the accusatory "Appendix" by Edward Christian, and Bligh's answer to Christian's assertions. Everyman's Library Series. London: J. M. Dent and Sons, 1938.

Maude, H. E. *In Search of a Home: From the Mutiny to Pitcairn Island (1789–1790)*. Washington, D.C.: Smithsonian Institution, 1960.

Morrison, James. *The Journal of James Morrison Boatswain's Mate of the Bounty describing the Mutiny and Subsequent Misfortunes of the Mutineers together with an account of the Island of Tahiti.* Edited by Owen Rutter. London: Golden Cockerel Press, 1935.

Rawson, Geoffrey. *Pandora's Last Voyage*. New York: Harcourt Brace Jovanovich, 1963.

Riesenberg, Felix. *Cape Horn*. New York: Dodd, Mead & Company, 1939.

Rogers, N. A. M. *The Wooden World, an Anatomy of the Georgian Navy*. Annapolis, Maryland: Naval Institute Press, 1986.

Villiers, Alan. *The War with Cape Horn*. New York: Charles Scribner's Sons, 1971.

ART CREDITS

National Portrait Gallery, London, England: Frontispiece.
National Maritime Museum, London, England: pages 8, 9, 10, 17,
    20, 22, 23, and 91.
Maps drawn by Alex Wallach, Kittery, Maine.
All other illustrations by Nathan Goldstein, Newton, Massachusetts.

INDEX

Diseases, 12, 51, 52, 55–56, 63, 114
Djakarta. *See* Batavia
Dolphin, H.M.S., 53
Drake, Francis, 35
Dripstone, 82
Ducie Island, 145
Duke, H.M.S., 159
Dutch East India Company, 123, 126, 156
Duty, shipboard rank and, 184–186

E

Edwards, Edward, 143–158; log of, 6
Ellison, Thomas, 23, 24, 85, 132, 136, 142, 145, 154, 159–161, 181
Elphinstone, William, 24, 76, 90, 181
Endeavour, H.M.S., 9
Equator-crossing ceremony, 30
Equivalents, table of, 30
Essex, U.S.S., 173

F

Fiji islands, 99–100
Folger, Mayhew, 173
Food. *See* Victuals
Fort George, 132–133
Foster, Gregory, 91, 92
Franklin, John, 174
Fryer, John, 24, 50, 64, 65, 67, 90, 112–114, 120, 124–125, 160, 168, 182; book of, 6

G

Gorgon, H.M.S., 157
Great Barrier Reef, 106–107, 110
Grog, 28, 42, 187–189
Gunner, duties of, 185

H

Hall, Thomas, 24, 40, 90, 125, 181
Hallett, John, 23, 24, 90, 125, 143–144, 152, 161, 167, 182
Hamilton, George, 6, 144, 151, 153–154, 156
Harrison, John, 9
Hawaii. *See* Sandwich Islands
Hayward, Thomas, 24, 66, 69, 77, 90, 143–144, 145, 147, 152, 160–161, 182
Hector, H.M.S., 158
Heywood, Nessy, 159, 161–163
Heywood, Peter, 23, 24, 59, 83, 88, 133, 136, 145, 159–163, 182
Hillbrant, Henry, 24, 29–30, 84, 132, 136, 142, 145, 151, 181
Hill Tribes of Fiji, The (Brewster), 100
Hoorn, (ship), 35
Horse latitudes, 35
Huggan, John, 24, 41, 51, 64

I

Interest system, 21

J

Jenny, narrative of, 169

K

Kupang. *See* Coupang

L

La Boudeuse (ship), 53
Lamb, Edward, 167
Lamb, Robert, 24, 65, 82–83, 87, 90, 115, 181
Latitude, 9, 35, 45
Lau islands. *See* Bligh's Islands
Lebogue, Lawrence, 23, 24, 90, 118, 119, 166–167, 182
Ledward, Thomas, 24, 90, 118, 119, 125, 181
Le Maire Strait, 36
Life of Captain James Cook (Beaglehole), 13, 21–22, 188
Linkletter, Peter, 24, 41, 90, 181
Longitude, 9, 100

M

Magellan, Ferdinand, 35
Maitea island, 52
Martin, Isaac, 24, 68–69, 77, 83, 84, 87, 136, 169, 178, 182
Master, duties of, 50, 67, 184–185
Master-at-arms, duties of, 185
Matavai Bay, 52–72
McCoy, William, 24, 74, 77, 84, 132, 136, 169, 178–180, 182
McIntosh, Thomas, 24, 85, 88, 136, 138, 139, 145, 159–161
Mewstone Rock, 46
Midshipman, duties of, 185–186
Mills, John, 24, 78, 84, 88, 136, 169, 178, 182
Millward, John, 24, 65, 68, 84, 87, 136, 138, 142, 145, 159–161, 181
Morrison, James, 4–5, 24, 67, 79–82, 83–84, 88, 128, 133, 136, 138–142, 145, 154, 159–161, 163, 182; journal of, 4–6
Muspratt, William, 24, 65, 68, 84, 87, 136, 142, 145, 159–161
Mutiny, 1–2, 77–85, 86–87
Mutiny on the Bounty (Barrow), 50, 89
"Mutiny on the Bounty" (movie), 1, 4, 14

N

Narrative of the Mutiny on board His Majesty's Ship Bounty, A (Bligh), 126–127

Watch system, three-, 13, 31
Williams, John, 24, 45, 77, 84, 87, 136, 169, 178,
182
Wooden World, The (Rogers), 32–33, 189
Wreck Island, 151–152

Y

Yangasu Levu island, 99
Young, Edward, 24, 83, 136, 169, 178–180, 182

COLOPHON

John Baskerville, who designed the typeface used to set the text of this book, was born in Worcestershire, England in 1706 (just 47 years before William Bligh was born in Cornwall). Baskerville was first a calligrapher and writing master, then a stone engraver, then a very successful producer of japanned ware. The fortune he acquired in that trade provided him with the capital to pursue his dream of being a type founder and printer. As he wrote, ". . . Having been an early admirer of the beauty of Letters, I became insensibly desirous of contributing to the perfection of them. I formed to myself Ideas of greater accuracy than had yet appeared, and have endeavoured to produce a Sett of Types according to what I conceived to be their true proportion . . ." His contemporary printers were startled by some of his innovations, and did not rush to purchase his fonts. Benjamin Franklin was an early supporter of the Baskerville types, and they steadily increased in popularity amongst the printers of fine editions; in fact 200 years after their introduction Baskerville was the overwhelmingly dominant font in award winning books. In the last 25 years Baskerville has been nudged aside by several faces enjoying their day in the sunlight of fashion. But for beauty and legibility it is hard to fault Baskerville.

The ornamental rule used throughout this book was designed by William Caslon, a British printer just 14 years Baskerville's senior. It was chosen for use in this volume because of its similarity to the carved and gilded quarterboards of British vessels of the *Bounty*'s time.

This book was designed by Richard C. Bartlett. Production direction was by Molly Mulhern. Graphic Composition, Incorporated of Athens, Georgia set the type, and page makeup mechanicals were prepared by Deborah Davies. The printing and binding were done by the Hamilton Printing Company of East Greenbush, New York. The paper is 70 pound eggshell offset, made by the P. H. Glatfelter Company in Spring Grove, Pennsylvania. The cover cloth is Crown Linen manufactured by the Holliston Mills of Kingsport, Tennessee.

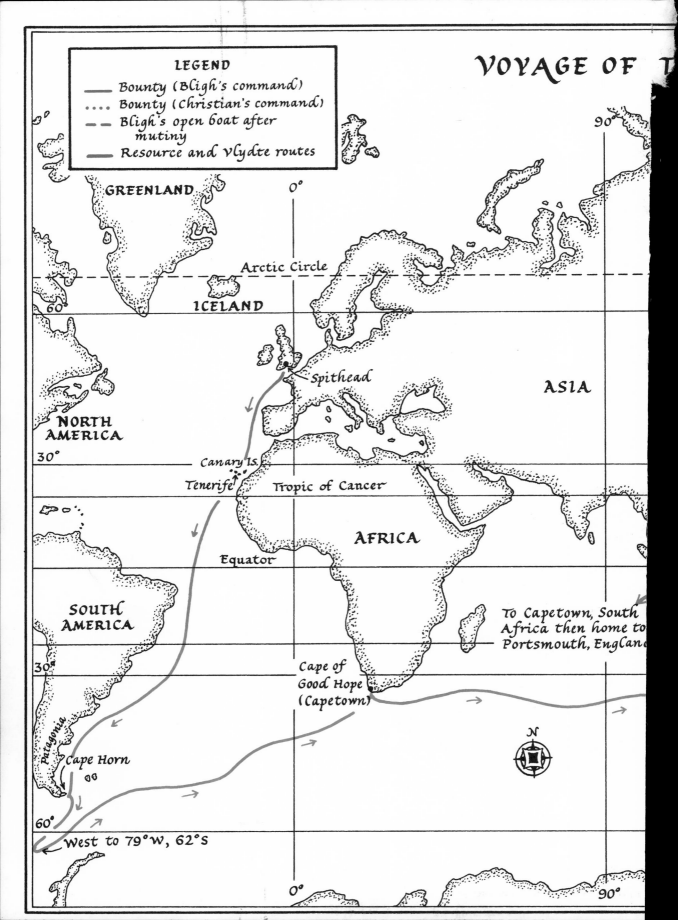